ENGLISH METRISTS IN THE EIGHTEENTH AND NINETEENTH CENTURIES: BEING A SKETCH OF ENGLISH PROSODICAL CRITICISM DURING THE LAST TWO HUNDRED YEARS

Published @ 2017 Trieste Publishing Pty Ltd

ISBN 9780649574810

English Metrists in the Eighteenth and Nineteenth Centuries: Being a Sketch of English Prosodical Criticism during the Last Two Hundred Years by T. S. Omond

Except for use in any review, the reproduction or utilisation of this work in whole or in part in any form by any electronic, mechanical or other means, now known or hereafter invented, including xerography, photocopying and recording, or in any information storage or retrieval system, is forbidden without the permission of the publisher, Trieste Publishing Pty Ltd, PO Box 1576 Collingwood, Victoria 3066 Australia.

All rights reserved.

Edited by Trieste Publishing Pty Ltd.
Cover @ 2017

This book is sold subject to the condition that it shall not, by way of trade or otherwise, be lent, re-sold, hired out, or otherwise circulated without the publisher's prior consent in any form or binding or cover other than that in which it is published and without a similar condition including this condition being imposed on the subsequent purchaser.

www.triestepublishing.com

T. S. OMOND

ENGLISH METRISTS IN THE EIGHTEENTH AND NINETEENTH CENTURIES: BEING A SKETCH OF ENGLISH PROSODICAL CRITICISM DURING THE LAST TWO HUNDRED YEARS

ENGLISH METRISTS

(18th AND 19th CENTURIES)

OXFORD: HORACE HART
PRINTER TO THE UNIVERSITY

ENGLISH METRISTS

IN THE

EIGHTEENTH AND NINETEENTH CENTURIES

BEING A SKETCH OF ENGLISH PROSODICAL
CRITICISM DURING THE LAST TWO
HUNDRED YEARS

BY

T. S. OMOND

M.A. EDIN. & OXON.
FORMERLY FELLOW OF ST. JOHN'S COLLEGE, OXFORD

AUTHOR OF
"A STUDY OF METRE"
etc.

HENRY FROWDE
OXFORD UNIVERSITY PRESS
LONDON, NEW YORK AND TORONTO
1907

PREFACE

THIS volume completes a survey which was originally meant to form an Appendix to my *Study of Metre*, and of which a small introductory portion has been already printed, as mentioned in the first paragraph of my text. As there explained, however, the present volume is practically independent and self-contained, since within its period comes all that constitutes our real criticism of prosody.

While regretting the delay which has unavoidably intervened between outset and completion, I am glad that this enables me to mention in my Postscript several recent works of importance.

It has been my endeavour not merely to enumerate and summarize treatises, but to trace the gradual development of sounder views about verse-structure. Writings which influenced this development are therefore considered somewhat more fully than others. No such report on the progress of metrical science has appeared, that I know of, in any modern European language; the necessary materials, indeed, have scarcely been brought together.

I am much indebted to several correspondents who, accepting an invitation now renewed on behalf of a volume which must need their good offices still more, favoured me with notice of errors or omissions in my previous pamphlet. Some particular obligations are acknowledged in Appendix A. But I would here especially thank three friendly contributors, Mr. E. L. White of Baltimore, Mr. E. P. Morton of Indiana University, and Mr. F. I. Carpenter of Chicago, for help which has enabled me to make my list of American publications less incomplete than before.

May I suggest to American writers on *metric* the expediency of forwarding a specimen of their work to the British Museum? Few people care to buy unseen books; a copy deposited there might attract some purchasers, and would at least advance knowledge. Our subject not being popular, the Museum authorities are apt to pronounce "unnecessary" even volumes that readers wish to consult.

When this book was planned, I seemed to have the field to myself. Now, a formidable competitor may be thought to have arisen in the person of Prof. Saintsbury. How far future volumes of his *History of English Prosody* will take possession of this field I do not know. Judging by what has already appeared, I incline to suspect that our aims diverge, and that students may profit by seeing the same matters treated from two very different points of view. However this turn out, I rejoice that a cherished design is being executed before "the night and the shadows" come to prevent; and shall hope that my narrower attempt may share some of the interest which, I trust, my friend's work is destined to excite in a subject too much neglected of late years by English scholars.

14, CALVERLEY PARK, TUNBRIDGE WELLS.
December, 1906.

CONTENTS

CHAPTER I
	PAGE
THE OLD ORTHODOXY: 1700–1750	1

CHAPTER II
RESISTANCE AND REBELLION: 1750–1800 . . .	17

CHAPTER III
THE NEW VERSE: 1800–1850	86

CHAPTER IV
THE NEW PROSODY: 1850–1900	145
POSTSCRIPT	226
APPENDIX A	243
APPENDIX B	255
NOTE	268
INDEX	269

CHAPTER I

THE OLD ORTHODOXY

1700-1750

ONLY during the last two Centuries has there been any systematic study of English prosody. The present volume, therefore, though it takes up a tale begun before, may be regarded as practically complete in itself. In a fragment printed three years ago [1] I sketched the faint beginnings of English prosodical criticism which preceded the opening years of the Eighteenth Century, and also made an endeavour (the first so far as my knowledge goes) to compile a bibliography of the subject. Such additions as have suggested themselves will be found in Appendices A and B. To these I refer readers for any bibliographical details not given in the text. My survey is confined to works written in the English language; to go farther would have immensely increased a labour already arduous, perhaps without satisfactory result. At any rate, the present volume deals only with criticism of English verse by English-speaking authors; and I believe that all which is of consequence in that criticism occurs during the period now to be surveyed.

It may be well to summarize results already reached. I have shown that, naturally enough, English verse as we know it was written long before any discussion arose about its nature or methods (with its origin and historical derivation we are not concerned); that when such dis-

---

[1] *English Metrists*, printed and published by R. Pelton, The Broadway, Tunbridge Wells (1903; paper covers, price 1s. 6d.).

cussion did arise it began without proper preliminaries, without enquiry into the actualities of English speech-sounds; that our first critics were wholly possessed by Classic precedent, and sought to interpret English metre in terms of Latin and Greek; and that contemporaneously with them a deliberate attempt was made to revolutionize our verse by substituting rules of Classic 'quantity' for native measures. This ill-starred attempt was followed to its foregone conclusion; a few *addenda* are mentioned in Appendix A. Thereafter were examined the scant records of English metrical study during the Sixteenth and Seventeenth Centuries, ending with Charles Gildon (1718). From that date, early in the Century before last, the tale is now to be resumed; all that is vital to the science of English prosody, as well as much that is quite other, still lying before us.

Most of the work which falls first to be examined is occupied by discussions of accent and quantity. Echoes of dreary controversy are roused by these words. Arguments about them seem as arid and as hopeless of solution as arguments about free will or the origin of matter. Nor can it be said that the writers we are about to take note of deal helpfully with the questions at issue. Their method is pre-scientific; they talk round and about their subject rather than really investigate it. We seldom find any thing like true analysis. Can we, then, before plunging into this dusty arena, get some clear ideas for ourselves as to the matters in dispute, to prevent entire confusion and bewilderment?

'Quantity' presents no great difficulty. I have already stated the meaning of the word in Greek and Latin verse, and need now only repeat that it referred solely to the time syllables took to pronounce; and that this was held to depend either on vowel-duration or on retardation by separately pronounced consonants. A long syllable was accounted equal to two short, and carried two time-beats as against the one apiece of the short syllables. In English we have nothing analogous to this fixed rule. Our ears are presumably not different from those of old Greeks and Romans, but our habits of speech are different. We have a powerful stress-accent, which reduces quantitative distinction to low and fluctuating values; they, apparently, had a very slight one. Were our language more like theirs—did it contain a large proportion of vowels, rarely separated by more than two or at most three consonants, and were it devoid of strong accentuation—we, too, might have made quantity the basis of our verse-structure. As it is, any attempt to write English quantitative verse seems vain and meaningless. Bearing in mind, then, that quantity refers solely to length of syllables, let us go on to consider what can be determined about accent.

Three elements must be distinguished in every spoken sound—pitch, force, and duration. I purposely use the least ambiguous terms. Pitch is synonymous with height of tone, force with loudness; duration represents what we have just called 'quantity'. These three elements are distinct and different, separable always in thought, separated often in practice. No analysis can be accurate which confuses them.[1] In the books before us accent is defined sometimes as one of these (each in turn by different writers!), sometimes as any two of them, occasionally as all three together. At present it is usually defined as consisting of force. The question which most exercised our metrists—the only question of consequence for the measuring of verse—is, does or does not accent also imply duration, does emphasizing a syllable necessarily prolong its utterance?

There is certainly a well-marked tendency this way. The typical Scot inclines to say *leemit, releegion, trayvel* and *trayveller, abohminable*. That is, he likes to prolong the accented vowel. The same tendency prevails farther south. When we shift stress from the first to the second syllable of *doctrinal*, we also lengthen that second syllable. We change the quality, and therewith the 'quantity', of

[1] This account is not put forward as complete. Other qualities, especially *timbre* or tone-quality, play their part. But the first necessity is to distinguish clearly between the three factors above named.

its vowel. Countless instances of this tendency might be cited. But it is, after all, only a tendency. Other influences create other tendencies, as when hurry leads us to scamp words, to reduce *fore-head* to *forred*, *cheer up* to *chirrup*, *don't know* to *dunno*. This influence will in most cases overpower the other. Careless talk may be to blame for it, but we must take facts as they are. It seems impossible to argue that, in our ordinary speech, accentuation necessarily implies prolongation.

I submit that, as a matter of fact, 'accent' with us does not necessarily imply either elevation of pitch, or increase of loudness, or prolongation of time. Normally we like to unite all three on one syllable, and this is probably our commonest type of accent. But it is possible to accentuate a syllable by lowering the voice instead of raising it, by uttering it more softly instead of more loudly, by shortening instead of prolonging its duration. Any device which thus distinguishes a syllable from its fellows makes it conspicuous, and this conspicuousness is what we really mean by 'accent'. This rendering conspicuous of some syllables more than others is highly characteristic of our speech. Compare, for instance, the ideal of French speaking. There no syllable must predominate rudely over its neighbours, and in French regular metre every syllable is accounted of the same value. With us it is quite the reverse. In common talk, as in oratory or verse, every second or third syllable is usually rendered conspicuous in some way, and a dead level of pronunciation is repulsive to us.

We carry this habit of speech into other languages. We read Greek and Latin verse as we do our own, and imagine that when we make 'long' syllables conspicuous we are reading by quantity. Conversely, we believe that in English verse a conspicuous syllable is necessarily protracted. Many will refuse to admit that the first syllable of words like *very, limit, busy, banner, muscle, cockle, patter, petty* is as short as the second. (Spelling is of course no guide.) To a musician this will seem incomprehensible. He knows that three crotchets with an accent on the first is not the same thing as a minim followed by two crotchets. Till we can similarly distinguish accentuation from quantity, conspicuousness from duration, the problems presented by English verse must remain insoluble. In what precise manner accent operates is a question for the philologer rather than the metrist. The one point of importance for prosody is to feel sure that accentuation does not by itself involve any change of duration.

If the definition of ours as a "force-accent" be meant to exclude other elements, it is certainly too narrow. Nine times out of ten, I venture to say, raising of pitch accompanies increase of loudness in our speech. The very term "accent", common to our earliest observers, properly means elevation of tone. Names do not always describe facts; yet the using of this one is significant. The words 'stress' and 'stress-accent', on the other hand, are conveniently vague, since anything which gives importance to a syllable may be said to lay stress on it. In any case, those who make accent synonymous with force cannot claim that it necessarily implies prolongation, since the length of a syllable and its loudness are clearly two different things.

The writers we are to deal with took for the most part no such broad view of their question. Each brought with him his own preconception. To one accent is pitch, and he will not admit any other element. To another it is length, and no short syllable can ever be accented. Yet a third makes it loudness, and finds in English verse such music only as attends the beats of a drum. Each view is partial, one-sided; built on *a priori* argument rather than induction of instances. In one point, however, they all agree. Unanimously they assert that accentuation plays in our verse the part that quantity did in Greek and Latin. Even this, surely, is but a half-truth. How can accentuation form a basis of metre? It is an intensive, not an extensive factor. The phrase "accentual foot" involves a misconception. The essential quality of a 'foot' is duration, and this is not created by accent. Without doubt, accentuation is the most salient feature of our verse, as 'quantity' of Classic verse. But to presume identity between their functions is illogical. The one records time, the other only illustrates it. With us, accent is mainly a signalizing element. It calls attention to periods, but does not and cannot create these. So far as it makes the voice linger on a syllable, it becomes a constitutive element in verse; but its main function is to emphasize recurrence. The old confusion between accent and time is perceptible again here, and turns the "half-truth" into "wholly a lie". Accent and quantity are incommensurate, and to draw elaborate parallels between them as in the same plane can only mislead.

The conclusions sketched in these last paragraphs are, I believe, in accord with modern phonetic science. They may at least serve as a clue through the mazes of prosodic controversy. Before entering these, let me record—as I omitted to do in its proper place—that Dryden, toward the end of the "Dedication" prefixed to his translation of the *Aeneid*, says : " I have long had by me the materials of an English Prosodia, containing all the mechanical rules of versification, wherein I have treated with some exactness of the feet, the quantities, and the pauses." As in the previous case of Ben Jonson, one feels regret that this project was not executed. Still more must it be regretted that Milton left no record of the principles which guided him. We should at least have known how these great poets viewed the subject-matter of their art. As it is, we are only told what critics think, until, toward the end of our survey, we find prosody discussed by singers such as Poe, Patmore, and Lanier.

Also, along with Bysshe (1702) and Brightland (1710) should have been mentioned two grammarians immortalized by a line in the *Anti-Jacobin*—

Dilworth and Dyche are both mad at thy quantities.

In my draft Bibliography I gave what I believed to be

their dates. But I have since discovered that the 1710 edition of Dyche's *Guide to the English Tongue*, though the earliest copy in the British Museum library, is only the second edition; while the 1751 [not 1761] edition of Dilworth's *New Guide*, though the earliest copy there, is actually the thirteenth edition. Both writers must therefore date from the beginning of the Eighteenth Century. Both *Guides* are elementary school-books, dealing mainly with spelling and pronunciation. Dyche has no section on prosody; Dilworth has a single page on it (Part III, Chapter 2), from which I take the following choice excerpt:

"What is an accent?
"A tone or accent denoteth the raising [*sic*] or falling of the voice on a syllable, according to the quantity thereof.
" How many accents are there?
"There are three accents; the long, the short, and the common."

Long and short are exemplified by *mīnd* and *lŏt*; then—

"The common accent hath no regard to the grammatical quantity of a syllable, but being placed over a vowel denotes the tone or stress of the voice to be upon that syllable; as, *plénty*."

This extraordinary confusion between two very different things is by no means confined to Dilworth, and may warn us to expect some loose writing. Both men were London schoolmasters, Dilworth at Wapping, and wrote other books of an educational nature; but that reference in the *Anti-Jacobin* now alone rescues them from oblivion.

Resuming chronological order, I must add a word more about Gildon, with whom we left off. Though he says very little about metre, what he does say is to the point. In his *Complete Art of Poetry* (1718) but ten pages (293-302) are given to versification. He maintains against Bysshe[1] that we have real "numbers" [a great word at this time to denote verse-structure], denies that they are formed merely by accentuation,

[1] Bysshe (*Art of English Poetry*, 1702) may be taken as standing for traditional orthodoxy of the most mechanical kind. See my previous pamphlet, p. 42.

represents feet by musical notes, distinguishes *high*, *loud*, and *long* as qualities of sound, and contends that Sidney's attempt failed through accidental causes. He thinks pronunciation might be noted by something like the "prick'd notes of Musick", and represents whole passages of verse by minims and crotchets. But "our Business is the Art of Poetry, not of Versifying". All this in these ten pages; the rest of the book does not concern us. *The Laws of Poetry . . . explained and illustrated* (1721) consists mainly of criticisms on Buckingham, Roscommon, and another from a general point of view, but in one place (p. 62 *seq.*) he touches on "numbers and rhime", and protests against too great uniformity of cadence. Milton and Dryden are styled "the greatest masters of English versification", Shakespeare a "great but very irregular genius", Ben Jonson "of the most consummate comic genius that ever appeared in the world, ancient or modern" (p. 33). Slight and sketchy as are his remarks, they show independent judgement; but "complete" is not the word one would think of applying to either book.

Pope and Addison, Bentley and Swift, were briefly referred to in my previous booklet, which also examined *An Introduction of the Ancient Greek and Latin Measures into British Poetry* (1737). To these may now be added *Letters concerning Poetical Translations, and Virgil and Milton's Art of Verse*, published anonymously, but ascribed to one William Benson. The edition I have seen is dated 1739, but I believe an earlier appeared in 1713. There is little to report on in these Letters. Their "art of verse" means merely management of rhetorical pauses. Milton's "bottomless pit" cadence is said to be introduced for variety's sake, as any one might be glad to do after writing thousands of regular verses (p. 50). Scansion (Letter VIII) is of the crudest kind, *e. g.*—

Arms and the man I sing.

We have here the "old orthodoxy" untouched by doubt.

These were followed by a group of able though unprofessional prosodists—Pemberton, Manwaring, Harris, Say, and Mason. Henry Pemberton, M.D., Professor of Physics at Gresham College, was author of several medical and scientific treatises, and in the "Advertisement" to his *Observations on Poetry* (1738) apologises for leaving "employments of a quite different nature" to play the critic. Most of his book deals with the substance of epic poems, and contains such excellent remarks as: "The essence of poetry consists so much in making a due impression upon the imagination, that a single word productive of that effect . . . shall give a poetic turn to the plainest thought" (Sect. V, p. 83). His sixth Section or Chapter is headed "Of Versification", and alone concerns us. With a fair show of learning, and much eulogy of "the power of numbers", that is, of "a just and harmonious measure of verse" (p. 106), he nevertheless lays down rules of the very narrowest kind. Like the other members of his group, he refers much to music. "All verse intended for rehearsal [recitation] consists of those species of measures which are directly divisible into a musical movement" (p. 112). He sees that we have in our ordinary English metres no quantitative structure, and notes that we read Sapphic measure to dactylic time, thus—

$$-\cup\cup\,|-- |\cup\cup\cup\cup\,|-- \text{ (p. 107).}$$

Salinas divided this measure into quintuple feet, which is "a division wholly unknown to the modern music" (p. 109; this is no longer true). Instead of quantity, we have only "such a rangement of the words whereby the syllables follow one another with a free and easy cadence" (p. 106). This free and easy cadence [the adjectives have been wickedly misused since his time] he afterwards calls *rhythmus* [*rhythm* was hardly yet an English word], and thus defines it: "rhythmus in speech is every orderly succession of long and short syllables, which will pass agreeably over the ear; but metre and verse is [*sic*] such rhythmus confined within a short compass, and successively repeated" (p. 123). What makes syllables long and short he does not say, and complains that " the measures [*sic*] or rhythmus of our verse has not been so much considered by writers on this subject, as it might have been " (p. 125); but he evidently identifies accentuation with length. Our accent " is constantly attended with an emphasis which implies greater length in the syllable " (p. 126). And his one demand is that every alternate syllable in our "iambic" verse should be accented (p. 130). "Two syllables placed together in the same foot, which must both of necessity be pronounced short, will certainly destroy the harmony of the verse." So he proceeds to suggest how several of Milton's lines could be made to run more smoothly, and censures that poet for ending lines with a syllable which is not "firm and stable" (p. 134). Even Pope's initial trochee violates his rule, for though "any error in the measure of the verse is least offensive toward the beginning of it", yet the error is greater when the second syllable cannot be lengthened (pp. 130–1). In fact, the critic's whole conception of verse is that it should be absolutely and regularly monotonous; the slightest variation of accenting is to him a positive blemish.

We have seen already, when dealing with Bysshe (1702), that this was the fashionable creed of the day. But I cannot refrain from pointing out that Pemberton exemplifies a very common failing of metrists, who are prone to think that any line which violates their rules must be bad. They forget that these rules are and can be drawn only from the prevailing practice of poets, and must be faulty if at variance with this. Modestly as Pemberton puts his criticism, he has evidently no doubt whatever that he is right and Milton wrong. His book originated in an examination of Glover's *Leonidas*, the versification of which is monotonously regular, and therefore—on Pemberton's showing—superior to Milton's. We can see that this position is absurd, because we have outgrown this particular view. But how often are similar mistakes made even now! How often are individual lines pronounced defective or unmetrical because they transgress some fancied canon! I do not claim that poets are infallible, that they never write bad lines. But the presumption certainly is that a great poet understands his business better than any critic. The burden of proof rests with the latter. Milton mingles 'iambic' and 'trochaic' beginnings in his young poems, 'iambic' and 'trochaic' cadences in *Paradise Lost.* This fact should have been made the starting-point of an enquiry which would have shown how and for what reasons English verse differs from Greek. Ample illustration awaits us of how critics persisted in arguing from supposed *a priori* laws, instead of by patient search ascertaining the facts of English prosody; it were well if we could believe this to be altogether a thing of the past. Dr. Pemberton at any rate had the courage of his convictions—convictions shared by very many among his contemporaries and successors.

Of Edward Manwaring, or Mainwaring, D.D., I know only that he was author of several books on Classic verse, one entitled *Stichology* [science of lines]. His treatise on *Harmony and Numbers* (1744) is dedicated to Pepusch the musician, who had introduced him to the writings of Mersennus on ancient poetry. Fired by these, and convinced that "modern music falls infinitely short of antient harmony", he turns to our verse, and finds that "English poetry is from the same principles of harmony as the Greek and Latin iambic metre" (Chap. V, beginning). His definition must be given *verbatim.* "Our Pentametre, or English Heroics, is a seventh in Music, which is made up of a Tierce Minor and a fifth. The Tierce Minor is a tone and a half, and the fifth has three tones and a half, equal in all to ten half tones in the Diatonic scale, or, to ten half feet in the Pentametre" (*ibid.*). What precisely this mysterious deliverance means, I must leave musical scansionists to tell. I gather that he thinks our heroic verse should always divide unequally, and note that a Tierce Minor is equivalent to a trochee or iamb, a Tierce Major to a spondee. He is ready to praise or blame Milton, "our incomparable poet," according as he finds agreement or disagreement with his rules. In an earlier Chapter he illustrates feet not amiss, rightly making *flattery* a tribrach and *slavery* a dactyl (Chap. II); but again (Chap. III) he makes *holy* and *blessèd* equally trochees, and the first word in "*let every man*" a long syllable. I do not think Manwaring's pages need detain us, even if musicians pronounce his formulas satisfactory and intelligible.

James Harris, author of *Hermes*, preluded his philological studies by *Three Treatises* (1744) in a lighter vein on the various Arts, including that "most important of them all", the Art of Happiness! The second treatise, divided into six Chapters, discusses music, painting and poetry in a sketchy fashion, dwelling mostly on their mimetic character. *Onomatopoeia* is noticed in Chap. III, where also he points out that music has at least five lengths of sound (semibreve to semiquaver inclusive), which may be infinitely compounded, while "poetry" has but two. Chap. IV deals with imitation by symbol ("sound significant"), and in Chap. V he concludes that "poetry is on the whole much superior to either of the other mimetic arts" since, while equally accurate as they, it takes subjects of a higher kind. In this fifth Chapter (p. 92, *note*) he contends that "there is a charm in poetry, arising from its numbers only", and illustrates this by quoting the first six lines of *Paradise Lost*, each of which consists of "ten semi-peds", while the natural pause or break varies in position from the third to the seventh half-foot. Beyond these not very profound remarks, I notice nothing whatever bearing on versestructure.

Samuel Say was a fellow-pupil at school with Watts, and dedicated his *Critical Essays* to Richardson the novelist. They came out in his posthumously published volume of Poems, in 1745, but had been written seven years earlier, after reading Pemberton's book, to which he refers without naming it (pp. 140–1). He is all for freedom and variety, for *Paradise Lost* as against *Leonidas*, ridiculing Bentley's contractions and the whole notion that a heroic line must contain only ten syllables. A couplet made up by him in imitation of Chaucerian and Spenserian cadences (quoted in my Bibliography) proved a rare bone of contention to contemporary and subsequent metrists. While thus sound about variations, he is less clear as to what they vary from, and ignores fundamental uniformity. Feet are simply "so many sounds as may be united together in one movement" (p. 102), four being the maximum, and of these he recognises in English six principal ones. Like the others of his group, he represents syllables by musical notes, and he recognises that our pronunciation of Latin substitutes accent for quantity, making two trochees of *miserarum* (p. 107). Still more striking is his description of ordinary English verse as "iambics in accent, yet in real Quantity of Time nearer to spondees" (p. 142). On the whole, Say strikes one as eminently sane and reasonable, while deficient in his conception of what actually constitutes verse. His width of view, and sympathy with Elizabethan liberty, are welcome amid so much that is narrow and perverse, though he omitted to lay any solid foundation on which to erect a definite prosody.

The last member of this group comes nearest to dealing with the actual mechanism of metre. Mason's two *Essays on the Power of Numbers* came out in 1749, but I quote the revised second edition of 1761. Its modest Preface disclaims profound enquiry; his work is merely practical, for the use of students. The Essay on "Poetic Numbers" comes first. These consist of "times, syllables, feet, measures, verse", each after the first being made by a combination of several of the preceding (p. 5). This use of "times" is evidently borrowed from Greek prosody, and he recognises that "custom and accent often ... contract a double Time into a single one, e.g. Th' Infernal Serpent" (p. 7), also that some "Times" are shorter than others, but this makes no "great alteration in the Harmony of Numbers" (p. 8). Into the pitfall of confusion between accent and quantity he tumbles headlong. "By Quantity I mean that space of time, whether long or short, in which any syllable is pronounced; which in English numbers is determined almost altogether by the accent" (p. 9). And so, again— "The proper Accent and Emphasis then is the chief rule that determines the English quantities" (p. 11). Acting on this view, he has no doubt that our ordinary verse is iambic, a short time followed by a long, and scans it by Greek symbols—

$$\breve{I} \text{ lift} \mid \breve{my} \text{ heart} \mid \breve{to} \text{ thee.}$$

Nevertheless, when later he comes to analyse the opening lines of *Paradise Lost*, he admits variations, this being how he renders the famous first line—

$$\breve{Of} \text{ man's} \mid \bar{first} \text{ dis-} \mid \breve{obe} \text{-} \mid \breve{dience,} \text{ and} \mid \breve{the} \text{ fruit.}$$

He sees, however, that our 'quantities' often differ from Latin ones, as when a vowel before another vowel remains long (p. 10). How entirely his English quantities depend on accent appears from his making *abominate* a double iamb (*cf.* pp. 17–19). His most interesting section begins with Chap. VII (p. 20 *seq.*; the Chapters are very short), on the musical proportion of feet. Again following Greek prosody, he classifies feet according as they divide equally or unequally. Equal feet (dactyl, anapaest, *etc.*) "are in proportion of the unison in music". Iambs and trochees are "in proportion of the Octave or Diapason, which is the most perfect chord in music". Feet of sesquialterate ratio (3 : 2 or 2 : 3) "answer to the Diapente or fifth in Music, which is the next most perfect concord". He lays down quite clearly (p. 22) that feet in verse correspond to bars in music, and that equal and unequal times in verse answer to the common and triple times of music. The musician's "beating time" thus represents the metrist's "arsis and thesis", which terms he uses in their true Greek sense,[1] referring for justification to "Chambers's Cyclopaedia" [for the Eighteenth Century, too, had its so-named repertory of knowledge]. By these he scans all lines, holding that a foot must not exceed one arsis and thesis, and that four-syllable feet are impossible in English [why?]. But he has no objection to trisyllabic feet in heroic verse, approves Say's couplet already referred to, and quotes as a parallel Milton's "many a dolorous groan". When, however, it comes to that other line of Milton's—

> In their triple degrees, regions to which ...

his indulgence is exhausted. Like any Dryasdust critic, he pronounces this "no verse, much less iambic" (Chap. XIV, p. 58). For the most part, however, he is liberal and reasonable. As against Pemberton, he maintains that trochee followed by iamb is legitimate in our strictest verse, and he recognises dropped syllables in triple-time verse, e.g.—

$$\overset{\wedge\;\;\smile\;\;-}{\text{My time,}} \mid \overset{\smile\;\;\smile\;\;-}{\text{O ye Mu-}}\text{ses, was hap-}\mid\overset{\smile\smile\;\;-}{\text{pi}}\text{ly spent,}$$

where he has no doubt that the feet are anapaests. *Caesura* (Chap. X) he thinks is as necessary in English heroic as in Latin hexameter verse, "and hath as many variations"; but he does not explain its rationale in either. Of natural quantity in English words he takes no account whatever; every accented syllable is long, every unaccented short, but when two long or two short syllables meet in a foot he simply records the fact, and does not offer any explanation of how their meeting is possible.

The second Essay, on "Prosaic Numbers", contains

---

[1] In Greek prosody, the *thesis* or down-stroke indicated a strong syllable, the *arsis* or up-stroke a weak one. Latin grammarians, oddly enough, inverted the terms. This mistake passed into English use, and still survives in many grammars, but is being generally discarded. Whenever the terms occur in an English treatise, it is necessary to know whether they are employed in the orthodox Greek or the heterodox Latin sense.

little that is material. In it he scans many passages of both verse and prose by – and ᴗ, and remarks that our modern verse is as much too strict in its rules as our "antient" verse was too lax (Chap. VII, p. 47). Incidentally he observes that Greek accent-marks were probably intended " to regulate the tone or key of the voice, not the stress or force of it" (Chap. III, p. 25). On the whole, Mason must be credited with recognising, more fully than any other of his group, the close analogy that exists between verse and music; and he is quite against the Bysshian attempt to reduce all feet to one pattern (*Poetic Numbers*, p. 52, *note*). He wants but a better fundamental theory of verse-structure to be a sympathetic and intelligent critic. Any theory which, like his, starts by assuming that every "unaccented" syllable in English verse is equally "short", every accented one equally long, is bound to wreck itself against the rocks of plain fact; and some of Mason's scansions are astounding. Yet, after all deductions, his two Essays (for the third, on "Elocution", is entirely negligible) stand out above the ruck of common prosodies, and must be remembered as one of the earliest attempts to vindicate for verse its rhythmical basis and relations.[1]

The relative shortness of this Chapter may excite surprise. Virtually, all that has gone before, from the little treatise of Gascoigne onward—setting aside quantitative verse as a thing by itself—may be regarded as belonging to it. Three Centuries of English verse did hardly more than produce the "old orthodoxy" of prosodical criticism, varied latterly by a few faint protests. Serious attempts to analyse that verse all date from after 1750, and will demand, when reached, examination at considerably greater length.

[1] He speaks of "rhythmus", whence our word "rhime", now assigned a special meaning of its own, though Milton used it to mean verse of any kind—

Things unattempted yet in prose or rhime.

Cf. Poetic Numbers, p. 13, *note*, with its Classic references.

CHAPTER II

RESISTANCE AND REBELLION

1750–1800

WE now pass into the latter half of the Eighteenth Century, far more fruitful and interesting metrically than the former. It will be remembered that already, by 1750, a new spirit was awakening in English poetry; life was stirring in the dry bones of Classicism. Gray, Collins, Warton and others were groping, however stiffly and sentimentally, after Romantic motives. Cowper was already writing his "Early Poems", among them a piece of 'sapphics' which I omitted to mention in its due place, but have now noted among *addenda* (see Appendix A). The way was being prepared for that great outburst and upheaval which is called the Romantic Reaction. In criticism, too, old creeds were being examined, old shibboleths discarded. Criticism, however, as a rule follows rather than precedes creation, and we need not be surprised to find the Bysshe school of prosody still potent for many a day. As a matter of fact, the first book that meets us in the new Half-Century is by one of its most uncompromising supporters, the great Dr. Samuel Johnson.

In my hurriedly arranged Bibliography, I erroneously stated that the first volume of Johnson's *Dictionary* appeared in 1749. That was the date when his prospectus was issued; the work itself, though he had hoped to complete it within three years, came out in two massive folio volumes in 1755. To Vol. I was prefixed a "History of the English language", and a "Grammar of the English tongue", the latter ending with a Section on "Prosody".

The Grammar underwent several corrections in subsequent editions, but I have not noticed any material change in the Prosody Section. It is short, clear, straightforward. The first part deals merely with rules of pronunciation, and one sentence alone in it requires note by us: "Pronunciation is just, when . . . every syllable has its proper accent, or, which in English versification is the same, its proper quantity." Then he comes to "laws of versification". Recognising only iambic and trochaic verse—except that anapaestic is mentioned by way of afterthought as a "very quick and lively measure", in which "a syllable is often retrenched from the first foot"—he makes syllabic uniformity the basis and ideal. "In all these [iambic] measures the accents are to be placed on even syllables [in trochaic on odd]; and every line considered by itself is more harmonious, as this rule is more strictly observed. The variations necessary to pleasure belong to the art of poetry, not to the rules of grammar." After exemplifying various lengths and combinations of rhymed and unrhymed lines (the latter being represented by one casual reference to Addison's blank verse), he concludes: "Our versification admits of few licenses, except a *synaloepha* or elision of *e* in *the* before a vowel, as *th' eternal*; and more rarely of *o* in *to*, as *t' accept*; and a *synaeresis*, by which two short vowels coalesce into one syllable, as *question, special*; or a word is contracted by the expulsion of a short vowel before a liquid, as *av'rice, temp'rance*."

That is literally all! No enquiry into facts, no historical or philosophical treatment, no appeal to either reason or authority. Had this dictator been asked whence his "laws" were derived, what could he have answered? Not that they were drawn from the practice of our chief writers; Shakespeare and Milton laugh them to scorn, and it is noteworthy that he neither quotes from nor refers to these poets. Nor from the inherent nature of verse; no such analysis was even attempted. Probably he would have said that they were rules observed by the "best wits" of his day. To these gentlemen our Elizabethan singers were barbarous and uncouth. Proper verse began with Denham and Waller, made great advance under Dryden, reached its climax in Pope. To us, such a view is almost unthinkable. But even granting its truth, Johnson's rule is still too narrow. It is by no means a fact that Pope's best lines, "considered by themselves," are harmonious in the ratio of their regularity of accentuation; rather is the contrary true. Johnson's own verse, vigorous and strenuous if not very highly inspired, belies his critical precept. No English poet (unless Glover deserve the name) ever sanctioned by his practice this monstrous canon, which owes its conception and promulgation to grammarians alone. So artificial and unreal had our theoretic prosody become. Divorced from fact, it invented imaginary "laws", which were broken by even our most "correct" verse-writers, and whose observance would have killed all life in our poetry. Since Johnson's ideas probably still sway a good many people's minds, and shape to some extent the teaching of our grammars, it is needful here to protest against them entirely. They are utterly fallacious as a test of good verse, and can produce no vouchers for their pretence of authority. Unfortunately, Johnson was neither the first nor the last critic to substitute assertion for argument and imagination for fact. In any other science such procedure would be scouted; one does not see why an exception should be made in regard of prosody.

I find nothing else to cite published during the decade 1750–60. But here should be mentioned some notes which may belong to it. When the poet Gray died in 1771, his posthumously published papers included certain fragments entitled "Observations on English metre". These had been written several years before, to form part of a History of English Poetry projected but abandoned by him, as related in Mason's *Memoir*, Section V. In spite of the title, they contain little which bears on our subject. Gray did, indeed, purpose to give a full historical sketch of our poetry, commencing with the "Scaldic, British, and Saxon" sources which gave rise to a literature whose actual beginning he dated from Chaucer; and he "made many elaborate disquisitions into the origin of rhyme, and that variety of metre to be found in the writings of our ancient poets". The fragments which were printed justify this description, and show Gray to have been a careful and sympathetic student of our early verse. But they contain nothing definitely bearing on verse-structure. He enumerates various forms of versification, and declares his inability to understand what is meant by the "riding rhyme" of older critics.[1] He abandoned his task on finding that Warton [*infra*, 1774] was similarly engaged, and made over some of his memoranda to him. Probably, therefore, the bulk of his notes may have been made shortly before or after the year 1760.

The second decade of the Half-Century, on the other hand, was marked by several publications important for us, particularly those which appeared in the year 1762. Foremost of these comes a book in which prosody takes only a secondary place. '*Foster on Accent*' was long reckoned a standard work, its first edition as above being speedily followed by a much enlarged edition a year later, while the most useful and accessible one, that of 1820, contains further additions as well as Gally's two Dissertations. Dr. Henry Gally, or Galley, a versatile and accomplished divine, had published in 1754 a *Dissertation* against pronouncing ancient Greek according to its accent-marks. Dr. John Foster, sometime head master at Eton, and a good Classical scholar, was at first inclined to accept Gally's view, but finally dissented, and wrote his *Essay on the Different Nature of Accent and Quantity* to prove that Greek should be so pronounced. Gally replied in a second *Dissertation* which appeared while Foster's

---

[1] This term was applied to 'ten-syllable couplets' like those of Chaucer's *Canterbury Pilgrims*, as distinguished from statelier quatrains and stanzas. For long such couplets were considered unfit for serious themes—an idea in Gray's time hardly comprehensible, though he himself wisely preferred quatrains for his famous *Elegy*.

second edition was passing through the press, but in time to let Foster append a "Review of some passages in the preceding Essay, in reply to Dr. G.'s second Dissertation". "Dr. G." is Foster's usual way of referring to his opponent, whose Dissertations were published anonymously after a rather tiresome fashion of the time, even when the authorship was no secret.[1] The dispute between the two authors, therefore, referred primarily to Greek and not to English. Foster contended that it was theoretically possible to accentuate a short syllable without lengthening it; Gally maintained the opposite view. I referred briefly to this controversy before (*English Metrists*, 1903, p. 46), and need not now dwell on it so far as Greek is concerned. For us the main thing to notice is how both disputants agreed that in English speech an acute accent involved prolongation of time. Foster, indeed, recognises that such an accent may rest on a short syllable, as in "privy" (1820 edition, p. 25, *note*; this note added in second edition); but even so he thinks it gives additional length to that syllable. He only maintains that it need not have done so in Greek; that there a short syllable might have its tone raised without any alteration of "quantity". He even believes that he can illustrate this in his own pronunciation of Greek (p. 269). But he entirely agrees with Gally that, in our ordinary English way of speaking, "*elevation* doth not commonly subsist . . . without a *prolongation* too" (p. 140, and *passim*); that all accented syllables in English "sound long to the ear" (Gally, p. 374).

"Accent," according to Foster, means merely elevation or depression of the voice (p. 3). All through his discussion he distinguishes between accent and quantity [pitch and duration]. These are closely united, yet quite distinct (p. 7); and "are equally founded in the very

---

[1] Sometimes no author's name is given on a title-page, though the Preface or dedication is subscribed with either initials or full name. And sometimes, to make matters worse, such a book will be referred to in other books by the publisher's name instead of the author's.

nature of the human voice, are necessary and inseparable from it" (p. 5). To the third element, *force*, he makes no reference, except in a passage toward the end of his first Chapter where he terms it "spirit or emphasis", identifies it with aspiration, and adds that it "is very distinct from accent and quantity, though occasionally joined with them" (p. 10). Our syllabic accent, according to him, has nothing to do with this last, but is a combination of higher tone and longer duration. Therefore the first syllables of *liberty, heavily, honestly, character* are all marked "long" by him; the second syllable of *solicit* equally with the second syllable of *mistaking*; the first syllable of *folly* is long, though less so than that of *dowry* (pp. 16-17). While asserting this of English pronunciation, he finds it different in Scotch, Welsh, and Irish. The Scot, he declares, accentuates (and thereby lengthens) the last syllable of *majesty*, while still prolonging the first syllable; and similarly deals with the last syllables of *human, subject, summons, monarchs* (pp. 25 and 35). The Scotch keep or rather increase our quantity, but alter our accent; the Irish observe both, but with a greater degree of "spirit or emphasis"; the Welsh keep our quantity and alter the accent, adding a peculiar manner of voice (pp. 38-9). He stoutly contends (Chap. II) that modern languages have "natural quantity", instancing the word *Chrultznitz* (p. 28; in first edition *Grotzky*); yet he says that the first syllable of *strengthen* "hath as quick and easy a pronunciation as the first syllable of *oozy*" (p. 25). On the whole, his view seems to be that length, in English syllables, depends mainly on accent. "Those syllables which I call long receive a peculiar stress of voice from their acute accent. .... They are elevated; but they are lengthened too. .... We English cannot readily elevate a syllable without lengthening it" (*ibid.*). Surprise must be felt that a writer who could so accurately distinguish pitch from duration, and so clearly see that the two were separable, was yet content to mark as alike "long" the first syllable of *private* and the first syllable of *privy*.

Foster's remarks on English verse will be found in his third Chapter (largely added to in second edition). He makes our common verse *iambic*, our heroic line "trimeter brachycatalectic", boldly scanning thus:

$$\breve{\text{An}} \, \bar{\text{honest}} \, \breve{\text{man's}} \mid \breve{\text{the}} \, \bar{\text{noblest}} \, \breve{\text{work}} \mid \breve{\text{of}} \, \bar{\text{God}}.$$

But he admits three-syllable feet, making *visible* a dactyl [!], while other combinations of syllables yield tribrachs and anapaests, as "would appear much oftener, with propriety and grace, if abbreviations were more avoided". He praises the "nervous springiness" of Pope's initial trochee, and in defiance of Johnson asserts that Pope's most regular lines are his weakest in point of versification. The trochee may occur anywhere save in the last foot [Milton would have had something to say to this restriction]; and he finds one even where his principles would seem to require a pyrrhic, *e.g.*—

$$\bar{\text{As}} \, \breve{\text{full}}, \mid \breve{\text{as}} \, \bar{\text{perfect}}, \mid \breve{\text{in}} \, \breve{\text{a}} \, \bar{\text{hair}} \mid \breve{\text{as}} \, \bar{\text{heart}}.$$

The pyrrhic he also recognises, as in the last two syllables of *eternity* or *philosophy* (all the foregoing in pp. 29-31). "The admission of so many different measures into our common verse gives it a variety... not to be exceeded, if equalled, in any of the ancient kinds of metre" (p. 32). But the comparative shortness of our heroic line, and the infrequency of dactyls in our language, not to speak of spondees, prevent our verse from reproducing the cadence of ancient hexameter. "For the most part the long and short syllables of our language are alternate" (p. 33). (Gally, on the other hand, thinks that English abounds in dactyls, but "hath no trisyllable that maketh an anapaest": p. 319.) Singularly enough, Foster thus scans a trisyllabic line (p. 34)—

$$\breve{\text{With}} \, \bar{\text{honour}} \mid \breve{\text{and}} \, \bar{\text{glory}} \mid \breve{\text{through}} \, \bar{\text{trouble}} \mid \breve{\text{and}} \, \bar{\text{danger}}-$$

where the cadence might equally well be termed dactylic or anapaestic, and where two short syllables intervene between each long one. With more consistency he makes (next page) the following line consist of *cretics*—

   – ᴗ –   – ᴗ –   – ᴗ –   – ᴗ –
O the sweet | country life | blest with health | peace and ease.

But his most remarkable contention (p. 35 *seq.*) is that the essence of English verse is "founded in quantity alone", not upon accent, though the latter "jointly with quantity doth direct it". In support of this he quotes the couplet—

> All human things are subject to decay,
> And when fate summons, monarchs must obey—

and makes the astounding assertion that, though a Scotsman should accentuate the final syllables of the words *human, subject, summons, monarchs*, the metre would still "essentially subsist". What metre would remain after such violation of rhythm I am as unable to imagine, as I am to pronounce on the accuracy of Foster's description of Scottish pronunciation in his day. It seems to me that the metrical cadence would be entirely destroyed by such mispronunciation, and that what "subsists" is only a possibility of restoring that cadence by proper pronunciation. In what sense "quantity" would be unaltered, either on Foster's showing or any other, I fail to see. Yet he goes on to say that while metre depends on quantity alone, "rhythm is in its nature more complex, and seems to comprehend accent with quantity"; justifying this by saying that an English line needs no caesural division, because with us "the long times and acute tones coincide", so that such a line as—

> Heroes, repel attacks, command success,

is good rhythmically as well as metrically. Even were this passage less hesitating and vague than it is, I do not think that any intelligible account of the basis of English verse can be extracted from it; nor, perhaps, is it altogether reasonable to look for one from a writer whose main concern was to teach the true nature of the ancient Greek accent.

It may be added that Foster freely uses the anglicised word *rhythm*, being one of the earliest writers to do so; and that Gally speaks several times of *stress*, though not identifying it with force. Primatt, another writer who joined the fray with a book called *Accentus Redivivi* (1764), writes the former word as "rythm". The further fortunes of the Greek-accent controversy do not concern us, though we shall find it obtruding itself in several later studies of English verse. The fashion of printing Greek without accent-marks had a very prolonged existence. After the end of the first quarter of the Nineteenth Century, it appears in a book by the Public Orator at Oxford [*vide infra*, 1827], and in publications of the Galignani press of Paris; at one time it bid fair to become universal.[1]

From Scotland came, in the same year 1762, a work of much larger scope, the first of many attempts to consider scientifically the whole field of artistic labour. Henry Home or Hume, a judge in Court of Session under the title of Lord Kames (sometimes spelt Kaims by his contemporaries), published in 1762 his *Elements of Criticism* in three octavo volumes. A second edition was called for two years later, and others followed; that of 1820, in one volume, can still be procured. The twenty-five Chapters of which the book consists are divided into Sections, and the whole arrangement is admirably clear. Whereas "Bossu, a celebrated French critic," rests his rules merely on the practice of Homer and Virgil, supported by the authority of Aristotle, Kames seeks to discover principles, working upward from facts (*Introduction*). The promise of this beginning is to some extent fulfilled, as a glance at the chapter-headings will show. The style may be somewhat stiff and dry, the matter somewhat verbose and platitudinous; but the scientific spirit is fairly awake. In each depart-

---

[1] I have since noticed that accent-marks are omitted in Leigh Hunt's *Imagination and Fancy*, published by Smith, Elder & Co. in 1844. Can a later instance be quoted? Peacock's *Gryll Grange* might furnish one.

ment the endeavour is to get at facts, not merely to repeat traditional phrases.

Our particular subject is reached in his Chap. XVIII on "Beauty of Language", particularly in its fourth Section on "Versification". Noteworthy hints occur in the other three Sections, as indeed throughout the book; in the second Section he assumes that *feet* are pronounced "with a sensible interval between each" (p. 249 of 1824 edition, to which my references are made), and the last paragraphs of the third Section deal with pronunciation. He distinguishes five qualities of sound, according to which it can be *harsh, long, high, loud, quick,* or the opposites. In syllables the first and second are fixed by component elements, the others are at the speaker's option. Such matters, however, belong chiefly to the delivery of verse; its actual formation is considered in Section 4. Here we find at first somewhat of Johnsonian rigour. The number of syllables in a line is assumed not to vary. Verse and prose alike please by intermixing long and short syllables; verse differs from prose only in doing this more perfectly, and is "subjected to certain inflexible laws". Pope's *Rape of the Lock* is held up as being, "in point of versification, the most complete performance in the English language." Five things are said to be of importance in all verse, *viz.* (1) the number of syllables in a line; (2) their different lengths, *i. e.* "the difference of time taken in pronouncing" each; (3) the arrangement of these syllables into words; (4) the "pauses or stops in pronouncing"; (5) "the pronouncing syllables in a high or low tone." The first three of these are "obviously essential to verse". Two short syllables are "precisely equal" to one long; and this rule holds good in all verse. The fourth and fifth "things" he also finds in both ancient and modern verse. Having thus laid his foundation (all this is in the first two or three pages of § 4), he next considers the structure of ancient hexameter verse, rejecting the usual division into feet—which he deems a mere invention of grammarians (p. 276, *note*)—and substituting a constructive canon of his own formulation. Then (p. 282) he comes back to English verse. Our heroic line he treats in the same way. While discarding feet, he demands absolute succession of long and short syllables, condemning such a line as—

This nymph, to the destruction of mankind,

because *the* is not a long syllable. Structurally considered, he allows only two variations from iambic uniformity: the initial trochee, and the final extra syllable. (*Cf.* p. 276, *note*, last paragraph.) The occasional use of an "Alexandrine" is also pronounced legitimate (p. 282). Variety he would have provided simply by dividing the line at different points, and he enumerates four types of heroic line, according as the "capital pause" comes after the fourth, fifth, sixth, or seventh syllable (p. 295). But, just as one has concluded that his view is wholly restricted to the Popian couplet he goes on to blank verse (p. 300), and surprises us by preferring it. Shakespeare's blank verse, indeed, he dismisses as "a sort of measured prose", "perfectly well adapted to the stage" (p. 301); but Milton's contains "the richest melody as well as the sublimest sentiments", and he exalts it not only above rhyming couplets but in some respects above Greek or Latin hexameter verse. The passage which he quotes, curiously enough, contains two instances of the very fault objected to in Pope; but these pass unnoticed. It need hardly be said that each of Milton's lines is made to contain ten syllables by writing *th' eastern, temp'rate, etc.*; yet *aëry* [*sic*] is not altered to *airy*. The "great defect of Milton's versification, otherwise admirable," is said to be a "want of coincidence between the pauses of the sense and sound" (p. 303). A short explanation of the inability of English verse to reproduce "hexameter" melody, and some sensible remarks about rhyme, conclude the Section.

This analysis is certainly too narrow. A view which sees in Shakespeare's lines only "measured prose", and in Pope's best verse habitual incorrectness, may safely be pronounced faulty. Yet, on the other hand, there is vigour and sense in Kames's criticism, despite its cramping theory. His *obiter dicta* are usually sound. He sees clearly that accent is not a structural but an illuminative element. Identifying it with tone (pp. 271, 275), he notes that "an accent considered with respect to sense is termed *emphasis*" (p. 293, *note*). He feels how vague is our perception of quantity. "Every language has syllables that may be pronounced long or short at pleasure; but the English above all abounds in syllables of that kind" (p. 282). Even his rigid doctrine of caesural pause, and the way it is reinforced by accent (p. 295), while too universally stated, is founded on observation. Our heroic line does naturally tend to break into two sections, less often equal than unequal; but we have no right to make this a law, for our chief poets often disregard it. So, too, even Pope sometimes neglects the pause or break at the end of a couplet; this licence, however, Kames does not wholly condemn (pp. 290, 291), while to the running on of sense at the end of a blank verse line he is altogether tolerant (pp. 300-1). Also, though recognising four regular places of capital pause, he admires the boldness with which this rule is disregarded by Milton, and occasionally by Pope (p. 292). He is ready to admit licences "where the sense or expression requires a variation"; but he regards them as cases where "the melody may justly be sacrificed" (*ibid.*), instead of as instances of a higher melody. English verse he considers decidedly superior to French, through its variety of pause (p. 302), and he censures Boileau for letting sentences end with the first line of a couplet (p. 300, *note*); but he admits the greater liveliness of French speech (p. 295, *note*). In one place he strangely professes not to know if our language contains any word of five syllables (p. 283). His prime contention that "a musical pause ought never to be placed where a pause is excluded by the sense" (p. 291) must be pronounced too sweeping, and his condemnation of scores of lines in consequence altogether too dogmatic.

With a better theory, Kames would have made a critic of high quality; but it is only too evident throughout his book that as yet English prosody had never faced the whole facts of verse as exhibited by our best poets.

Ireland vied with Scotland in study of our subject. Sheridan published in 1762 some remarkable theories about accent, but as his chief work on English verse appeared in 1775 I reserve consideration of him till then, asking readers to remember that his influence as writer and teacher was at work during the years which intervened. A fourth book dated 1762, however, also had Hibernian antecedents. Daniel Webb, Irish-born though Cambridge-bred, published his *Remarks on the Beauties of Poetry*, as two years earlier he had published *An Inquiry into the Beauties of Painting*, and as seven years later he published *Observations on the Correspondence between Poetry and Music*. All three were reprinted, with other papers not to our purpose, in a quarto volume entitled *Miscellanies*, by the late Daniel Webb, Esq. (London, 1802; my references are to this edition), and may be considered together; the more so, as the interval between 1762 and 1769 produced no outstanding work on our subject. The first two are in dialogue form, not without dramatic liveliness, especially in the second, which opens with an entirely imaginary reference to "a gentleman who has just left us". Seven dialogues discuss Painting, in the first treatise; in the second, on Poetry, there are but two. Beginning with a spirited defence of Shakespeare and Milton, he ridicules the monotony of Pope, and extols the superior variety of blank verse (pp. 103-14). Then, after some censure of sibilants, he goes on to treat of expressiveness in verse; the remainder of the first dialogue, and the whole of the second, deal either with this or with the more general attractions of verse.

But much more important, in itself and for us, was Webb's volume of 1769. In this Essay—for such is its form—he makes a real attempt to consider verse-structure. Beginning with more general questions, he reaches this subject in pp. 197-222. There must, he thinks, be quantities in verse; but whether these "are governed by an invariable prosody, or flow from the impression of the sense and accent, the effects will be much the same in all parallel movements". Therefore English and Greek lines of similar length produce identical effects[1], even though in our case "the quantities of syllables are but the variations of accent". Greek verse, like ours, founds on contrasting grave and acute accent; a dactyl does but repeat the second stroke of a trochee, an anapaest the first of an iamb. Like Kames, he thinks no language is incapable of metre, unless there be one whose syllables are all pronounced in equal times, which some say is the case in Hebrew, but this he does not believe (p. 200). On the contrary, he thinks the root of "natural prosody" is the same in all known languages (p. 203). In English verse (p. 204 *seq.*) he recognises feet, but will not admit a dactyl where such scansion would leave an adjacent foot of one syllable, as in "And | vindicate". He praises the spirited effect of trochee followed by iamb. "When an enforced or ascending accent strikes on a monosyllable, the vibrations continue, as in the chord of a musical instrument, after the impression or articulation hath ceased; especially when the stroke is succeeded by a pause." "As our accents are modes of expression," sound is influenced by sense; "where accent and structure co-operate," they may give some additional length to a syllable. "It should seem that the mechanism of the Greek verse took its rise, and derived its advantages, from the opposite principle." (p. 205). For this reason monosyllables are not necessarily heavy with us; "the feeblest and heaviest lines in our language are those which are overcharged with polysyllables." (*ibid.*). So, later (pp. 212-13), he says that two monosyllables are as good as any dissyllable, and two dissyllables as any quadrisyllable; we

[1] Webb's illustrations of this thesis—"I fain would sing of Cadmus," *etc.*—are quoted by almost every subsequent metrist of the Century.

have subdued our polysyllables, in verse, to the tenor of a monosyllabic rhythmus, although music tends to shorten the mid-syllable of a trisyllabic word. Dealing with "imitation of classical rhythmus", he remarks that with us "the accent governs the measure, while the sense, in conjunction with the laws of musical succession, governs the accent" (p. 209).[1] Before we could write hexameters of Classic type, we must recast our language. Finally, dealing with the "separation of Music from Poetry", he is puzzled "how their union could have subsisted after the institution of measures founded on artificial quantities" (p. 212). ("The movements of prose hold a middle course, between a total neglect, and an absolute strictness of measure": *ibid.*, *note.*) All artificial prosody thwarts musical accent. "Modern lyrical poesy is a school for painters, not for musicians" (p. 215). As the spirit of expression declines, a taste for description begins; this is seen both in verse and music. Imitative description is only good when striking; "procumbit humi bos" is trivial, Milton's Behemoth sublime. The more syllables we can get into the same time, the greater impression is produced of lightness and rapidity; but an "Alexandrine" is not lighter or swifter than a "pentameter".

Webb's ideas seemed upsetting to his contemporaries, and are often animadverted on by later critics. To us they seem amateurish and tentative, yet possessed of a certain freshness and individuality. There is an attempt to look at verse with his own eyes, not through pedantic spectacles; to recognise that verse and music are akin, and that metre is something more than a mere counting of syllables. He does not define accent, rather takes it for granted, and does not spend time over caesural pauses. It is the actual structure of verse, not merely its delivery, that engages his attention, though he is aware that sound is often regulated by sense. If he does

---

[1] "Strong passions . . . were never destined to creep through monotonous parallels; they call for a more liberal rhythmus" (p. 208).

not do much to determine the questions he raises, he at least deserves the credit of raising them for others to settle. He is a pioneer in the search for a more rational prosody than that which made verse be mainly an exercise in arithmetic. The frequent references to his books show that they made their mark on men's minds.

Little of consequence can be cited between 1762 and 1769. Three publications only during this time need be named. Dr. John Brown, Vicar [according to the British Museum Catalogue] of Newcastle-on-Tyne, printed at Dublin in 1763 a small book entitled *A Dissertation on the Rise, Union, and Power, the Progressions, Separations, and Corruptions, of Poetry and Music*. Though this learned treatise begins and ends with a poem by the author, and though its erudition ranges from Greek and Latin writers to Snorro Sturleson and Lafiteau's Iroquois, it is taken up almost entirely with ancient and modern music, and deals very little indeed with verse,[1] though he does speak of "rythm [*sic*] or measure" (p. 29, and elsewhere). In the same year, 1763, the *British Magazine* contained a paper by Oliver Goldsmith now included among his "Miscellaneous Essays", on "Versification", to which I have before referred [*English Metrists*, 1903, p. 50] on account of its allusion to pseudo-Classic metres. Otherwise there is little new or noteworthy either in this Essay or in its neighbours, which merely repeat current ideas, and utter vague phrases like "the words we term *emphatical* are such as by their sound express the sense they are intended to convey" (Essay XV, on "Poetry distinguished from other writing"). In this same Essay he observes that versification is not the sole criterion that distinguishes poetry from prose, another being "its own peculiar expression"; and in the preceding one (on the "Origin of poetry"), after starting with the doubtful axiom "poetry sprang from ease", he goes on to draw a vigorous picture of the tribal emotions and

---

[1] It is, however, very often referred to by subsequent metrists.

acts of worship in which verse almost certainly had its origin, whatever we may say about the origin of "poetry". But these are commonplaces, as are most of his remarks on *metaphors* and *hyperbole* (Essays XVI and XVII); while the short paper on versification (Essay XVIII) contains no outstanding feature. Verse is still "an harmonious arrangement of long and short syllables", our verse containing feet similar to those of Classic verse; " to assert that modern poetry has no feet, is a ridiculous absurdity." The real difference is merely that "rhythmus or number" in ancient verse relates to the feet, and in modern to the syllables. So with his remarks on "pause and accent". It is all just what others have said, expressed with Goldsmith's delightful ease and clearness, and without any apparent misgiving. The speculations of heterodox critics have left no trace on his teaching, which repeats with tranquil assurance doctrines much more familiar than convincing.

In 1765 was published a treatise [not mentioned in my Bibliography] by one John Rice, of whom I know nothing, entitled *An Introduction to the Art of Reading with Propriety and Elegance* (8vo, London, Tonson). This might be supposed a mere elocutionary manual, but several Sections deal with prosody. Say, "Kaims," Mason, Harris, Sheridan are referred to by name and criticised, the last with severity, though Rice agrees with him in dissociating accent from tone. English verse is discussed in the last three "Sections" of Chap. II more especially, without very definite result, except to protest against pedantic rules. Johnson's tenet is directly challenged; "from what Principle of Nature" does it follow that regular alternation is preferable to irregular (pp. 110-11; *cf.* 153)? Classic laws of prosody do not apply in English; to measure our verse by dactyls and spondees reminds him of an Oxford wag "selling strong beer by the ell" (p. 116). Milton's harmony is exalted above the "mechanical form of versification" used by Dryden, Pope, and Addison (pp. 156-7). When, however, he passes from criticism to construction, his teaching is indefinite. "The harmony of verse principally consists . . . in the consonance or affinity which the words of such verse bear to their meaning" (p. 115). Accent does not determine quantity, yet quantity is a compound of accent and time (p. 116). "Accent and emphasis do not actually give time, but supply the want of it in the composition of metrical feet" (*ibid.*). Feet, however, need not be equal, except when accompanied by music (p. 137). The mechanism of English verse is a mixture, "founded on heterogeneous principles" (p. 165); he does not even think that equal lines are necessary to blank verse (p. 179), and makes its harmony depend on "the quick succession of a few flowing syllables" (p. 176). In fact, he ends by almost denying the necessity of any structural form at all. These revolutionary ideas seem to have excited less notice than might have been expected, but the fact of their being put forward at all is remarkable, and contrasts curiously with Goldsmith's easy conservatism.

The third last decade of the Eighteenth Century was richer far than its predecessors as regards metrical criticism. In passing may be mentioned a *History of the Science and Practice of Music* (5 vols. 4to, 1771), published anonymously after the prevailing fashion, but known to be by Johnson's biographer Sir John Hawkins; mentioned, merely because its "Preliminary Discourse" is so often referred to (generally without naming the author) by metrical writers when treating of the "principles and power of harmony". And then we come to a bright little book on *Vocal Sounds* (1773), written by Abraham Tucker under the pseudonym of "Edward Search". This I have already mentioned [*Metrists*, 1903, p. 50 *seq.*] in connection with its author's attempts at quantitative verse. Of ordinary English measures he says little, being content to regard them as mainly "iambic" (pp. 50-2). His merit and originality depend on his clear statement of phonetic principle, that indispensable basis of a true prosody. He is, indeed, bewildered by the false doctrine that a vowel followed by two consonants was sounded long in Latin, and troubles himself about this to no purpose. But he states plainly that we have quantitative difference of vowel-sound in English, instancing *wood* and *wooed*, *have* and *halve*, *Mary* and *merry*, *etc.* (pp. 9, 21). He reprobates our method of teaching spelling, since *a. n. d.* should stand for *aind*, *g.o.n.e* for *jony* (p. 11); and desires symbols like those since invented. He sees that speaking, not writing, determines quantity, and that a doubled consonant produces no sensation of length in English (p. 65). Later (p. 89 *seq.*) he deals with prose, which also has measure, but in it " the art of periodic measure consists ... in approaching as near as possible, without falling into, direct verse " (p. 93). Pope's Homer he finds " cloying " (p. 98), and he notes that " we can still make shift to read Chaucer " (p. 115). Further quotation is needless, but Tucker must always be remembered as one of the first, if not the very first, to apply phonetic method to our verse, to point out that verse-structure depends on sound not on spelling, and thus to pave the way for a more adequate and helpful conception of metre.

Very different is another little book, also published in 1773, and also referred to by me before [*Metrists*, p. 52]. *The Elements of Speech*, by John Herries, A.M., has an ambitious title, which its 259 pages hardly justify. The first part deals with voice-formation and organs of speech, the second with qualities and " command " of speech. In the third Chapter of this Part II he remarks that " an absurd notion has long prevailed " according to which accented syllables are long and unaccented short (p. 123); but the hopes raised by this promising dictum prove illusory. He frankly admits that he does not understand what 'quantity' means, either in Latin or English (*ibid.*), and excuses himself from discussing the nature of accents in either tongue (p. 171), his aim being wholly practical. Reading Latin verse entirely by its prose accents, he finds no fundamental difference of metre. " I see no reason why the same accents, intervals, pauses, and cadences that occur in any Greek or Latin verse may not be introduced into the English" (p. 185). Accordingly, as an equivalent for

Te, dulcis coniux, te solo in litore secum,

he proposes the following—

Thee, lovely partner, thee only he constantly chanted;

and similarly travesties two Sapphic stanzas from Horace. "Upon the whole, it appears a very easy task to reduce into English the exact measure of every verse or stanza in Homer, Sappho, Anacreon, Horace, or even Pindar, so far as it [*sic*] regards the arrangement of the accented syllables"; but he does not think this "would greatly promote the harmony of our compositions" (p. 187). The purport of quoting these remarks is to show that their author, like most people still, read Latin verse to English measure, his total ignorance of quantity bringing about the same result as their substitution of accent for quantity. It was natural that he should think our triple-time verse represented the flow of ancient hexameter; but it is extraordinary that trained scholars should think so. Otherwise there is nothing noteworthy in this book, and we must pass on to matter of greater importance.

James Burnet, Lord Monboddo (his title derived, like that of his elder colleague Lord Kames, from a seat on the Scottish bench), has left a somewhat bizarre reputation. Pre-Darwinian theories as to the simian origin of man, our ancestors having worn off their tails by sitting on them; suppers after the manner of the ancients, satirised by Fielding in his novels; rides from Edinburgh to London, coaches being despised as effeminate—these and other eccentricities are associated with his name. His latest biographer[1] does not seem to take his writings seriously. It will surprise many to hear that his book *Of the Origin and Progress of Language* contains acute analysis and powerful reasoning. It is deficient in the

[1] *Lord Monboddo and some of his Contemporaries*, by William Knight, LL.D. London (Murray), 1900.

method and lucid order of Kames's treatise. Its six volumes came out irregularly from 1773 to 1792, with no name or dedication, and by different publishers. The later volumes unblushingly repeat the former, traversing the same ground, often using identical language. A student of metre need hardly go beyond the first and second volumes, with perhaps the beginning of the third. Vol. I, treating of primitive man and the origin of speech, contains the speculations which so amused his contemporaries; in Vol. II (published in 1774) he comes to the "Art of Language". This second volume is divided into three "Books", of which the first deals with the formal part of language (nouns, verbs, *etc.*), the second with the material part ("language considered as sound," p. 226), the third with "the composition of language" (*i.e.* syntax). It is therefore to Vol. II, Book II, that our chief attention must be directed. Its first three Chapters treat mainly of articulation, of letters and alphabets; with Chap. IV begins his examination of accent and quantity as elements of spoken sound.

Monboddo was a devoted Grecian, and with him accent means variation of pitch. He argues at great length that this was so in ancient Greek, but when he comes (p. 298) to consider English accent, maintains that our change of tone is on words or sentences only, not on syllables, which are simply pronounced louder or softer, the music of our language so far as syllables are concerned being "nothing better than the beating of a drum" (p. 300). Such alternations of force hardly exist in French, and probably did not in Greek or Latin, since "no antient grammarian speaks a word of [*i. e.* about] it" (*ibid.*). This doctrine excited very much comment. I do not think Monboddo was first to use the metaphor of a *drum*. Herries refers to it (*op. cit.*, p. 173), and there may be earlier instances.[1] But Monboddo made it his own, returns to it over and over

[1] I had imagined Sheridan its inventor, but cannot find that he uses it in print before 1775.

again, and no idea is more often referred to by others in connection with him. It seems to me that all who make English *stress* purely and simply a matter of "force-accent" are bound to endorse Monboddo's description. He himself, however, was driven to modify it later, as will appear when we come to Steele [1775].

In his next Chapter he takes up 'quantity', conceived of as absolute duration of motion. His elaborate analysis of the five possible forms of rhythm—"it does not appear that the nature of the thing admits of any more" (p. 317)—with its clear distinction between frequency of percussions and continuance of one percussion, may be passed by, since he confines attention to this last-named, which he says is called *time* in music and *quantity* in speech, though it really forms only a part of the whole 'quantity' of a language (*ibid.*, *note*). Excellent are his remarks on the phenomenon so defined. Not for him the vulgar error that a Latin vowel became long when followed by two consonants, or the equally common fallacy that a doubled consonant in English means a double sound. The length of a syllable, he points out, even in Greek verse was relative and not absolute; the proportion was taken as two to one, minor differences being neglected (pp. 318-19). Length depended either on the vowel, or on the consonants which follow the vowel, and which "retard the pronunciation so much, as to make the syllable long" (p. 319). "And so nice were the antients, that they distinguished by their pronunciation whether the vowel, in a syllable long by position, was of itself long or short" (p. 320). But he recognises that neither quantity of this kind, nor accent such as theirs, is necessary or essential. What, then, of English verse? If we alter the quantity of particular syllables in a line, it does not change the metre (p. 326). Some syllables are long in themselves, but even these can be pronounced short without essential change; and most are indifferent. Accented syllables are not longer than others, only louder, and "pronounced with more violence" (pp. 322-5). Foster was wrong in assigning absolute quantity to English syllables, just as in not keeping separate the rhythm of Greek verse from the tone-melody of its words (p. 322, *cf.* 329 *seq.*). Two things are essential to English verse: accent, and number of syllables. And by their combination we make the best verse of any nation in Europe (p. 325). French verse, owing to want of accent, needs the aid of rhyme; their blank verse he thinks "miserably unsuccessful". On the other hand, " there is a certain hardness or want of music in all the languages of Gothic or Celtic extraction" which disqualifies them from reproducing Classic metres (p. 327).

At the beginning of Chap. VI he shows how we substitute accentuation for quantity in reading Latin and Greek, making for example the first syllable of *Tityrus* louder and stronger, but not longer. Omitting this, and the earlier part of Book III, I come to Chap. VIII in the latter, " Of the composition of accents in English, and of English verse." Applying his former analysis, he defines our verse as a " species of rhythm", concerned with loud and soft syllables, these occurring at intervals which must be " equal or such as have some other ratio to one another" (pp. 384–5). This implies "a certain [*i.e.* fixed] number of syllables". Here again he drags in his *drum.* Yet presently (p. 388, *note*) he distinguishes between " the accent, which is the elevation of the voice upon one *syllable* of the word, and the emphasis, which is the same elevation upon a *word* of a sentence ". So he does seem to recognise the function of *tone* in verse, as he recognises the existence of pauses " such as the sense requires" (p. 396). He praises Milton for securing variety by "breaking the measure", and approves the cadence of

Burnt after them *to the bottomless pit,*

which was so often censured (p. 388, *note*). The remainder of this Chapter enumerates various forms of English verse, characterizing them in the usual way as iambic, trochaic, anapaestic, though he seems to use these terms with some reluctance. At the end he recurs once more to his drum, and rebukes the heresies of "one John Mason" (p. 401, *note*). Succeeding Chapters wander off into other subjects, the "feet" of prose, the artistic development of language, Chinese, and Bishop Wilkins's "philosophical language"; and the volume ends with three Dissertations on Greek. Throughout these pages, and in Vol. III (1776), which deals with *style*, there are many shrewd sayings, and Milton is quoted (often in unexpected places) as a model and master. A note on p. 409 in Vol. III refers to Steele, and distinguishes "syllabic tones, or accents, properly so called" from "tones of passion and sentiment". Otherwise I have noted nothing of importance to add to the foregoing, though I cannot pretend to have read carefully the subsequent volumes, which seem mainly to repeat their predecessors. The gist of Monboddo's view I believe to be stated above.

That view, it will be seen, differs from the orthodox one mainly in substituting loudness for length; and even this may have been suggested by Sheridan. Otherwise he does not seem to transcend the common notion of verse depending on a fixed number of syllables. His excellence is in phonetics rather than prosody. Yet he never objects to additional syllables; and his glorification of Milton above Pope, blank verse above rhyme, together with his independent view of what constitutes 'quantity', must have helped to encourage new conceptions. Had his six volumes been compressed into three, with more strict relation of ideas and merciless excision of digressions and repetitions, they might have ranked among the institutional works of our language. As it is, they remain a storehouse of vastly mingled materials, out of which may be picked some really sound and excellent stuff. I do not think they have ever been reprinted[1], but a selection of their best passages might have advantageously been made.

[1] Vols. I and II went into a second edition almost immediately, but I fancy that was all.

Perhaps *A New Dictionary of the English Language*, by William Kenrick, LL.D., (4to, London, 1773) should be added to our Bibliography for the sake of its "Rhetorical Grammar" (pp. 1–57). The Dictionary indicates pronunciation by elaborate symbols, anticipating a cherished design of Sheridan's. Prosody is considered briefly and generally in Chapter I, Section VI, of the "Grammar", and somewhat more minutely in the last three Sections of Chapter II. But little definite doctrine can be extracted from these. As a critic of others, Kenrick is acute, and will not admit that our syllables form "what the ancients called a foot" (p. 48). Yet in lieu of this conception he offers nothing but vague talk about the "easy flow" of what he indifferently terms *feet* or *measures*, which are constituted by alternation of accented and unaccented syllables. Of any thing conditioning that alternation he seems unconscious, or of any need for a theory of metre. That this attitude was not peculiar to him my next paragraph will show.

In 1774 appeared the first volume of Thomas Warton's great *History of English Poetry*, in favour of which Gray had abandoned his own projected one. It was completed in four volumes, the last a posthumously published fragment. Long the standard work on its subject, it was reprinted several times during last Century, and still holds the field in W. C. Hazlitt's edition of 1871. Students speak with respect of its survey of our elder literature, and at the time it was thought wonderful. But to us the most astonishing fact about it is that it contains absolutely no discussion of verse-structure. This erudite and accomplished historian of our poetry never asks himself what is the actual nature of the verse he is describing. Even when, in Vol. IV, he records the Elizabethan attempts at quantitative verse, he dismisses them with a remark on their "unnatural and impracticable mode of versification" (p. 289, Hazlitt's edition; said of W. Webbe). Historically, his survey is admirable; philosophically, it is naught. I do not think a more striking instance could be found of how entirely English scholarship had blinked the question of prosody, taking for granted a traditional view which applied Latin rules to English verse without ever enquiring whether as a matter of fact such application were possible and justifiable.

But the work left undone by Warton was taken up by others. The same year which saw his first volume issued saw also published, really anonymous, *An Essay upon the Harmony of Language, intended principally to illustrate that of the English Language.* Thirty years later it reappeared as *An Inquiry into the Principles of Harmony in Language, and of the Mechanism of Verse, modern and antient. By William Mitford, Esq. The second edition, with improvement and large addition.* In its original form, the *Essay* was chiefly a criticism of Foster. The enlarged *Inquiry* follows the same material arrangement, but leaves out much detailed criticism, replacing this by more general statement. It is much fuller, and more authoritative. In many respects, however, the earlier *Essay* seems to me preferable, being simpler and clearer and more concise. Chronological fitness also makes it desirable to quote mainly from it, while reserving the right to refer to the later edition. Mitford being an acknowledged authority, his book deserves careful study. The *Essay* is divided into thirteen " Sections " or Chapters, the *Inquiry* into eighteen.

At the outset, Mitford complains of prevailing ignorance about the factors of speech, particularly of our own speech; some make accent its efficient principle, some quantity; "some affirm that there is no such thing as quantity in our language, and most hold that what quantity we have is always determined by accent" (p. 7). A little later he denounces the errors of "all who have written on English prosody, and their utter inability to form any system for analysing English verse" (p. 19). For himself, he distinguishes in language *melody, cadence,* and *articulation* (p. 10). The third adds beauty to speech, as does the tone [*timbre*] of a violin to sound ; by attention to it the French and Italians have improved their languages. But the first and second form his subject. "Melody, in language, arises from the various tones of the voice, which are called accents. Cadence is determined by the quantity of time employed in the pronunciation of syllables" (pp. 11-12). Hence arises a third incident to the harmony of human speech called *meter* [*sic* throughout] or *measure*. Following Foster into the question of ancient accentuation, he notes that the Greek accent-marks " are daily growing more out of fashion " (p. 19). For the most part he accepts Foster's view, but complains that its author does not apply it to any living language. He (Mitford) will therefore try to explain " the particular nature of accent and quantity in the English language" (p. 28).

What we commonly call accent, he says, is really *principal accent*. "Every trisyllable" which has a strong accent on its first syllable has "some" also on its last, and *vice versa*; e. g. *cónfidènt, èntertáin*. The principal accent he calls acute, the other grave, and omits minor varieties. Accent being "nothing more than the tone of the voice", its " more minute modifications are indeed almost infinite" (p. 30); for practical purposes the above-named two suffice. Quantity is more complex, depending either on vowels alone or on "the connexion of vowels with consonants " (p. 31). Most dogmatically he lays down that there are *six* degrees of quantity, three of which were reckoned short in ancient verse and three long; "we shall probably not err if we do the same" (pp. 39-41). At great length he applies this to English speech, claiming that a short vowel followed by two distinct consonantal sounds makes a long syllable with us as in Greek, this being a rule " founded on nature and necessity ". Mute and liquid are not distinct sounds, but coalesce; we say *re-gret*, but *con-tend*. And our doubled consonants represent usually one sound. This last assertion he makes in capital letters, saying it will startle the learned, and seemingly unaware that others had anticipated him. As exceptions he notes *wholly* [pronounced *wholely*], *overrun*, and with careful speakers *irretrievable* but not *irritate* (pp. 41-4; cf. 55, 225; and *Inquiry*, p. 44). So *ng* is one consonant in *singer*, but two in *anger*; and *dg* is a single sound in *sedgy*. As to vowels, he maintains that there is palpable difference of length, as in *fathom* and *father*, *pepper* and *paper*, etc.; but that spelling is no guide, witness the last quoted pair of words, while others use the same letter for wholly different sounds (*ibid.*). Later he contends that vowel followed by vowel is short, except the diphthong *oi*; *being* is as short as possible (p. 72), and "*die* of a rose" would be short but for the emphasis (p. 76). Thus he recognises emphasis as altering quantity, a fact which increases confusion.[1] We are scrupulous about our accented vowels, careless about our unaccented. This prolonged analysis occupies Sections III and V, Section IV being a protest against Foster's confounding accent with quantity. Then, in Section VI (p. 79), he proceeds to analyse English verse in accordance with the principles he has laid down.

"Meter," he says, is irregular with us. "A certain rhythmical or measured disposition of the accents," however, is necessary to the "very being" of English verse (p. 90). "Accent is the fundamental efficient [these two words in capitals] of English versification" (p. 91). The fact that "rhythmus", with us, resides only in the "disposition" of accents makes our verse inferior to the "metrical versification of Greeks and Romans" (p. 93). Therefore trisyllabic feet are quite legitimate in heroic verse, and elision is condemned. He scans verse by feet, using symbols to show length and accentuation. In Sections VII and VIII Milton is exalted as the great model, his "inverted accents" giving all necessary variety; yet he wrote "many harsh lines", which "cannot be defended" (p. 102), while

[1] In the *Inquiry* he makes emphasis moveable, accent immoveable (p. 64). He also admits that accent includes force as well as tone, while still contending that the latter is necessary, which he illustrates by our pronunciation of the imaginary word *Alalal* (p. 57).

Shakespeare's verse was "calculated not to be read, but to be acted" (p. 118). Thus he condemns (p. 131) a line which he thus represents—

Gămbōl'd | bĕfóre | thĕm : th' ūnwíel-|dў ĕ-|lĕphānt,

[the colon being meant to show *caesura*, while four accents are made to replace the usual five]. Similarly, in Section IX, where he deals with [oratorical] pauses and "cesura", he declares that Milton's "bottomless pit" line "is to my ear not an English heroic verse" (p. 155). Section X is historical, and here the *Inquiry* (Section VII) is certainly fuller. In Section XI he comes to lyric measures, distinguishing between "common and triple cadence" (p. 181)—I will return to this immediately—recognising dropped syllables in the latter, and affirming that "the triple measures are wholly unfit for the sublime" (p. 190). Section XII deals mainly with Classic verse, asserting that "to an English ear a certain disposition of accents, without any regard to quantity, will raise the idea of a Latin hexameter" (p. 219), and that we read Latin verse "by an accentual rhythmus only" (p. 220). Finally, in his last Section, he deals more explicitly with the question of time, and makes what is perhaps his most important contribution to the subject under discussion.

This last Section deals with "Poetry and Music". Both possess "rhythmus", both exhibit common and triple time, and sometimes notes agree with syllables. But our iambic verse does not move to triple time, nor our dactylic to common (pp. 261-2). "The even and the triple foot can no more appear in the same verse than common and triple time in the same musical strain" [*query* as regards music?], but a syllable can be added to an even foot or retrenched from a triple one, while the converse rarely happens (pp. 262-4). Triple-time verse is suitable for either riotous mirth or tranquil melancholy, as in music for either jig or "Sicilian movement", but not for any thing intermediate (p. 266). Should the accented syllable begin the bar, as in music?

The other way is "more proper" and more convenient (p. 267). These remarks are interspersed with comments on "Anglo-Saxon" verse, on Greek metre, and on Greek music. Continuing to discuss this last, he thinks that it had no bars, or at any rate these were not distinguished by accent or emphasis as in modern music (p. 280). The Greeks measured cadence by length of time only, we by emphatical accent also. Therefore they could subdivide verse into many "meters", while we have but two [common and triple]; for their syllable divided the cadence definitely, ours does not (p. 281 *seq.*). Therefore, also, the relations of verse to music in modern times are quite different to what they were in ancient; the two have grown apart. "What connexion subsisted between the accents of music and those of speech among the Greeks does not, that I know, appear from any of their writings;" but their music "had no connexion with language but by means of versification" (p. 284). The power of their poetical measures we cannot understand, not knowing the just pronunciation; they clearly admitted of more variety than ours. A few concluding sentences (pp. 287–8) express, though modestly, a belief that he has cleared away some difficulties regarding Classic verse, as well as thrown light on our own.

This belief was not wholly unfounded. Mitford does not, indeed, seriously modify the conceptions of his time. Much that I have quoted is common to him with others; much more, not quoted, repeats traditional formulas. The same ideas, the same quotations and comments, appear in all writers of this epoch. But Mitford handles them with freshness, and does throw new light on them. He distinguishes accent from quantity as carefully as Monboddo; both wholly reject the view of Bysshe and Johnson that accent makes quantity. In his recognition of "time" as conditioning verse Mitford has the advantage of Monboddo, and takes a distinct step forward. Most valuable of all, perhaps, was his explicit declaration that English verse-structure presents a problem to be solved; that critics were wrong in thinking they knew all about it, or could explain it by Classic rules. This declaration alone counts for much. It is disappointing to find that between 1774 and 1804 Mitford made little progress. The *Inquiry* does not really carry us farther than the *Essay*, though it amplifies his argument and—especially in its earlier half—introduces some new ideas, *e.g.* "The poetical or metrical syllable is not precisely the same with the grammatical syllable" (p. 105). But he remains substantially at his earlier standpoint. To Steele he makes but one patronizing reference (p. 213), and his later "Sections" digress into cognate matters such as "euphony and cacophony", grammar, *etc.* The last Section, with the Appendix which follows, can only be called a hodge-podge, but in the former he remarks that *jig* is a duplication of triple time, *minuet* a triplication of common time. Some remarks on foreign languages should be read with caution, as his knowledge hardly extended beyond the Romance tongues. On the whole, what is valuable in his views will be got most easily from the *Essay*, which has the directness and sharpness of a first sketch, and which—after all deductions—entitles Mitford to an honourable place among the pioneers of a rational system of scansion.

The year 1775 is memorable in the history of English prosody. Three books of note had birth in it. Of these Sheridan's *Lectures on the Art of Reading* must come first, for we have already neglected him too long. Thomas Sheridan, son and namesake of Swift's friend, father of Richard Brinsley Sheridan, Irish by birth and upbringing, retired actor and fashionable teacher of elocution, was a figure of some prominence in his day. Readers of Boswell should not be misled by Johnson's ridicule of "Sherry" the second, or by the repeated phrase "old Mr. Sheridan" used to distinguish him from his famous son. He was some twelve years junior to Johnson, from whom he was estranged by a foolish quarrel. Settling finally in London shortly before 1760, at the age of forty or thereabouts, he had lectured in the Universities and elsewhere on the need of better speaking, had published a *Dissertation* on the imperfections of our alphabet and *Lectures on Elocution* (both in 1762), was engaged in compiling his *Pronouncing Dictionary* (to be published in 1780[1]), and taught a peculiar theory of accent to which attention must now be given.

From the first, while styling accent "that grand master-key to the pronunciation of our tongue, whose nature has hitherto been little understood, or grossly mistaken" (*Dissertation*, pp. 31-2[2]), and contending that "it is by the accent chiefly that the quantity of our syllables is regulated" (*Lectures*, 1762, p. 41), he had rejected with scorn the idea that accentuation necessarily lengthens sound. On the contrary, when accent falls on a consonant it shortens the preceding vowel, as in *hat* and *habit*; only when it falls on a vowel, as in *hate* and *hater*, does it lengthen that vowel. This is Sheridan's great idea, repeated in his *Dissertation*, in both sets of *Lectures*, and in the "Prosodial Grammar" prefixed to his *Dictionary*. He claims to have discovered it, and from it to have deduced this further "invariable rule" that when accent falls on and lengthens a vowel, all other vowels in that word are short, while if it falls on a consonant, no vowel in the word has its full long sound (*Dissertation*, as above). In the *Lectures* of 1762 he further develops this view, defining accent as "a peculiar manner of distinguishing one syllable of a word from the rest", either by dwelling longer on it, or by "giving it a smarter percussion of the voice in utterance" (pp. 40-1). "There can not be any thing more false" than to say

---

[1] Not 1789, as stated in my Bibliography. That is the date of the second edition, inadvertently taken by me for the first. Sheridan's Dissertation contains his plan for a Pronouncing Dictionary, but Kenrick (as we have just seen) anticipated him in execution.

[2] This Dissertation is reprinted in the *Lectures* of 1762, being the last of several in that volume (pp. 223-62; the above quotation, p. 258). It was reproduced by Pitman in his *Phonetic Journal* for 1856, and issued as a twopenny tract. Its exposure of the shortcomings and inconsistencies of our alphabet makes good reading still.

that accent always lengthens a syllable, though "all who have written on the subject" declare it does (p. 41). Only when accent rests on a vowel is this true; when it rests on a consonant, the syllable is either short or doubtful—short, if the consonant itself be a short one, such as *k, p, t*; doubtful, if the consonant be long, such as *l, m, n, r, v* (*ibid.*). Besides thus regulating quantity, accent is useful as dividing syllables into words, which the Greeks did by variety of tone, and "many modern nations" by pausing after each word, neither of which is necessary in English (pp. 44-6). Greek accent he understands to have been tone merely ("certain inflections of the voice like musical notes"), though the grammarians who say so do not tell us how to put it into practice (p. 39). At any rate, English accent is different. They distinguished three accents, we have one only[1], and its operation is as stated above. The difference between English and Scottish pronunciation is chiefly that the latter accentuates the vowel where the former accentuates the consonant (p. 42). "Nothing is of more moment in our tongue than to know when the accent is on the vowel, and when on the consonant" (*Dissertation*, as above).

These quotations are from the Third Lecture in the 1762 volume. The other Lectures deal mainly with elocution, the First and Second treating of letters, and the Fourth of emphasis, which "is to sentences as accent to words". The Fifth and Sixth discuss "pauses or stops" as bringing out the sense, and tones as ministering to expression; the Seventh and last is on gestures. For us, therefore, Sheridan's contribution so far consists of his teaching about accent. I fear this cannot be deemed quite satisfactory. Do we really accentuate the *t* in *hat* any more than in *hate*, or is the difference not entirely in the vowel-sound (the final *e* is of course merely a typographical sign of a long vowel)? We do certainly dwell longer on the vowel in *all* than in *add* (p. 44); but the

[1] No distinction is made, as by Mitford, between principal and secondary accent.

difference is surely one of quantity alone. I do not gather that Sheridan's view satisfied critics at the time, or would pass muster with philologists now. His "invariable rule", also, is by no means an absolute one. Does the second syllable of *twilight* lose any of its length, or the second syllable of *wayfarer*? The first and third syllables of *privateer* are usually both sounded long.[1] Sheridan's rule usually holds good, simply because we love to emphasize one syllable and subordinate others; but this usage is not invariable. These, however, are questions which scarcely affect prosody. What does make Sheridan's contribution metrically valuable is its clear perception that accent may shorten as well as lengthen a syllable. Whether his explanation of the fact be mistaken or no hardly matters. He saw clearly the difference between *ha-ter* and *hatt-er*, and invented a formula to account for it. Whatever we think of the latter, his recognition of the difference stands to his credit, and one looks with interest to see how it will affect his view of verse. This is not given in the earlier volumes. They are practical, concerned with the oratorical delivery of verse, not with its structure. Beyond a statement that "by the variety of the seat of accent, our words easily and naturally fall into all sorts of metrical feet" (Lecture III, p. 52), I do not think he refers at all to questions of prosody. When, however, we turn to the *Lectures* of 1775, the case is different.

The "First Part" of these later *Lectures*, indeed (Lectures I–IV), is taken up with how to read prose. Here the old ground is traversed, the former volume referred to, and accent again dealt with on the same lines. Foster's account of it leaves him "as much in the dark as before" (Lecture II, p. 73[2]). Ancient accent was "an elevation or depression of the voice", ours is a "mere stress of the voice, without any change of note"; ours is the drum, theirs the trumpet (pp. 74–5). Scot-

[1] Many other instances will suggest themselves, while in words like *edify, arrogate, emulate*, accent has deserted the long vowel.
[2] My quotations are from the third edition (1787).

tish speech has three accents like Greek, but irregular and without proportion; English has but one, and "is utterly unacquainted with the circumflex" (pp. 76–8). In emphasis he now recognises a change of tone (p. 87). While unaltered in essentials, this later presentment of his view is more precise than the former; he has profited by reading other definitions and discussions. But it is in "Part II" (again comprising four Lectures) that he comes to "the art of reading verse", and begins with a characteristic flourish. "The principles and laws of our versification are either buried in obscurity or falsely seen through the mists of error" (p. 191). Our rules of prosody are taken from French or Classic verse. Because the French count syllables, we suppose that our heroic line must contain exactly ten syllables, which is absurd; who says *ech'ing* for *echoing* (p. 192)? A well known line of Milton's contains thirteen syllables. And "a couplet of as fine sound perhaps as any in our language" [*viz.* Say's concocted one] disproves such numeration (p. 193). On the other hand, "not many years since, some essay writers showed [tried to show] that" English verse "was formed by feet, like that of the ancients", and "boldly applied most of the rules of Latin prosody to our versification; though scarce any of them answered exactly, and many of them would not square at all with the genius of our tongue" (pp. 193–4). Both views are wrong. "The Latin poetic feet are formed by quantity, the English by accent" (p. 194). He will explain the difference, and after doing so will conduct his hearers by "an unfrequented path" to "our part of Parnassus" (p. 212).

Such an exordium raises our hopes. Nor are they wholly disappointed. Sheridan still clings to *feet*, but these are conditioned by time.[1] "Numbers ... consist

[1] He also invents a distinction, afterwards adopted by Lindley Murray [1795], between quantitative and accentual feet, according as the accent falls on vowel or consonant. This gives us duplicates of the eight usual feet. "We have all that the ancients had, and something which they had not." *Cf.* pp. 230–1 *seq.*

in certain impressions made on the ear at stated and regular distances" (pp. 225, 230); "the other circumstances of long and short in the syllables, or diversity of notes in uttering them, are not essentials" (p. 230). Quantity is always variable in our syllables, depending on emphasis (p. 208); and is not necessary to verse. Regular proportion is necessary, but our poets are justified in introducing "heterogeneous feet" for the sake of variety, as Milton does often. Two such feet following each other, however, are fatal to melody, wherefore Milton's double trochees are unhesitatingly condemned (p. 346). Heroic verse need not consist of iambs alone, but the feet should be proportionate; trochee followed by iamb is just measure, so is spondee followed by pyrrhic (pp. 239-40). Yet this proportion may be sacrificed to expressiveness occasionally, that being "higher than mere melody" (p. 242). Melody, Variety, and Expression are all good, and he considers them at length. He distinctly recognises monosyllabic feet (p. 245), contends that Say's lines occupy exactly the time of pure iambic ones (p. 249), and asserts that a dactyl may always be substituted for a trochee, an anapaest for an iamb (p. 256). This variety, he had before said (p. 216), gives our heroic verse an "amazing advantage" over that of the ancients. Excellent are his criticisms of Dr. Forster [*sic*] (pp. 205 and 209), Pemberton (217), Kames (224). Of Pope he says that he "knew more of the art of versification than any of his contemporaries, though he seems not to have dived deep into the science of numbers" (p. 279); and evidently thinks him too monotonous. He insists on a "suspensive pause" at the end of every line, and claims that no one else has noticed this (p. 258 *seq.*). A recapitulation occupying pp. 298-304 concludes the Second Lecture, and summarizes his whole view. Two remaining Lectures treat of "expression", and illustrate his attitude toward verse. Milton's description of Hell-gate is "exceedingly expressive, but cannot be called verses"; his " Me, me only " would have read better as "Me, me alone" (pp. 350-1). He is naïvely surprised "in reading Milton, who was so perfect a master of numbers, to find so many lines that have not the least air of verse, and which could not have slipped from the pens of our middling poetasters" (p. 347); but this suggests no doubt of his own criteria. In these final Lectures he enumerates and characterizes various metres, on fairly familiar lines, the chief novelty being a contention that "amphibrachic" is a common type with us. On the whole, however, it is in the First Lecture of Part II that his most distinctive doctrine occurs. Its leading features are defence of variety as against monotony, and insistance on "Compensation" as the law by which one foot is shortened and its neighbour lengthened (p. 240); coupled with a sense of the importance of time as compared with mere syllabic numeration.

Had these views been proclaimed in 1762, Sheridan would have ranked high as a reformer. We do not know how far he may have taught them orally before 1775, any more than we know his attitude toward prosody in those earlier days when Johnson was a frequent guest at his house, and such questions must surely have been discussed. Published when they were, his Lectures only show that he shares a general movement, has assimilated its principles, but not advanced beyond them. To Johnson he refers once (p. 220), censuring him for calling "*most good, most fair*" iambs; but he himself says (p. 299) that "all unaccented syllables are short", so that the question between them is merely one of accentuation. In advocating variety, and approving trisyllabic feet, he duly follows where others had led, though he states the ground of his approval better and more convincingly than they. His indebtedness to Mason, Webb, Kames, Monboddo, is palpable; I do not think he refers to Mitford. As a supporter of 'accentual feet', Sheridan undoubtedly stands high; later grammars copy him largely, and his authority carried weight. Most of his exposition would probably still commend itself to orthodox metrists, though in some points we have outgrown his standard. I had marked many more passages for quotation and favourable comment. But to me the surprise is that, having gone so far, he went no farther. Had he been more of an original thinker, less of a merely judicious critic and adapter, he might have seen for himself that English verse does not depend wholly on an ordered succession of syllables. That discovery he did not make. It was made—as will appear almost immediately—by a writer of much less note and authority, whose use of it, moreover, was by no means so successful as it might have been, and probably would have been in Sheridan's hands.

In 1775 was also published *The Canterbury Tales of Chaucer: to which are added, An Essay upon his Language and Versification . . . etc.* The author was Thomas Tyrwhitt, a well known antiquary, but as usual the title-page bore no name. The original edition comprised four volumes, the Essay and other introductory matter being in Vol. IV; a fifth, containing glossary, *etc.*, came out in 1778. Often reprinted, it can be had in modern editions complete in one volume; as the Essay is divided into short Sections, with numbered *notes*, references to these will suffice. Tyrwhitt was a writer of the same type as Warton, to whom he refers with high esteem, and his work is mainly historical. He holds our verse to be of Norman origin, copied from late Latin accentual metres, and owing nothing to "Saxon Poetry", in which he can find practically no verse (§ 1, and *notes* there). He takes the usual view of the constitution of our metre, feet being composed of "syllables strongly and less strongly accented" (*ibid., note* 42; *cf.* first sentence of § 10). Yet he refuses to require an absolutely fixed number of syllables. While unable to conceive "that an heroic verse which wants a syllable of its complement can be musical, or even tolerable" (§ 8, *note* 60), he has no objection to "superfluous" syllables, quoting five lines from Milton in support of this, and laying down "one general principle, that an English verse, though chiefly composed of feet of two syllables, is capable of receiving feet of three syllables in every part of it, provided only one [*i.e.* one only] of the three syllables be accented" (§ 14, *note* 66). On this principle he scans Chaucer's lines, emphasizing the necessity of pronouncing "feminine *e*" and other dropped sounds. Previous writers had done this to some extent. In the extracts from Chaucer prefixed to Johnson's Dictionary accents were marked on "sweté breath," "allé night," *etc.* Tyrwhitt carried this immensely farther, while stipulating for an "obscure evanescent sound" (*note* 68) of final *e*, and restored proper accent to various words, thereby rendering Chaucer's rhythm intelligible to many who before had only "made shift" to read him. This, and his sanction of trisyllabic feet, are often referred to by his contemporaries. Yet his 73rd *note* shows him still trammelled by Johnsonian ideas; at the best we can only say that, like a good many people, he practised better than he preached.

But the third book was far the most remarkable as touching prosody; more remarkable, from that point of view, than any other book of the Century. In 1775 appeared *An Essay towards establishing the Melody and Measure of Speech, to be expressed and perpetuated by peculiar symbols.* Four years later followed a "second edition, amended and enlarged," under the title of *Prosodia Rationalis: an Essay ... etc.* Its author was Joshua Steele, an Irishman, and Fellow of the Royal Society. The two editions are practically identical to the close of the first (p. 193); what follows in the second is headed "Additions" and dated September 1779. It looks as if the unsold sheets of the first edition had been used for the second, and new matter added. The leaf of *errata*, subjoined to the first edition and prefixed to the second, is in the latter revised and extended; the index is enlarged to include the new matter, and the title-page is new. Otherwise I detect no change; dedication[1],

---

[1] Or rather *inscription*, to Sir John Pringle (see next paragraph). The British Museum copy contains also a formal dedication to the Royal Society, but this is absent from my copy.

preface, and text (pp. 1–193) seem unaltered. As most of my references will be to the earlier pages, it is immaterial which edition is used. To meet with either is not easy, and the book has never been reprinted.

It began as a reply to Monboddo. The then President of the Royal Society, Sir John Pringle (to whom the book is inscribed), asked Steele to write remarks on Monboddo's view of verse (*cf.* p. 2). These—forming Parts I and II of the book, pp. 4–46 or possibly 55—were circulated in manuscript, and the author thought of printing them privately (p. 64). But Monboddo, to whom they had been sent, wrote frankly admitting some points and querying others; Steele wrote Part III (pp. 65–84 or 89) in reply, and determined to publish (p. 92). The friendly correspondence continued, and in answer to further comments Steele wrote his long concluding Part IV (pp. 113–73). Meanwhile, proofs of the first three Parts had been sent to Monboddo, and his remarks on these rendered it necessary to add a Postscript (p. 174). Finally the book was published in stately quarto, the whole correspondence printed in full, Steele's reply to Monboddo's last observations concluding it (pp. 181–93). The additions to the second edition similarly contain criticisms by other correspondents, with Steele's replies, both sides being given fair play by his printing in full the remarks replied to.

The Essay, in either edition, is therefore less a consecutive treatise than a series of tracts, points being taken up as they are suggested by others. The correspondence between Steele and Monboddo is honourable to both. It is amusing to see that neither addresses the other by name; the letters are always "to the author of", *etc.* Yet there is no concealment; Steele says "your l——p", and Monboddo sends Steele a copy of his book. The anonymity was a mere etiquette. Monboddo gets decidedly the worst of the argument, and admits defeat on several points with engaging candour. The critics replied to in the "Additions" of 1779 are not named; one of them (p. 208) seems to have written *Remarks on*

Mr. Steele's Treatise, but I cannot find that these were ever published. The concluding pages of the second edition (226-36) deal with Pemberton and Foster, the former of whom he had not read before (pp. 208 and 226). It is, however, in the earlier pages of the Essay that we get Steele's own view most distinctly stated, and a very remarkable one it is. For the first time (I believe) in the history of our literature a writer proclaims that verse is essentially matter of musical rhythm, and applies musical methods frankly and fully to the notation of metre.

These ideas had been 'in the air' throughout the Century. Gildon had desiderated "prick'd notes" like those of music. Say and the others of his group had referred much to music, and had represented "feet" by notes. Mason, as Mitford later, recognised common and triple time in verse. Foster asserted that "every sentence uttered ... is ... capable of musical notations" (*op. cit.*, p. 254). Kames contended that for accurate recording of pronunciation "notes must be invented, resembling those employed in music" (*op. cit.*, p. 272). It was felt that, in modern England as in ancient Greece, verse and music had been artificially separated, their close kinship lost sight of; and it was desired to bring them together. But, while earlier writers merely played with this notion, Steele put it into practice. What they only desiderated he tried to perform. Discarding the whole doctrine of *syllabic feet*—a doctrine, as we have seen, which was taken from Classical prosody, and had never been shown really applicable to ours—he substituted for this the conception of "*cadences*", similar in all respects to musical bars, and to be similarly treated. For their analysis he originally invented a "staff" even more elaborate than that of music (p. 6), but came ultimately to regard the latter as practically sufficient (p. 30). As regards time, he was content with four lengths of note, answering to semibreve, minim, crotchet, and quaver in music, any one of which could be made one-half longer by "dotting"; [1]

[1] This makes "eight different proportions of quantity" (*cf.* p. 144, *note*).

and, correspondent to the four lengths of note, he postulated four "rests or pauses" of like duration, with symbols to match.

This last idea was wholly new. The "pauses" spoken of by earlier writers were merely caesural divisions, affecting the delivery rather than the substance of a line; Steele was first to treat them as factors of metre. That this should be so is truly surprising, and shows the artificiality of previous prosody. For, surely, it is a self-evident proposition that in any ordered succession of articulate or inarticulate sounds an interval of silence may on occasion be substituted for utterance, and may count toward the total result; just as in dancing a measured interval of quiescence may form part of the 'steps', or as in music 'rests' are an integral part of the bar. Incredible as it may seem, this obvious fact had escaped notice, and was not admitted even after Steele called attention to it. Succeeding metrists, except a few avowed followers of Steele, ignored it in their teaching, as to this day it is ignored in the "Prosody" Section of our grammars. Coleridge never mentions it in his references to metre. Poe does not notice it in his protest against scholastic scansion, not even when it would seem impossible to avoid doing so. As lately as 1870, Prof. Sylvester appears to claim it as his own peculiar discovery. During recent years not a few writers have, as they were well entitled to do, recognised its obvious reality. Yet when in my *Study of Metre* I took it more or less for granted (as I have done since the first day I began to think about verse-structure), many of my reviewers pronounced this revolutionary. I should have deemed it a matter hardly needing demonstration that pauses as well as syllables go to make up a metrical unit.

The word *pause* is not free from ambiguity. In music, I understand, it denotes a prolongation at pleasure of either sound or silence, rhythmic movement being temporarily suspended. In ordinary English it is more loosely used. We speak of pausing on a syllable or pausing after a syllable, the first being analogous to the 'dotted notes' of music and the second to its 'rests'. That both of these exist in verse seems clear ; probably it is more or less optional which we employ in any given line. The first might be called 'dwelling on' a syllable ; no convenient synonym suggests itself for the other. Personally, I use *pause* for both, following ordinary usage, and distinguishing when necessary by adding the musical equivalent. Even writers on music, I find, do not always restrict the term as above, but speak of "rests or pauses", as Steele himself does (p. 8). The pause which follows a line of verse I regard as extra-metrical, when it exists at all ; the 'rests or pauses' which occur during a line I regard as integral to structure, proved to be so by their taking places occupied in other lines by syllables or parts of syllables.

But Steele's notation was not restricted to expressing time. It was designed to show all the five "properties or accidents belonging to language", viz. *accent, emphasis, quantity, pause,* and *force* (Preface, pp. viii and xvii). These, with their respective symbols, are explained in Part I. Accent is confined to tone, emphasis to pulsation and remission, in Greek phrase *thesis* and *arsis* [these words used in true Greek sense] ; the other terms explain themselves. With the ordinary division of verse into accented and unaccented syllables he has no patience (p. 20, *cf.* 86);[1] nor do "modern musicians" escape censure for a similar misuse of terminology (p. 11). The alternation in both cases is really between emphasis and remission, *thesis* and *arsis*, setting down the foot and raising it up. In verse, he proposes to express this by the terms *heavy* and *light* syllables, distinguishing this from accent on the one hand and on the other from force or loudness (p. 20). Remiss or light syllables may be highly accented and loudly uttered, but verse is not affected thereby. A general term is wanted to cover both *heavy* and *light*, as 'accent' covers *high* and *low* and 'quantity' *long* and *short* ; let that word be *poise* [spelt

---

[1] The popular use of these terms is "solecismatical" (p. 86).

poize], and then "the poize of syllables is the most determined accident in our language" (pp. 77 and 144). The five sets of symbols are summarized and shown on p. 24. I cannot attempt to reproduce these here; they must be studied in the book itself. "Heavy poize" is represented by △, "light" by ∴, very light by ∵. These, with the marks of quantity, he finds sufficient for ordinary scansion; it is only sometimes that he adds symbols of accentuation [in his sense][1] and of *forte, piano, crescendo, diminuendo*. He notes, however, that "the meaning of a sentence may often be entirely altered by changing the accent from acute to grave, or *vice versa*" (p. 30); he does not say the same about loudness. It is interesting to know that he found in English intonation "at least as great" a range as the Greeks allowed to their accents, *viz.* a fifth (p. 17, *cf.* 149); also that, like them, he makes voice *slide* (as a general rule) from tone to tone in ordinary speech, but *jump* without intervening gradation from one to another in music.

This elaborate notation—which yet may be thought more complex than it really is—Steele applies to both prose and verse. Both move to either common or triple time (pp. 11, 25, *etc.*). The prose sentence on which he first illustrates his scansion gives his own view (p. 28), running thus—"Every sentence in our language, whether prose or verse, has a rhythmus peculiar to itself; that is, in the language of modern musicians, it is either in common time or triple time; videlicet, minuet time, or jigg [*sic*] time, or mixed." With this statement I cannot agree. All musical scansionists of prose seem to me apt to read into it a factitious regularity; Steele's scansion of this passage is itself a case in point. No doubt in all speech there is a tendency to be rhythmical, and by exercising a little compulsion we can force prose words to keep time. But the true beauty of prose is lost when we do so. Fundamental irregularity is the law of prose,

[1] In one place, however (p. 150), Steele employs *accentuation*, "for want of a better word," in a wider sense, *viz.* as a general term to include *accent, quantity,* and *poise*.

as fundamental regularity of verse. Certainly, good prose has its musical movements, which in ordinary parlance are vaguely called "rhythmical", in obedience to which a sentence rises or falls, swells or dies away. Isolated phrases will form rhythmical passages, just as isolated words will form 'feet' in our speech as in Greek; but these are not therefore necessary or fundamental. Metre may exist in prose, without being more than an accident; prose may be *metric* without being *emmetric*. Too great metrical regularity, we all know, is fatal to good prose; I contend that too great rhythmical regularity is equally fatal. Irregularity of rhythmic impulse is its distinctive note. In verse, syllables are set to equal time-measures, in prose to unequal. We can constrain them to act otherwise if we like; but in doing so we destroy their proper effect. Add to this that no two readers will 'poise' prose sentences in at all the same way, and it will appear how futile it is to force upon prose the temporal regularity which belongs only to verse. Those who seek to obliterate the dividing line between prose and verse must be somewhat insensible to the prime beauties of either.

With regard to verse, I accept Steele's principles of analysis, but not his application of these. He seems to recognise no law but his own ear. Our heroic line he makes consist sometimes of six cadences, sometimes of eight (*e.g.* p. 31). To an ordinary 'octosyllabic' line he gives five cadences (*ibid.*), but only four to the same when 'trochaic' (p. 32), and five to (p. 33)

> My time, O ye Muses, was happily spent.

His scansion of Hamlet's speech (pp. 40–6) ignores line-division, but Garrick's delivery of its first line (p. 47) is made to contain seven cadences. All this seems to me utterly wild, as wild as the division of Greek and Latin hexameter into eight cadences (pp. 80–3, and elsewhere). To place pauses wherever we choose to fancy them is to make verse a chaos. Steele was right in thinking that pause forms an integral part of every normal English line, wrong in thinking that this left him free to insert stops of any length at will. Temporal uniformity is the first law of verse. It might be possible to argue that every heroic line contains six periods; it is clearly wrong to say that it contains sometimes six, sometimes eight. Steele's error comes partly from his libertine use of pause, partly from failing to see how the natural "heavy poize" of syllables was altered by metrical relation. Thus in his oft-repeated scansion of Pope's line—

Oh, happiness! our being's end and aim!

he assigns *thesis* or "heavy poize" to both the first and second syllables, which entirely destroys their metrical character. Throughout the book, one feels that his scansions are frequently forced and unnatural. His synthesis is not equal to his analysis. The admirable skill with which he dissected our complex speech fails him when he comes to reconstruction, and the monstrosities which he presents as specimens of scansion are enough to make careless readers reject his scheme entirely.

It was probably these extravagances which blinded contemporaries to his real merit. Enough has been said to show how profoundly original, how subtle and penetrating, was his analytic work. Nothing like it had been seen before. It might well have been "epoch-making"; but it failed to become so. Monboddo accepted correction on some points; other writers praised "the ingenious Mr. Steele"[1] with dubious compliments. Most of them evidently thought his attempt impracticable and useless. He himself went off to the West Indies, and devoted himself to philanthropic work there. Prosody knew him no more, and forgot his teaching. A few followers, indeed, kept his name alive, and systematized his doctrine. Of these will presently be mentioned Odell [1806], Thelwall [1812], Chapman [1818], Roe [1823], of whom the first and last were the most valuable as regards theory. Through Thelwall, Coleridge may have profited by his teaching; but he never mentions him. Guest

[1] Mitford, *Inquiry*, p. 213; *cf.* Nares [*infra*, 1784]; *etc.*

[1838] refers to him or his followers with contempt, not naming Steele. Poe seems never to have heard of him; Sidney Lanier surprises us by a slighting reference in his preface. On the other hand, Coventry Patmore gives him high praise, and students of phonetics have recognised his value. Rush [1833], an American writer on the voice, excepts him from his general strictures on prosodists; Alexander John Ellis, our highest authority on vocal physics, praised and adopted his analysis. Of late, Steele's star is certainly in the ascendant, but perhaps he is more often quoted than read. Even a meagre summary like the foregoing has not, to my knowledge, been attempted elsewhere. His work was professedly tentative. The subject had occupied his thought for years (*cf. Dedication* and p. 1, also p. 204), and he aspired to lay a foundation for others to build on (pp. 3-4, *etc.*; *cf.* on pronunciation, pp. 166, 216). This at least he certainly did, faithfully and well. No "rational prosody" of the future, no prosody based on the actual facts of language, can neglect Steele's analysis. Those who substitute deduction for induction, theory for fact, may pass it by unnoticed; those who judge only by results may turn from him in disgust. The real student will hail Steele as a master, however widely differing from his metrical conclusions, and will pronounce his the first really living work in the evolution of English prosody.

A few special *notanda* may be subjoined. The *thesis*, or heavy syllable, Steele of course makes begin the bar (p. 27, *etc.*); or rather, as he puts it more accurately later, the *thesis* rests on the "first sound or silence" of every cadence (p. 184). This idea would be new to most of his readers. He began his researches by attempting to devise a musical accompaniment for speech (p. 1), which he concluded must resemble the drone of a bagpipe, giving keynote and fifth (p. 46); our "speakers to the psaltery" may think this worth attention. He deprecated elisions in verse, taking the true ground of their non-necessity (p. 75). He recognised many forms of circumflex accent (p. 85), here anticipating later critics.

He thought quintuple time impossible; "a division into five equal parts nature will not admit" (p. 114). Recent music, as before said, disproves this assertion. The beginning of Part IV summarizes his analysis, but introduces an attempt to determine the absolute duration of measures (pp. 118–24) which seems to me both useless and hardly intelligible. Pp. 136–44 give representations of accent, *etc.* on isolated words, a very doubtful procedure. His view of *appoggiatura*, referred to by Guest, will be found on p. 145. In answer to Monboddo, he admitted that accent does not always slide by imperceptible gradations, but sometimes "rises or falls at once" (p. 192). There are some quaint scansions on p. 213, and on pp. 226 and 228. Steele's style throughout is clear, and his tone modest. He disclaims much knowledge of Greek (pp. 171, 200, 235, *etc.*), yet seems to read and translate it fluently. To Monboddo he is always polite, though sometimes firm (*e.g.* p. 168); and his "I——p" is the same, once apologising for the length of his remarks by saying he "had not time to make them shorter" (p. 93) [had this phrase been used before? [1]]. To me it is particularly interesting that Monboddo was converted on the subject of pause forming part of rhythm (*cf.* pp. 110, 177). His gradual adoption of Steele's views on accent and "weight" does him very much credit. With such desultory remarks and imperfect appreciation we must leave the author of *Prosodia Rationalis*, certainly the most independent and acute enquirer into the phenomena of verse-structure whom we have yet encountered.

As a pendant to these three books I may name one of slighter content [not in my Bibliography] entitled *The Art of delivering Written Language; or, an Essay on Reading, in which the subject is treated philosophically as well as with a view to practice* (Anonymous: 8vo, London, 1775). It is said to have been written by one

[1] Parallel phrases are common enough, *e.g.* Locke, introductory "Epistle" to his famous *Essay*, "I am now too lazy or too busy to make it shorter." But Monboddo's expression is neater.

William Cockin, a teacher in Lancaster, highly esteemed though not widely known,[1] and is dedicated to David Garrick. Quoting and following Sheridan, its author defines accent as "stress, energy, or force of utterance" (p. 22), but also recognises modulation of tone, consisting of "such restless inflexions of voice, through the smallest part of a note, as can by no means be suggested by the notes of a musical scale" (p. 121) [the contrast with Steele is curious]. Also, on p. 72 (*note*) he represents the actor's traditional delivery of a heroic couplet thus:

> Ti ti dum dum, ti ti dum ti dum de,
> Ti dum ti dum, ti dum ti dum te

[I quote *verbatim*, not professing to understand]. And in his last Chapter (pp. 135-6) he says that "Poetry" is to ordinary speech as dancing to walking, and is akin to music, though "modern refinement has in a great measure destroyed this union". Beyond these rather suggestive remarks, the book makes little or no reference to verse.

I may also be allowed to mention that I possess a manuscript Essay entitled *An Enquiry into the principles of English versification, with some analogical remarks upon the versification of the Ancients*, which begins by controverting Monboddo and contains references to Steele. Internal evidence shows it the work of Allan Ramsay, junior (son of the poet), a painter, author, and fine gentleman of those days; Johnson's affection for him will be remembered. He wrote miscellaneous articles, some of which were collected into a volume in 1762[2]; but this is later, and has apparently never been published, or finished for publication. It is evidently a draft copy, with many excisions, additions, and alterations; part is in a bound volume, part in loose sheets of the same size, these latter coming at the end. It is divided into sixteen Chapters or Sections [both words are used].

---

[1] See obituary notice in *Gentleman's Magazine* for June, 1801 (Vol. 71, pp. 575-6).
[2] *The Investigator* (anonymous); contains four papers on widely differing subjects, not relating to verse.

There is a title-page, but no preface, index, or table of contents. In its arrangement the book follows familiar lines, quoting largely from Classic verse [Greek words have no accent-marks], but the writer's fundamental conception is original. As against the Grammarians, he contends that division into feet is nugatory, unless we know the time which governs these. Metre is nothing without rhythm. "The natural sensation of rythm [*sic*, but elsewhere otherwise] gave the first rise to Poetry, and must always continue to be the directing soul of it." Practically, therefore, his main view is Steele's, but he explains matters differently. Besides objecting to Steele's "heavy" and "light" as merely metaphorical, he takes the more solid ground that the three qualities of *loud*, *acute*, and *long* really exhaust the possible properties of sound, and leave no room for Steele's fourth dimension. Monboddo had tried to make out that Steele's "heavy syllables" were *loud*; he (Ramsay) contends that they are *long*, instancing "soil" and "toil", which Steele (p. 166) had declared to be heavy by nature. Unluckily, however, he adds that all "important" syllables are long in virtue of their importance, which is merely the old confusion between accent and quantity. His analysis, therefore, cannot be called successful, and his examples are sometimes grotesquely wrong, as when he makes the first syllable of "contribute" short and the second long. But when he comes to the rhythm of verse he is decidedly good. *Thesis* and *arsis* he explains correctly, and identifies them with beating of time. [It must be remembered that this view was not then the commonplace it is now; Böckh and his successors were still in the future.] By these he really scans all verse, ancient and modern, explaining the former by the latter. Feet are in all respects like musical bars. Iambic and trochaic are one measure, as also are anapaestic and dactylic. The Classic pentameter must either be two lines or contain six feet. Pause is thus recognised as constitutive of metre. Little is said of our heroic line, except that its fifth foot must be an iamb; most of his English examples are taken from songs and comic rhymes. The best Chapter is on "the connection between Musick and Poetry", where however he commits himself to the statement that "*accent* either means *quantity*, or it does not mean anything relative to the construction of verse". Two final Chapters deal with "some doubts and difficulties", mainly about Classic verse, and take up the cudgels against Bentley. On the whole, except for its view of rhythm, and its amusing examples (which I regret not having space to quote), this Essay hardly deserves to be rescued from its manuscript limbo. What is remarkable, and will seem surprising to many, is that at this time—different indeed from ours—prosody was a study that engaged the attention of men who were by no means pedantic; that a court-painter to George III (for such Ramsay was), or a President of the Royal Society like Sir John Pringle, gave their hours of leisure to considering its meaning, and quoted Greek grammarians and English poets with equal gusto and with true apprehension.

We next reach books of greater celebrity but less value for our purpose. Dr. James Beattie, Professor in Aberdeen University, poet and philosophical critic, another friend of Johnson's ("we all love Beattie"), published in 1776 a volume of *Essays*[1] containing one on "Poetry and Music as they affect the mind", written fourteen years earlier, but not previously printed. There is nothing novel in its subject-matter, but some interesting footnotes (*e.g.* on p. 90), a short account of rhythm in general (p. 158 *seq*.), and a final Chapter on the sound or harmony of verse. Even this last Chapter deals mainly with sounds which imitate sense, but metrical form is pronounced necessary to the perfection of poetry (p. 274), and in the last half-dozen pages Beattie compares the structures of English and Latin

[1] There are two editions, both dated 1776. One, a fine quarto, includes his Essay on Truth, followed by the above and two other Essays, while the octavo edition contains only the last three. My references are to the third edition of the octavo (1779).

verse, treating both by accent, and opining that a Latin dactylic hexameter line is rhythmically represented by

> Multitudes rush'd all at once on the plain with a thundering uproar.

The concluding sentence refers to a "Treatise of Versification and English Prosody, which I began some years ago, but have not yet finished". This was apparently never completed in the form here proposed, but his later *Dissertations Moral and Critical* (4⁰, London, 1783) include an Essay on "Language",[1] the fourth Chapter of which probably summarizes the treatise in question. He there discusses English verse-structure, making it depend wholly on "emphasis" [the term *accent* he keeps for tone, see Chap. V, where he mentions having heard of but not seen Steele's book], yet claiming the right to use Latin names of feet and the symbols – and ◡ (pp. 72, 73). He rejects numerical uniformity of syllables, but postulates regularity of stress, any departure from which makes verse not "well tuned" (pp. 68-70). Much of his matter comes straight from Sheridan, including quotations; the examples of versification which conclude the Chapter are more fresh, but the scansion frightfully wooden. Even "anapaestic" verse must not drop a syllable except in the first foot (p. 83), though it may sometimes add one (p. 84). Heroic verse, however, is said to be capable of thirty variations (p. 76). The whole Chapter is largely a compilation, and declines to "enter into the niceties of English prosody" (p. 84). Its mechanical view of verse prevents any regret being felt for this, or for the non-completion of the larger treatise, which would probably have contained nothing distinctively original, though its conclusions would doubtless have been expressed with characteristic clearness and elegance.[2]

[1] Also published separately. I quote a "new edition" of the separate Essay (1788). My draft Bibliography omitted to mention this Essay.

[2] In case a reference by Beattie, or elsewhere, should suggest to any one the idea of consulting a work by Beattie's co-Professor and

In 1776 appeared also the first volume of a *History of Music* by Dr. Charles Burney, father of "Evelina" (a Doctor of Music, not of Divinity like his namesake who wrote on Greek metre). This volume was devoted to ancient music, especially Greek, of which he had the lowest opinion, citing passages to show that they beat time with bones and oyster-shells—"what a noisy and barbarous music!" (p. 75)—and concluding that their tunes might have suited "Cherokees or Hottentots" (p. 103). The preliminary Dissertation (pp. 1–194) from which these remarks are quoted contains one or two references to verse, especially in § VI on "Rhythm", often mentioned by contemporaries. "A poetical *foot* consists of a certain number of syllables, which constitutes a distinct part of a verse, as a *bar* does of an air in music" (p. 77). This is said of Greek verse, but he adds that we too have dactylic lines, and scans his example thus—

$\smile$ | $-$ $\smile$ $\smile$ | $-$ $\smile$ $\smile$ | $-$
My | banks they were [are?] | furnished with | bees.

Later, speaking of modern verse—"We no longer know Rhythm now under its ancient name," but as "time, measure, movement" (p. 82); and he seems to hold that common and triple time exist in verse (*ibid.*). His remarks, however, do not concern prosody in itself, but merely the setting of words to music. He is credited with saying that metre can exist without rhythm, but I have failed to identify this passage, or indeed to find much directly bearing on our subject. Apropos of a point already mentioned more than once, I note that he represents Tartini as saying—"Music has been composed of five equal notes in a bar, but no musician has yet been

Principal, Campbell's *Philosophy of Rhetoric*, it may be well to mention that this contains no allusion to verse. Published in the same year as Beattie's earlier Essay, it is occupied wholly with the substance and rules of rhetoric, and does not even, like the Greek rhetoricians, separate prose sentences into 'feet'.

found that is able to execute it" (p. 82).[1] I find nothing else in the volume to quote.

A correspondent directed my attention to *Essays Moral and Literary*, by Rev. Vicesimus Knox, 2 vols. (1778 and 1779), but I have failed to find in them anything relating to prosody. Personally, my search was rewarded by lighting on a passage where this "Master of Tunbridge School and late Fellow of St. John's College, Oxford", spoke of "the blissful region of the Common-room . . . where never female showed her head since the days of the Founder" (Vol. II, p. 287). But my readers will scarcely value such excerpts, and I can assure them that Knox's pages yield nothing germane to our purpose, and have no right to appear in a bibliography of prosody.

The next book on our list is dated seven years later, but its true chronology is earlier. In 1783 Hugh Blair, D.D., an Edinburgh Professor, published the *Lectures on Rhetoric and Belles Lettres* which he had been delivering to students for the last twenty-four years. They ran through many editions; I quote from that of 1830, in one volume. Blair is often called wordy and shallow. The same ideas, the same stock comments and quotations reappear in his pages as in so many others, and there is nothing original in his view. Yet it is sensible in its way. Of forty-seven Lectures the last ten are concerned with poetry, and nothing could promise better than the title of the first of these (Lect. 38)—"Nature of Poetry: its origin and progress: versification." Rightly finding the origin of verse in music, he (p. 462 *seq.*) accurately describes Classic quantity, though his view of *feet* is too mechanical (p. 463, *note*). He points out our quantitative vagueness, and says that "the only perceptible difference among our syllables arises from some of them being uttered with that stronger percussion of voice, which we

[1] Burney refers to Benjamin Stillingfleet's *Principles and Power of Harmony* [Anon.: 4to, London, 1771], which expounds and comments on Tartini's musical theories. Verse is not mentioned in this book.

call accent" (p. 464). "This accent does not always make the syllable longer, but gives it more force of sound only" (*ibid.*). Our heroic verse "is of what may be called an iambic structure"; a succession, "nearly alternate," of accented and unaccented syllables. "The number of syllables is ten;" where there seem to be more, "some of the liquid syllables are so slurred in pronouncing as to bring the verse, with respect to its effect upon the ear, within the usual bounds" (*ibid.*). Here he follows and quotes Monboddo, as on music he had followed and quoted Dr. Brown. It is all excellent of its kind, but does not go deep; facts are stated, not their reasons. So with the usual exposition of "pauses" which follows, where he refuses to go farther than Pope allows. With Pope's versification he is entirely satisfied (p. 467). "Some liberty is admitted for the sake of variety," in accentuation, but "in general there are either five, or four, accented syllables in each [heroic] line" (p. 464). This is as far as Blair takes us; I do not think any thing more definite can be found elsewhere in the Lectures. The Thirteenth contains some remarks on prose feet (p. 141 *seq.*), the Thirty-third some hints on delivery of verse (pp. 400-1). If one had read no other book on the subject, these *dicta* would appear suggestive, if not quite satisfactory; but one has met them often before. Blair's statements put the popular view pleasingly and moderately, but neither add to it any thing novel nor discuss its meaning or authority.

Elements of Orthoepy, by R. Nares, A.M., "containing a distinct view of the whole analogy of the English Language, so far as it relates to Pronunciation, Accent, and Quantity," appeared in 1784. Rev. Robert Nares was an accomplished scholar, well up in his subject, not afraid to think for himself. He refers to Mitford for the "laws of English versification" (p. 142, *note*), to "the learned Dr. Forster" [*sic*] and Monboddo for the nature of Greek accent (p. 144, *cf. note*, where he thinks Steele's system "too obscure to be of general service"). But on English accent he speaks confidently, in Part II of his book (Part I deals with letters, *etc.*), and claims novelty for his view. "It is to this hour disputed what accent is," yet no one who sees an accent-mark placed on a syllable "feels any doubt in regulating his voice according to that accent-mark" (pp. 140-1). So begins Chapter I of Part II, and its second paragraph may be quoted entire. "Accent, in English, is only a species of emphasis. When one word in a sentence is distinguished by a stress, as more important than the rest, we say that it is *emphatical*, or that an emphasis is put upon it: when one syllable in a word is distinguished by a stress, and more audible than the rest, we say that it is *accented*, or that an accent is put upon it. Accent, therefore, is to syllables what emphasis is to sentences; it distinguishes one from the crowd, and brings it forward to observation" (p. 141). In monosyllables, accordingly, accent and emphasis are obviously identical. "So exactly is accent, in English, the same as emphasis," that it changes with meaning, as Ben Jonson pointed out (p. 143). Inflections, with us, affect sentences rather than single words (p. 145). Particles have usually no accent, therefore are "generally disposed in the unaccented part of each foot", *e.g.*

Fár as the sólar wálk or mílky wáy (p. 142).

Ancient speech, on the other hand, as Monboddo shows, was "more nearly allied to recitative than ours" (p. 146).

If this view is not so entirely novel as he supposes, it still deserves attention. The long sentence quoted from p. 141 shows the word "stress" passing from its older meaning of *importance* to its later meaning of *force*. With force accent was being more and more identified, notably by Sheridan and Monboddo, followed undoubtingly by Blair and others; Nares is somewhat more cautious. His solitary allusion to verse in Part II [it is here that he refers to Mitford] shows him concerned only with its accentual structure; of other elements he says nothing. The remainder of Part II (which contains ten short Chapters) is taken up with practical rules of accentuation. He recognises the "unstable" character of English accent (p. 147), therefore will point out the "general analogy" of our language, and frame rules for guidance. After going fully into these, he proceeds in Part III to deal with Quantity, which he well defines as "relative length of syllables" (p. 204). Here, unfortunately, he is misled by supposing that a short vowel implies a short syllable, so that *a, bad, barb, stands, strands*, are all to be classed as short syllables—though he admits "retardation of voice" by "concurrence of consonants" (pp. 205-6). On this, therefore, we need not dwell, except to note that he sees "how erroneous the common opinion is, that our accent always lengthens the syllable on which it falls" (p. 221); as just before he had remarked that, with us, even syllables apparently long by position are so "hurried on by the predominating force of our accentual emphasis" that they have neither the stability of long syllables nor the fluency of short ones (p. 220). Such criticisms lead one to expect a liberal prosody. But when, in the tenth Chapter of Part III, he deals with "syllables suppressed in poetic use", we find him an uncompromising supporter of elision. Of Milton's boldest experiments he can only say that the poet "melts two concurrent vowels of different words into one syllable" (p. 252).[1] Numeration of syllables is evidently his creed; *prayers* and *powers* "are now always monosyllables in poetry" (p. 253, *note*). So clear-sighted can a man be in subjects which he has studied for himself, so purblind when he merely accepts without challenge views dictated by others.

A book whose acquaintance I have but lately made contains nine "Critical Essays" by John Scott, of Amwell, posthumously published in the following year.[2] From the Introductory Memoir by "Mr. Hoole" I gather

---

[1] Cf. Part I, Chap. VII (p. 67), where in the line
   Thou diest, and all thy goods are confiscate,
diest is said to be a monosyllable [like *died*].

[2] *Critical Essays on some of the Poems of several English Poets.* By John Scott, Esq. 8vo, London, 1785.

that their author was of Quaker family, lived a retired and studious life, but occasionally visited London, there meeting Johnson and "the elegant Mrs. Montagu". He wrote poems of no great mark (*cf.* Boswell under date April 10, 1775), and Hoole notices "his predilection for laying an uncommon accent on words or syllables, which he thought gave strength to the line" (p. lxv). The nine Essays deal with nine separate poems, *Lycidas* being sandwiched between *Cooper's Hill* and *Windsor Forest*, while two Essays deal with Dyer, the other authors criticised being Gray, Collins, Goldsmith, and Thomson. The criticism is mostly on matter, but in Essay V (pp. 120–1) he makes some remarks on Milton's elisions such as "glory obscured" or "the only", which are "connected in pronunciation, so as to destroy the hiatus"; while of a rugged couplet by Dyer he remarks that "it has not the structure of any English verse, consequently has no melody", but admires its onomatopoeic character. Also, in the previous Essay (near the beginning), he finds fault with *Grongar Hill* for its "irregular mixture of iambic and trochaic lines; a circumstance rather displeasing to a nice ear". I have not noticed any other comments bearing on prosody, nor does it seem as if much of importance from our point of view were likely to come from this writer.

A striking and original paper "On Rythmical [*sic*] Measures" was contributed to the Royal Society of Edinburgh *Transactions* (Vol. II, Part II, p. 55) in December, 1786, by Rev. Walter Young, of whom I know only that he was a beneficed clergyman in what Southern writers call the "Kirk" of Scotland. It is a real study of the relations between verse and music. "Rythm, cadence, and measure" are shared by both; "tone" is peculiar to music. Our power of dividing sound is very limited; multiples of 2 and 3 are easy, of 5 extremely difficult, of 7 probably impossible. Unaccented initial syllables in verse are like notes preceding a bar [*anacrusis*], but in music these are always compensated. A pause is assumed after each bar. Our heroic rhymed verse contains three pairs of "times", the sixth being silent. Blank verse, omitting this silent space, comes nearer prose. This makes it specially suitable for narrative; it is enough if an occasional line in strict measure reminds us of the rhythm. Dactyl and spondee were the oldest feet, "march measure" being the simplest form of rhythm; here he quotes Burney's account of a young prodigy named Crotch. Ancient hexameter (though the fifth and sixth feet may have been added to an original shorter line) divided naturally into three pairs, these again suggesting triple or "minuet" time, which in verse produces a heavy effect by itself. On the other hand, when each unit is divided by three, we get tribrachs (or iambs and trochees), "gig measure" [jig?], light and airy. In Greek trochaic verse a spondee is admitted in each even foot, that being unemphatic. In iambic the opposite is apparently true, but if we regard it as trochaic with extra syllable prefixed, both agree; this is therefore probably the true view, but even so the combination is unintelligible to us, and he queries whether here the music did follow the verse. The object of "caesura", in all verse, is to break a line into unequal segments. My notes on this paper are several years old, and may easily have missed valuable points. Even this short summary, however, should show how far this paper is from merely repeating traditional ideas, how practically it considers questions of structure. Would that there were more such Essays to cite, and that the author of this one had given more of his attention to our own verse. At least we may hail here, for once, a direct contribution to prosody.

Last of the great Eighteenth Century grammarians and lexicographers comes John Walker. Of humble birth and limited education, Walker's abilities and industry forced him to the front after a career rather like Sheridan's in a somewhat lower sphere. About as much junior to Sheridan as he to Johnson, Walker cherished toward Johnson an almost idolatrous veneration, while toward Sheridan his attitude was more critical. As early as 1774 Walker printed his proposal for a Pronouncing Dictionary, and in the next year published his useful *Rhyming Dictionary*. *Elements of Elocution* followed in 1781, and his *Rhetorical Grammar* in 1785; a tract called *The Melody of Speaking delineated* came out in 1787, the *Critical Pronouncing Dictionary* in 1791, the *Key to the Classical Pronunciation of Proper Names* in 1798. Even these do not represent all his productions, and most of them were largely altered in later editions. This makes it difficult to 'place' Walker chronologically, but from 1785 to 1791 embraces his chief constructive work. The *Melody of Speaking* introduced one of his pet ideas; the "Principles of English Pronunciation" prefixed to his *Dictionary* are mainly practical. His fullest discussion of accent and quantity is affixed to the *Key to Proper Names*.

On two "discoveries" Walker specially plumed himself; viz. (1) that tones of speech proceed by *glides*, not by abrupt leaps; (2) that there are two forms of circumflex accent. In both he had been anticipated by Steele, to say nothing of others; but only in his later books does he seem to know aught of Steele. The Preface to his *Melody of Speaking*—in which the two circumflexes are first mentioned—claims absolute novelty for a method which falls far short of Steele's. His doctrine of *glides* seems clearly laid down by Greek grammarians, whom he ignorantly despised; but it is certainly strange that these grammarians knew but one form of circumflex, since there can obviously be several—Walker's two do not exhaust the number. As regards accent in general, he differs from most of his contemporaries by insisting that it includes tone as well as force. "If the word be pronounced alone, and without any reference to other words, the accented syllable is both higher and louder" than others (*Key to Proper Names*, "Preparatory Observations" to Accent and Quantity; *cf. Elements of Elocution*, Part II, § 1, and *Rhetorical Grammar*, section "On accented force"). As a rule, however, he deals only with words in a sentence, distinguishes rhetorical emphasis from mere verbal inflection,[1] devotes to the former his whole attention, and prescribes absolute laws for its regulation—laws which seem to me apt to create what Sheridan called a "reading brogue". His aim is elocutionary; nine-tenths of his discussion deals with the delivery of sentences and the way to pronounce particular words. When he comes to deal with *quantity* (which I think he does only in the Essay affixed to *Proper Names*), he is as far from truth about English syllables as about Latin and Greek. Having "no conception of quantity arising from any thing but the nature of the vowels, as they are pronounced long and short" (§ 2), he naturally does not understand what quantity means in either ancient or modern speech. His remarks on matters of scholarship can always be safely neglected, while in regard of his own language his native good sense has in this instance been led astray by the same fallacy that imposed upon Nares.

All this, of course, matters to us only as it affected his view of English verse. But on this subject he is curiously silent. Apparently he accepted in the main Johnson's ideas. The "Directions to foreigners" prefixed to his *Dictionary* assume that accentuation is regular, "though a different position of the accent is frequently to be met with in the beginning of a verse." The "Rules for reading verse" which will be found in both his earlier books (see their tables of "contents") are intended for the actor or reciter. He recognises "regularity of feet", and "that measured harmonious flow of sound" which distinguishes verse from prose; and even proclaims that "verse is a species of music"; these phrases occur in the sections just referred to. But he does not go beyond such generalities. In the *Rhetorical Grammar* ("Of the accent and emphasis of verse," Rule I) he asserts that "in verse, every syllable must have the same accent, and every word the same emphasis, as in prose"; a most disputable proposition. In *Elements of Elocution* (as

[1] In this way he admits degrees of stress, but without defining these as primary or secondary.

above, Rules IV and V) he refers to Sheridan's definition of " numbers " and to that writer's " pause of suspension " at the end of a line; but his remarks apply only to delivery, and assume that two syllables may be added to or subtracted from a line "without any indication of false quantity to the ear"! In both books he refers with praise to Lord "Kaims"[1] on pauses, in both pronounces against elision because "the syllable it forms is so short as to admit of being sounded with the succeeding syllable, so as not to increase the number of syllables to the ear, or at all to hurt the melody". On the other hand, every case of an 'inverted foot' implies that we "let the metre of the line shift for itself" (*Rhet. Gram., loc. cit.*, Rule II). These *obiter dicta*, however, are never woven into a statement of principle. To all speculations on the nature of verse, to all the discussions which exercised his contemporaries, Walker turns a deaf ear. None other of our leading grammarians has made so slender a contribution to debated questions of prosody.

Nearly the same criticism, yet with a difference, may be passed on Lindley Murray's *English Grammar* (1795). This—which long held the field, passing through countless editions,[2] and from which, or successors based on it, most of us probably imbibed our first notions about English grammar in general and English verse in particular—is professedly a compilation, and in its " Prosody " Section acknowledges indebtedness to Sheridan, while Beattie is also drawn on for examples. This section is divided into two Chapters, one on pronunciation, the other on versification; neither contains any thing that can be called novel. The former deals with "accent, quantity, emphasis, pause, and tone", adopting unreservedly Sheridan's view of accent, but recognising a distinction between principal and secondary (p. 225). Quantity is made to depend on accent, and to

---

[1] Foster he always calls "Mr. Forster".
[2] I quote the common (undated) 12mo "new edition". The 8vo edition, in two volumes, which came out first in 1808, adds nothing material as regards prosody.

be regulated by emphasis. "Though the quantity of our syllables is fixed, in words separately pronounced, yet it is mutable when these words are ranged in sentences;" it is "not fixed, but governed by emphasis" (pp. 234, 235). Pauses and tones are treated merely from an elocutionary point of view. The second Chapter follows Sheridan implicitly as to feet, in respect both of number and of their formation by either accent or quantity; and repeats the complacent remark "We have all that the Ancients had, and something which they had not" (p. 242). In scansion, however, both kinds of feet are marked by − and ᴗ, without any explanation, and with such appalling results as—

How lov'd, how valued once, avails thee not.

Be wise to-day, 'tis madness to defer.

From the low pleasures of this fallen nature.

On the warm cheek of youth, smiles and roses are blending.

Similar machine-like regularity is postulated throughout, relieved only by occasional intrusion of "secondary feet" (pp. 243, 248), which answer to Sheridan's "heterogeneous" ones. That writer's lead is followed in considering "poetical pauses" and "melody, harmony, and expression" (see under these headings), and the Chapter ends by referring "the ingenious student, for more extensive information on the subject", to the *Art of Reading*. As Murray adopts (p. 245) Johnson's creed about the melodiousness of a line, "considered by itself," depending on regularity of syllabic accentuation, we may describe his teaching as Johnsonian orthodoxy expressed mostly in terms of Sheridan.

Such is the travesty of fact put forward by our principal Grammar. Accent, quantity, and emphasis are jumbled up together and confused with metrical *ictus*, while verse is scanned not as it really is, but as the critic thinks it should be, written. The artificial nature of our traditional prosody receives striking illustration; if facts do not square with rules, so much the worse for the facts. General principles are never mentioned; even Sheridan's "stated and regular distances" are omitted by his pupil, and *time* is wholly ignored. Is it surprising that people turned in disgust from a theory so narrow, so frigid, so out of contact with reality—that prosody became a byword among readers of taste? I anticipate by saying so, for the discrediting process was gradual; sufficient for the day was the doctrine thereof. But an analysis of verse so crude, so rudimentary, so limited in its purview, was suited only to the mechanical age that produced it; before the onset of new forms and new ideas it crumbled into hopeless ruin.

The chief Eighteenth Century critics having now been passed in review, it may be well to take stock of results. Discussions on prosody have had to do with details rather than with general conception. Our verse has been assumed to consist merely of clustered syllables, and the main question has been how the syllables in each cluster are related to one another. At first it was held that there was alternation between long and short syllables, as in Greek or Latin verse. Gradually this view lost favour, alternation of emphatic and unemphatic syllables taking its place; some tried to amalgamate these views. The idea that an unemphatic was necessarily a short syllable, in particular, lingered long; arguments about quantity were vitiated by confused theories of what created relative length, due mainly to the mistaken belief that a Latin vowel became long when followed by two consonants. The importance of accent to our verse was admitted by all who identified it with force or quantity; those to whom it meant pitch found other terms to express the same conviction. Widely divergent views were held as to the function and operation of accent, but these were matters of phonetics rather than prosody, indeed mainly of nomenclature. Structural differences between English and Classic verse were mostly ignored; from Webb onward, a succession of writers maintained that by arranging accented syllables in the order which they followed in a Greek or Latin line we should obtain, in English, all the effect of that line. Our poets were not quick to adopt this view; when they did, as we shall see, the impulse came from abroad. Its adoption was but one incident in a revolution alike of theory and practice which set up accent as the sole factor to be regarded in English metre—a revolution whose progress we shall trace during the Century which follows. Eighteenth Century criticism paved the way for this revolution both positively and negatively; positively, by its gradual substitution of accentual for quantitative groups; and negatively, by failing to provide a theory which explained the variety and elasticity of our best verse. It was superseded by a criticism not less partial and one-sided, but which at least took the highest achievements of our verse as its subject-matter; the stages of this supersession must be described as we come to them.

At present we need only notice that in the *Monthly Magazine* for June, 1796, appeared a "transversion" from Macpherson's *Ossian*, by William Taylor, of Norwich, the well known "Address to the Sun" being rendered into accentual hexameters, avowedly on German models. This is memorable because it set Southey and Coleridge working on the same tack. I do not know whether Southey's "Sapphics" and "Dactylics", published in his *Poems* of 1797 and satirised by the *Anti-Jacobin* next winter, were suggested by Taylor's performance; his later hexameters certainly were. These, however, and the far more important poems published by Coleridge and Wordsworth, will be more suitably noticed in the beginning of the new Century. Before passing from the old one, there are still two or three names to mention, belonging in every way to it and its methods.

Peter Walkden Fogg, a teacher residing at Stockport, published there in 1796 *Elementa Anglicana; or, The Principles of English Grammar displayed and exemplified, in a method quite original* (2 vols., 8vo). The second volume contains twenty-seven miscellaneous Essays which were also issued separately (the only difference being the page-numbers) in a thin volume entitled *Dissertations, Grammatical and Philological* [my references are to the separate edition]. Of these, No. XI (pp. 55-7) is on "Prosody," No. XII (pp. 57-72) on "Versification". I do not find much novelty in Fogg's view of verse; indeed, in the Preface to Vol. II (p. xi) he makes humorous complaint of the way in which his ideas have been anticipated by other writers. Sheridan and Steele, both mentioned by him, were probably the chief offenders this way; for his explanation of syllabic length (pp. 55-6) follows Sheridan's line of thought as to "dwelling on a final consonant", and his division of syllables into "heavy, light, and very light" (p. 56) is avowedly taken from Steele. He does not, however, distinguish weight from force, but identifies both with *thesis* or stress, and says "By this force, thesis, or weight, is the prosody of English conducted" (*ibid.*). In dealing with versification, he makes two feet the shortest possible line (p. 57), whereas Herrick has lines of one foot; and his limits of length (*ibid.*) are too precise, as is his statement that "a single line is not acknowledged as verse" (p. 58). Rightly, however, he makes feet and not syllables constitute measure (*ibid.*), and regrets that "Our modern versifiers have endeavoured, too successfully, to lay aside the trisyllabic feet in heroic metre" (p. 59). The "elegancies" of verse are "melody, harmony, and expression" (p. 63), and harmony includes variety (p. 66); but "a mixture of feet is prejudicial to simple melody" (p. 65). Beyond these general remarks, I have noted nothing which demands reproduction. Even if "original", they are far from constituting a new departure; and one must regret that study of Steele did not prompt to bolder parting from old methods, and recognition of temporal rather than syllabic structure as the basis of our verse.

In 1796 was also published a famous treatise *On the Prosodies of the Greek and Latin Languages*, which we need only note in passing as dealing with accent in

English verse as well as Classic. Though published anonymously, it was known to be by Samuel Horsley, Dean of Westminster and Bishop of Rochester, and was dedicated to Lord Thurlow. While denying that accentuation necessarily lengthens sound (p. 18), he still contends that in English "quantity and accent always go together", and that "we have no other rule of quantity, but to lengthen the accented syllable" (p. 4). He does not deny that, when a word contains no long syllable, accent may rest on a short one, as in *honey, clever, luckily*; but if there be a long one, accent chooses it, so that *grátify* is more natural than *gratífy* (pp. 4–5). We need not follow him into Greek questions, nor into his criticism of Primatt (see his "Appendix"), whose book—published thirty-two years before—he had only just come across. His main assertion about English verse is that "we give the sharp stroke of the voice upon the syllable which, by its place in the verse, ought to be long" (p. 5). Beyond this *dictum*, which points toward unbroken regularity of accentuation, I find nothing which need detain us.

No one interested in the accent-quantity question should fail to read *Metronariston* ["best measure"]: *or a new pleasure recommended*, published anonymously in 1797, but ascribed to a "Dr. John Warner", whom I cannot otherwise identify. This most amusing writer urges that "there is nothing in common between Accent and Quantity" (p. 53), that "elevation without prolongation" is impossible to us (p. 6), that we read Latin and Greek as if they were English—an Italian priest said to him, "You dactylize and trocheeize every thing" (p. 13)—and that we should substitute for this reading by quantity. Incidentally he pokes fun all round, at Jacob and Bryant (in his Preface), at "Mr. Sheridan . . . who, I thought, when I was his scholar, could not exemplify his own very good rules" (p. 22, *note*), at Scotchmen (p. 27, *note*), Bentley (p. 53, *note*), "unhappy Homer," who rarely made quantity and accent agree (p. 88), Handel (p. 108, *note*), and Bishop Horsley (see

Postscript, pp. 113, 120). His opponents he makes say *Nolumus stupiditates Angliae mutari* (p. 100). English verse is often referred to, and paralleled with Latin in couplets like—

> *Ades, Pater supremè,*
> Thy head with glory beamy;

or,

> *Beatus ille qui, procul negotiis,*
> Can to sweet lore apply, and live in letter'd bliss (p. 40).

As a pure dactylic hexameter he proposes—

Come we in pity now from the low palace of old Father Ocean (p. 23).[1]

Every accented syllable he marks *long*, even in the line (quoted from Sheridan)—

> The busy bodies flutter, tattle still,

while asserting that "our rhythmus" never lengthens short syllables, though it shortens long ones (p. 19). Quantity by position our language "utterly disclaims" (*ibid., note*); the first syllable of *constrains* is short. So again, "we have syllables which are short . . . where the vowel precedes no less than four consonants"; and "some of the more northern languages", he believes, extend the number to six (p. 112, *note*). The book is a medley of sense and nonsense, the latter largely predominating, since his fundamental position is that we cannot accentuate a short vowel without lengthening it! But the wit and versatility of the writing make it unique among the dreary tomes of this controversy.

Lastly, in 1799 appeared [2] *An Essay on the Nature of*

---

[1] Before this is objected to, the reader should remember that this line is made up from two of Dryden's (in *Albion and Albanius*) which our common prosody would call dactylic, *viz.*—

> From the low palace of old Father Ocean
> Come we in pity, your cares to deplore.

Possibly the popular nomenclature may now be felt not wholly appropriate.

[2] Omitted in my Bibliography.

the English Verse, with directions for reading Poetry. By the Author of the Essay on Punctuation. This connotes Rev. Joseph Robertson, writer of many small books, and of "near 3000 articles in the Critical Review" [see leaflet following Essay], that jejune periodical which laid down laws of taste to the readers of this time. The Essay may be shortly described as worthy of the *Review*. Rightly beginning with a statement that our verse does not depend on quantity—whence it follows that *iambic* and *trochaic* can only be applied to our verse in a figurative sense (pp. 3-4 and 15)—he spoils this by showing that to him quantity means only length of vowels (pp. 1-2). And then he proceeds to dogmatize in the old irrational way. A "short final syllable is want of harmony" (p. 6). "For the sake of variety, the [heroic] line sometimes begins with an accented syllable" (p. 11); but if this is too often repeated, as by Pope, it becomes monotonous (p. 13). Whenever accent is misplaced, "the verse is lame and inharmonious," and he follows Kames in censuring

This nymph, *to the* destruction of mankind (p. 25).

As for Milton, while praising his "pleasing variety in pauses" (p. 10), he objects to "some archaisms and peculiarities in his versification", censures his double inversions, and declares that many of his lines are "mere prose", words being "protracted and extended in an arbitrary and capricious manner" (pp. 61-2). In an Appendix (pp. 124-6), while blaming Bentley's attempt to rewrite the concluding lines of *Paradise Lost*, he modestly suggests that it would be better if the last two pairs of lines were transposed! The best thing in the book is its many quotations; but nearly thirty pages (76-104) are occupied by a list of the Classical proper names that occur in English verse. Of any thing beyond mechanical criticism there is no trace. Leaving this typical specimen of self-contented Eighteenth Century dogmatism, we now at the same time bid farewell to the Century itself.

CHAPTER III

THE NEW VERSE

1800—1850

CHRONOLOGICAL divisions are seldom exact, and the revival of English poetry by no means waited for the dawn of a new Century. If in Gray and Warton and Collins and Cowper novelty showed itself rather by substance than by form, yet Burns with his bold simplicity and Blake with his pure though singularly artless melody had definitely set aside Augustan canons of "correctness". Delight in old ballads, ever since the publication of Percy's *Reliques*, told against artificial elegance; and Macpherson's *Ossian*, here as well as on the Continent of Europe, produced an impression hardly credible by us. Besides, the very men who should inspire the new Century were already at work during the closing years of the old. Walter Scott was "making himself" in his Liddesdale excursions; Wordsworth and Coleridge, Southey and Landor, were thinking and writing and publishing. Their impressionable years of youth and early manhood, with all these writers, belong to the Eighteenth Century. The first edition of *Lyrical Ballads* was published in 1798, the second—with Wordsworth's weighty Preface—in 1800. No work that Coleridge did in the new Century equals what he did in the old. For practical purposes, however, the new departure may be regarded as beginning with the new Century, which was well under way before the general public became aware of any change. Prosody always lags behind poetry, so not for many years shall we find the new methods recognised in books on metre.

However we may rank these writers otherwise, Coleridge

was the most potent as regards form. *Christabel* was not published till 1816; but its First Part was written in 1797, its Second in 1800, and both were freely read and handed round in manuscript. From them Scott avowedly took the metre of the *Lay*, as from Scott's poems Byron unquestionably derived that of his Oriental Tales.[1] The seed of *Christabel* grew to flower and fruit in these and other writers. All the "Lake Poets" were experimenters in metre as in matter. Southey carried Coleridge with him into hexameters on Taylor's pattern, and several fragments, including a prelude to their projected poem on Mahomet, survive as a record of that attempt. But neither there, nor in Southey's own elaborate verse-schemes, nor in Wordsworth's ponderous rhythm, nor even in the *Ancient Mariner* (which, metrically, is but a prolonged ballad), can the new inspiration be found. This came, so far as metre is concerned, particularly from *Christabel*. When the Preface to that poem was written does not appear. It may represent ideas as old as the Somersetshire days, ideas which—as I have already suggested—may have been partly shaped by Thelwall's account of Steele's views. In any case it affirms a "new principle" for prosody, which the poet had put into practice in those early days, whether or no he then formulated it explicitly. This principle was, in his own words, "that of counting in each line the accents, not the syllables." By the gradual adoption of this

---

[1] Many people—including Moore, his biographer—credited Byron with knowledge of *Christabel* prior to 1815. But his own *note* to his *Siege of Corinth* [published early in 1816], § 19, negatives this, and is confirmed by Scott, who in a letter to Mrs. Hughes says "It was I who first introduced his Lordship to the fragment". Byron and Scott never met before (or after) 1815, and it was probably at their first meeting that Scott repeated part of *Christabel* as well as *Hardyknute* (Lockhart, Vol. III, Chap. X). The earlier Tales therefore derive from Scott, not directly from Coleridge, though I feel some doubt whether Byron's abovementioned *note* is accurate as regards the lines to which it is appended. As to this, *cf.* Introduction to *Siege of Corinth* in Murray's new edition of Byron (Vol. III).

principle our verse, and later our theories of prosody, have been revolutionized.

Coleridge, of course, did not invent this principle. He may rather be said to have rediscovered it. Certainly it was "new" to the critics of his day. None of the Eighteenth Century metrists whom we have been studying—not even Steele or Mitford—had been aware of it. The whole discussion on 'trisyllabic feet' ignored it. In essence, however, it was a return to older standards, observed by our poets, neglected by our prosodists. It recaptured for the coming Century Elizabethan freedom and melody. Whether the description just quoted from Coleridge properly represents its nature and operation is, perhaps, open to argument. What, precisely, did he intend to convey by it?

Everything turns on what Coleridge meant by "accents". If he meant 'accented syllables', in the ordinary sense of that phrase, his definition is at fault. That he did mean this has been commonly assumed, theories of "stress-rhythm" have been built on the assumption, and lines of *Christabel* which do not comply with these theories have been roundly censured. For, on this view, the poet's assertion that "in each line the accents will be found to be . . . four" is quite incorrect. So, unfortunately, is his other assertion that the syllables "vary from seven to twelve". In the first five lines of the poem, one line has only four syllables, another six; and similar ones occur again. There are also lines of an entirely different pattern from what he has described, *e.g.*

> Amid the jagged shadows
> Of mossy leafless boughs,
> Kneeling in the moonlight,
> To make her gentle vows.

We may conclude that these had escaped his remembrance, and that his description applied only to such representative lines as—

> From her kennel beneath the rock
> She maketh answer to the clock,
> Four for the quarters, and twelve for the hour.

Even here, it must be owned, the words "From" and "to" do not fulfil his conditions. They are not primarily accented syllables, and the lines containing them have but three such apiece. If we wish to look facts in the face, this must be frankly admitted.

Coleridge's description being in any case faulty, let us see for ourselves what his verse was. The novelty of *Christabel* lay in this, that it subordinated syllabic structure to temporal. Orthodox metrical criticism had forgotten this latter element of verse. A few timid references to the *time* of a line, a few assertions of identity between *feet* and *bars*, with a vague consciousness that verse and music had drifted too far apart, show dissatisfaction with prevailing theories rather than any attempt to mend them. Coleridge's practice, if not his definition, restored *time* to its true pre-eminence. He does not say that his accents occur at equal intervals, but our ears tell us that they do. The 'feet' are uniform in length, though diverse in the number of syllables they contain. That is what his somewhat loose description means; that is what his magical verse builds on, with a charm all its own. In lesser hands the attempt might have failed, the result have been feeble, or harsh, or heavy. Coleridge, a master of verbal melody, carried it victoriously through, and in so doing vindicated for English verse its natural inalienable birthright.

It is possible to say, in another sense, that every normal line of *Christabel* (leaving aside for a moment those of a different pattern) carries four accents, because consisting of four equal bars or periods, each of which must theoretically have an accent appertaining to it. This is the musical view, and would be true of musical bars. But, firstly, there is no reason to think that Coleridge used "accents" in this sense; and, secondly, the analogy is imperfect. If in music a note occupied the place which "From" or "to" occupies in Coleridge's lines just quoted, it could not fail to be accented. The fact that these words are *not* accented shows that verse has laws of its own. For, assuredly, the plain truth is

that Coleridge meant these words to be devoid of accent.
Even to style them 'metrically accented' is fallacious;
they carry no accent whatever. Why should we force
the laws of one art on the material of another, and
imagine that spoken syllables must obey the same rules
as musical symbols? Let fact replace imagination. The
actual fact is that our poets sometimes substitute a weak
syllable for an expected strong one. Inferior writers
doubtless abuse this liberty; but our best poets use it,
and it is not likely that they are all of them wrong. I do
not think it is difficult to see why they do it. An
occasional weak accent relieves the oppression of a too
insistent beat, and makes welcome variety. However
this be, the fact is indubitable. Musicians may talk of a
"silent accent", but the term hardly applies here. The
theoretic rhythmical accent is not merely omitted, it is
deliberately contradicted, in a way for which music seems
to yield no parallel. Yet our perception of rhythmical
uniformity persists; persists, even though the syllables
transgress instead of enforcing it. This reveals the
fundamental law of English verse, opposition between
syllabic and temporal structure. It is Coleridge's glory
to have discerned this law, in practice if not altogether
in theory. His verse obeys it, though his Preface does
not clearly state it. His ear led him right, in this matter
of omitted accents, where I maintain that he is nearer the
truth than his critics. For, in our verse, time can be felt
even when not signalized by accent, and every period
need not necessarily contain a syllable of dominant
stress. If we say otherwise, we condemn the work of
(without exception) all our chief poets; we must, like the
Eighteenth Century critics, find fault with every line
containing such cadences as

This nymph, to the destruction of mankind.

But from theory I return to history. Coleridge's "new"
metre, through the medium of its admirers, spread its
influence far and wide. For long, indeed, it was considered a "light horseman" sort of affair, unsuited for the

highest poetry ; just as triple-time verse was so regarded down almost to our own day. Only by degrees was it perceived that Coleridge's "principle" held good for all verse, that even our heroic line was subject to its sway. Still longer was it before these ideas found their way into manuals of prosody. It need not surprise us to find no mention of them in the books we have next to examine. Even at the present time they are imperfectly assimilated by our grammarians. Prosody is made a mere matter of accented and unaccented syllables; the fundamental reality, the string which holds these together, passes unnoticed. Much less need we look for adequate views of verse in the prosodists of the earlier Nineteenth Century; with a few remarkable exceptions, these writers continue laboriously to turn the old treadmill.

The exceptions were chiefly followers of Steele, who were already at work when the Century began. Thelwall has been named; he printed tracts illustrating his scansions, but his one book on the subject will come before us under date 1812. Roe is credited with publishing a treatise on metre in 1801, but no copy is in our chief libraries and I have seen no account of it, so must reserve him till 1823, when his one extant study was published. Odell, whose book appeared in 1806, tells us it was written four years earlier ; and Chapman, whose two volumes came out in 1818 and 1821, had been teaching his views for many years before. All these writers, therefore, might be grouped at or about the outset of the Nineteenth Century; and they form a group by themselves. But their work was little known, their influence small, so it hardly matters where we place them. Chronological order of publication has been my rule hitherto, and I propose still to follow it unless there is reason otherwise. The medley of widely differing authors thus presented is, after all, a fact of history not to be disregarded.

In 1804, as has been already noted, Mitford published his *Inquiry*. Next year it was caustically examined by the *Edinburgh Review* (Vol. VI, No. 12, Article X). This paper is reprinted, with an added note about accent, and a Supplement of three pages written much later, in the *Works* of Dean William Herbert (Vol. II, pp. 31-78 and 212-15). If Classic instead of English prosody were our subject, this paper would need careful study. It propounds interesting views about the place of accent in Greek and Latin verse [anticipating those of Spedding, *infra*, 1861], while in the Supplement occur some good quantitative lines, for description of which see Appendix A. The young Oxonian—for such was Herbert when he wrote this review, though he adopts the standpoint of his periodical, calls the Scotch his countrymen, and speaks as though he lived in Edinburgh, " the metropolis of false quantities"—taxes Mitford with imperfect knowledge of his subject, and lays down the law about Classic, French, Celtic, Icelandic, and English verse with equal decisiveness. The last alone, fortunately, need engage our attention.

"The laws of English accent and versification . . . have perhaps never been rightly considered" (p. 377: 65).[1] So begins his analysis, but it contains little that is really new. It is restricted to verse of Popian type, and blames even that when it transgresses his rules. Two accented syllables must never come together in a foot, and when they adjoin must always be separated by a pause (pp. 377-8: 65-6). Three syllables may occur in any foot, so the above rule is observed ; the extra syllable "shall not be reckoned in scanning the verse". Words like *heaven, prism, etc.* must be monosyllables in heroic verse, but must be dissyllables in "verse of the triple cadence", in which no aberration of accent can be allowed (p. 379: 68). Pope errs, therefore, in beginning a line with the words " Heaven's whole foundations " ; but "All heaven's foundations " would be " good metre, because the adjective remains grave before its substantive " (p. 380: 69). In heroic verse "the tenth syllable shall be accented ; but the accent may be occasionally drawn back to the eighth" (p. 378: 66). He scans specimen

[1] I quote pages *first* of the *Edinburgh Review*, *second* of the *Works*, to facilitate reference.

lines by both accent and quantity, but his accents come quite irregularly and his quantities are those of Latin verse. To these latter he attaches importance; "quantity neither is nor ought to be entirely disregarded in our versification" (p. 380: 70). In proof of this he compares the line—

> O liquid streamlets to the main returning,

with this other—

> The headlong torrent from its native caverns,

and asserts that the former would be objectionable in blank verse to a Classically trained ear (*ibid., seq.*). I doubt if one such ear in a hundred would feel any difference, and certainly as English verse both lines are equally valid.[1] With more justice he says that in Greek and Latin verse the difficulty was to prevent too many short syllables coming together, while with us it is just the opposite; with them variety had to be restricted, with us it is to be encouraged (p. 381: 71, and *passim*). Yet his notion of variety is less wide than that of our chief poets, and his rules would restrict the freedom of even our most "correct" writers. If, finally, we ask whence these rules are drawn, the answer can only be, from the writer's imagination. No proof of them is offered, no justification of their authority; the author's *ipse dixit* is their sole foundation.

While, however, no adequate view of the basis of English verse can be found in these pages, they well deserve reading on other accounts. The scholar will pause over the assertion that "the metrical rules observed in the South of Europe [*e.g.* in modern Italian verse, with which he parallels our own] were not modern inventions, but the old accentual laws of Latin verse, which survived those of quantity" (p. 376: 63). Classic accent Herbert believed to have been nowise different from our own, and "the acute accent certainly does not induce length of time" (p. 367: 48). "The theory of

[1] *Cf.* criticism by Guest (Skeat's edition, p. 109).

Sheridan [about accent] was so unintelligible, that it scarcely requires notice" (p. 368 : 48). On every branch of his subject the young writer is equally dogmatic. Klopstock's hexameter is a "disgusting abortion", which "has in a manner destroyed all sense of good poetry in Germany" (p. 369: 50). French verse, through lack of accent, "affords little gratification to other European nations"; their Alexandrine is really two lines, not one (p. 381 : 72). A final Summary (pp. 384–5 : 77–8) resumes his chief conclusions. Students of Classic verse should read also the "Note on Horatian metres" which follows in Vol. II of the *Works* (pp. 79–90; dated 1841), and the "Additional Note" (pp. 151–8). In the latter he repeats his "position, that modern metres are accentual forms of ancient temporal verse with little regard to quantity" (p. 157), thus in mature age reaffirming conclusions at variance with those of most critics, but which he maintains with no little force and ingenuity.

This same year, 1805, saw published Scott's *Lay of the Last Minstrel*, which first popularized what we have called the new verse; and it also gave birth to *An Analytical Inquiry into the Principles of Taste*, by Richard Payne Knight. Little time need be spent over the latter, though it makes not infrequent reference to verse-form. Shallow and sceptical in philosophy, it applies Eighteenth Century canons to poetry as to other arts, and finds Pope "the best versifier that ever lived" (p. 112). Very little sensual gratification, however, is afforded by even the most melodious versification (p. 51). He ridicules pseudo-Classic structure in English (*ibid.*), and echoes previous writers as to our violations of Latin quantity (pp. 53, 127–31). Verse is well defined as being to prose as dancing is to walking (p. 111); but his only notion of prosody is that "English verse arises from a limited and regulated distribution of accents and pauses, as well as of quantities" (p. 112)—which really tells us nothing. Admitting the "great and transcendent merits of Milton's poetry", he yet blames the "rugged anomalies" of his music, and devotes pages to pointing them out (*cf.* pp. 112–

20). Later, treating of the sublime and pathetic, he pronounces our blank verse, "like Greek iambic, too near the tone of colloquial speech" (p. 395). Other remarks on metre are scattered through the volume, but I have noted nothing that requires mention. To all the higher side (as we now deem it) of verse this author seems insensible. His theory of art, and indeed of life, leaves little room for the nobler emotions; and his view of verse is as mechanical as the rest of his thought.

After Knight comes the first published book of the Steele school. "J. Odell," author of *An Essay on the Elements, Accents, and Prosody of the English Language*, was an M.A. of Cambridge, beyond which fact my knowledge does not go. His moderate-sized Essay has a modest preface, but no index or table of contents; it is not divided into Chapters, but takes each of its three subjects in turn. The *Elements* (pp. 1–54) are rightly defined as sounds, not letters merely, and his analysis of twenty-nine elementary sounds (p. 44) in English speech is original and suggestive. Six out of seven pure vowels, he says, may be either long or short. On *Accents* (pp. 55–123) he avowedly adopts Steele's view, regarding them as tone-inflections (of which there is an excellent description, with diagram, on p. 80), and constantly distinguishing them from emphasis. Monotony, in English speech, even for a single syllable, creates "intolerable dissonance" (p. 121). Steele's doctrine is summarized on pp. 93–102,[1] and Walker's discussed on pp. 104–23, as also in a "Postscript" (pp. 195–205). But it is the *Prosody* portion of this Essay (pp. 124–90) which specially appeals to us. Here he dissents markedly from Steele's teaching, both as to the difference between verse and prose, and as to the function of 'pause' in verse-structure. Prose, he maintains, does not possess "rhythmical cadences in regular succession" (p. 152); non-metrical

---

[1] While adopting Steele's principles, he criticises his practice. "I confess that some of the examples of accentuation specified in his book seem to have been incorrectly noted" (p. 101). *Cf.* his remarks on a passage cited from Dionysius Thrax (pp. 89–92).

pauses affect the recitation of verse merely, not its actual structure (p. 156). Nor does he distinguish between force and 'poise', like his master, though he bids us discriminate between "rhythmical and oratorial [*sic*] emphasis" (pp. 158-9). Moreover, he flatly rejects Steele's eight degrees of quantity, necessities of intonation limiting us to a proportion of four to one (pp. 154-5). In essentials, however, he adopts Steele's view, making "cadences" commensurate (p. 148), and actual time-beating the test (p. 151). Syllables possess quantity, but verse does not depend on these, but on "emphatic pulsations", regular as the beats of a pendulum; "without such isochronism, there can be no regular rhythmical modulation" (p. 148). On syllabic quantity he is unsatisfactory, inclining to believe that "nothing but lengthening the vowel can possibly make the syllable long" (p. 137), though in the Postscript he ridicules the idea that a vowel changed its sound according to its position. Even Greek verse did not depend wholly on quantity, a trochee sometimes taking the place of dactyl or spondee (p. 149); while in "our iambic verse" tribrachs, spondees, dactyls, and double pyrrhics "are equalised with the leading iambic feet; and sometimes a single syllable is made to fill a whole cadence" (p. 168). Common and triple time are, of course, distinguished; "the first is the rhythmus of a march, and the second of a minuet"; either may be quick or slow, and have "more or fewer steps" (pp. 130-1). Both occur in our heroic verse, but "without affecting the regular equality of the cadences" (p. 169). His excellent general principles, however, do not save him from supposing (pp. 173-4) that lines in *Paradise Lost* may consist, now of only three "cadences" or feet, now of four, now again of six, *e.g.*—

  (Im-)|mutable, im-|mortal, | infinite.
  Fountain of | light, thy-|self in-|visible.
  Hail, | Son of | God, | saviour of | men, thy | name—

(the first and third feet of the last line being shown as

eked out by a 'rest'). This, it need hardly be said, is simply flying in the face of fact. There can be no shadow of doubt that Milton intended every line of his poem, without exception, to be read as composed of five feet.

Toward the end of his Essay (p. 175 *seq.*), Odell maintains that Classic measures are quite possible in English, and have failed hitherto only because their writers violated natural accentuation, as in the 'sapphics' by Watts, or those others "I know not by whom" which were the work of Herries. And he gives some specimens of his own [for which see Appendix A], which are certainly neater and smoother than those of his predecessors, though not quantitatively exact. He makes no allusion to German verses, nor to those of Coleridge, Southey, or Thelwall, and seems to have worked entirely on lines of his own. These, it is interesting to note, are—careful compliance with accent, coupled with avoidance of clumsily crowded consonants. Their basis is accentual, but quantity is not wilfully neglected, as was done by most of his successors. If Odell's lead had been followed, we should have been spared many jaw-breaking lines by authors of more note. The book ends with a lament over the cacophony introduced into our words by omission of the vowels in *-est*, *-ed*, *etc.*, and some verses on "the old English language" (pp. 191–4) followed by the Postscript already mentioned.

Odell's Essay was originally written as an introduction to a Dictionary, and was primarily a criticism of Johnson's views. It replaces *a priori* dogmatism by study of facts. Our "numbers" consist of syllables in harmonious combination, under "a system which has never yet been fully investigated" (p. 125). Toward this investigation he makes a substantial and valuable contribution, though misled by false ideas as to the syllabic basis of verse. His criticism is always telling. The monotony of our heroic couplet he finds frequently "tiresome and disgusting" (p. 161); Milton's variety may sometimes be excessive, yet "less often than a cursory reader would imagine" (*ibid., seq.*). To Elizabethan writers he seldom if ever refers. His work has never been reprinted, though its freshness and vigour deserved longer life; its teaching would now be old-fashioned. Yet no student of our prosody should omit glancing through it, so suggestive is it both in its truth and its error. To suppose it a mere repetition of Steele would be a great mistake.

[1] From the *Letters on Literature, etc.*, of Dr. George Gregory (2 vols., 1812) little of direct interest can be quoted. Posthumously published, they belong to the Eighteenth rather than the Nineteenth Century, surveying general questions of style and composition quite on the lines of Blair or Beattie, not without grace and liveliness. In Vol. I, Letter VIII, pp. 93-4, he touches on prose form. "Something like a metrical arrangement may be traced in the style of our best prose writers." "The harmony of prose numbers depends on the judicious admixture of long and short syllables, and the musical or perhaps metrical conclusion of the periods or sentences." Macpherson's *Ossian* "is throughout metrical, and even monotonous". In the Bible, and Prayer-book Psalms, "you will find almost perfect hexameters." A grave uniform style abounds in iambs and trochees, as does English verse, while French verse "is all in dactyls". Again, in Vol. II, Letter XXIV, pp. 186-94, he points out the difficulty, not of distinguishing prose from verse, but of delimiting their boundaries, and defines the latter as "a metrical composition chiefly addressed to the passions", to which must be added that a poem is essentially a work of creation. For quantities of syllables, and rules for feet, he refers his reader to grammar, but warns him against supposing that English syllables are devoid of quantity, though in practice accent is more regarded. Our iambic verse he makes depend on number of syllables and management of pauses, "very little attention" being

[1] For Carey (1809) see under 1816.

paid to quantity. All this, it will be seen, is merely what has been often said before, nor does Dr. Gregory put it forward as novel; we need not, therefore, dwell on these volumes.

Next we reach "Citizen" John Thelwall, Radical and suspected revolutionary, friend of Coleridge and Wordsworth, editor of the *Champion* newspaper, where "Sapphics" by Coleridge and himself appeared [see my Bibliography],[1] lecturer on elocution, and disciple of Steele. His one book is usually cited by its half-title *Illustrations of English Rhythmus*, but the copy which I have seen—that in the British Museum—has a much longer title indicating that the book contains " Selections for the illustration of a course of instruction in the Rhythmus and Utterance of the English Language, with an Introductory Essay . . . *etc*.", the date being 1812. This copy, however, is a patchwork affair, parts of another book, and sheets which had evidently been separate tracts, being bound up with it. The "Introductory Essay " is the only part with which we are concerned, and I take it that this belongs to the title-page, and appeared in 1812. The " Selections" are merely samples of prose and verse, in a few cases illustrated by Steele's symbols, but usually without these, though some are barred and characterized by hand as if at the teacher's dictation.

The Essay (pp. i-lxxii, but I shall use Arabic instead of Roman numerals for my quotations) adopts Steele's terminology throughout, and begins by saying that Steele, Odell, and Roe had alone had a " conception of the true nature and characteristics of a cadence, or English metrical foot"; while even they had not " gone to the bottom of the subject", through ascribing to mere

[1] Thelwall's "Song without a sibilant" used to be famous. I give the first stanza:—

> No, not the eye of tender blue,
> Though, Mary, 'twere the tint of thine,
> Or breathing lip of glowing hue
> Might bid the opening bud repine,
> Had long enthrall'd my mind.

taste what is really due to "indispensible [*sic*] necessities of organic action". [The reference to Roe must be to his missing volume of 1801.] In all vocal efforts, the progress is from heavy to light, not *vice versa*, where there is alternation at all; a duck utters heavy sounds only, but the single animal that reverses the above rule is a guinea-pig! Therefore in English speech, and English verse, the rule is invariable. [Yet English sentences most often begin with a "light" syllable, *e.g.* "To be or not to be".] "A cadence is a portion of tuneable sound, beginning heavy and ending light;... a foot is a syllable or syllables occupying the space or duration of such a cadence,... and must be measured from the commencement of the syllable in thesis or heavy poise" (p. 6; *cf.* a fuller statement on p. 44). "Six proportional but varied cadences constitute (in its simplest form) an English heroic line" (pp. 3-4). General principles are thus laid down in pp. 1-20; then follow Sections on "praxis", definitions, organs of speech. A beginning must be made with simple lines; those of Shakespeare and Milton "can scarcely be treated thus in mechanical outline" (p. 22). "Appogiatura syllables" are mentioned (*ibid., cf.* p. 47); *caesurae* " sometimes do, and sometimes do not, increase the primitive number of the cadences" (p. 23). Pulsation and remission are explained (pp. 37-44), and are distinguished from long and short on the one hand, loud and soft on the other. But the most important Section of all is that on "Principles of Metrical Proportion, and of Rhythm" (pp. 44-58). Here he re-states his general theory with greater exactitude and more detail. Common and triple time are distinguished, also quick triple and slow triple (p. 45). These are recognised mainly by the number of syllables in a foot, which, if not constant, should be at least " so prevalent as to give its primary denomination to the measure" (p. 46). Feet of one syllable are freely admitted; they must always contain "a single protracted syllable, beginning heavy and ending light". Thus he scans—

Arms and the | man I | sing, | who, ʌ | forced by | fate.

[the *caret* indicates a "rest", which Thelwall represents by the musical symbol defining its duration] (*ibid.*). Comparative quantity is fixed, absolute quantity is "latitudinary"; "there is therefore no difficulty in giving to a trochee, or an iambus, the same entire quantity with a spondee, or to a spondee the same with a trochee, etc., though differing in the proportions of their integral parts" (p. 49). Moreover "some trochaics may be *inherently* as long as some spondees", and spondees may be pure or impure; "syllables are not meted out by a Winchester measure" (p. 51). Accepting Steele's eight possible degrees of quantity, he yet finds *three* suffice in practice, and notes that poise and quantity are often confounded (pp. 48, 51, 52). The Section ends with the following "Definitions of the Rhythmus of Verse and Prose", printed mainly in italics. "(1) Rhythmus consists in an arrangement of cadences, or metrical feet, in clauses more or less distinguishable by the ear, and of more or less obvious proportion, in their periods and responses. (2) Verse is constituted of a regular succession of like cadences, or of a limited variety of cadences, divided by grammatical pauses, emphases, and caesurae, into obviously proportioned clauses; so as to present sensible responses, at proportioned intervals, to the ear. (3) Prose differs from verse, not in the proportion, or in the individual character of its cadences; but in the indiscriminate variety of the feet that occupy those cadences, and the irregularity of its clausular divisions. It is composed of all sorts of cadences, arranged without attention to obvious rule, and divided into clauses that have no obviously ascertainable proportion, and present no responses to the ear at any legitimate or determined intervals" (pp. 55-6).

The remainder of the Essay deals with other subjects. From the foregoing it will appear how rigorous and logical is Thelwall's analysis. I cannot, myself, endorse it throughout. The claim with which he begins, that the divisions of cadences can be written out exactly "in score" (p. 7), is practically abandoned later in view of the difficulty attaching to syllabic analysis (p. 50); and his treatment of single-syllable feet seems to me arbitrary. Imperfect views of periodicity lead him to hold that "pauses and emphases increase the number", though they do not alter the proportion, of cadences, so that the following line contains *seven* cadences preceded by an anacrusis (the third foot being constituted, and the fourth supplemented, by a pause of the voice)—

(Ye) | airy | sprites | — | who ᴀ | oft as | Fancy | calls (p. 55).

To contend that every heroic line contains six cadences is reasonable, whether right or wrong; to suppose that the number of cadences is immaterial cuts away the foundation of prosody. This heresy, we have seen, originated with Steele himself; his followers unfortunately adopted it. But, after all deductions, and even questioning his fundamental postulate of progress from heavy to light, how much there is to admire in Thelwall's work! How actual, how close to reality, it seems after the *a priori* dogmatism of the Classical school. His ideal, too, is lofty; Shakespeare and Milton, not Denham and Waller and Pope, are his models. "The divine Milton," especially, was the idol of his boyhood (pp. 4, 18, *etc.*), and remains his master. In the opening lines of *Paradise Lost*, it may be mentioned, he finds the prevailing cadence spondaic (p. 49). Surely it is discreditable to English prosody that work like Odell's and Thelwall's remained almost entirely unnoticed; unanswered, not because unanswerable, but because unread. So it was, however; we shall find the high-priests of criticism sublimely unconscious of their contribution to metrical science, resolutely repeating old formulas which had lost what little truth they ever possessed.

My Bibliography next mentions a book or books that have wholly vanished. The titles are given in Watt's *Bibliotheca Britannica*, the author's name being Richard Edwards, the date 1813. No copy is known to exist; advertisements have failed to procure one. Guest mentions having tried to find the third; he does not refer to the others. My impression is that the three may have been parts of one production, possibly a school-book, issued together or separately. What creates interest is that the author professes to give specimens of verse measured solely by quantity, as well as of verse measured solely by accent. The former, however, are not said to be taken from *English* verse, while the latter are. Possibly, therefore, the contrast is merely between Latin verse and English, on familiar lines. Till a copy turns up, if one ever does, nothing further can be said. The author's name is otherwise unknown to me.

Dr. John Carey, author of treatises on Latin prosody and the well known *Gradus ad Parnassum*, published in 1816 a "new and improved edition" of his *Practical English Prosody and Versification* (the first edition, said to have come out in 1809, I have not seen); also a separate *Key* to same. As might be expected, both keep wholly to Classic lines. "Prosody teaches the proper quantity and accent of syllables and words, and the measures of verses;" but "the quantity or length of syllables is little regarded in English poetry, which is entirely regulated by their number and accent" (p. 1). Accent he defines as "emphatic tone" (*ibid.*), and explains that the symbols – and ᴗ, in his book, denote accented and unaccented syllables respectively (p. 4, *note*). Of any real basis of verse, beyond mere numerical limit of syllables, he is unconscious. Rejecting Lindley Murray's absurd scansion [borrowed from Beattie] of

From thĕ lŏw | plēasūres ŏf | thĭs fāllĕn | nātŭre,

he proposes to substitute

From thĕ | lŏw plĕas-|ūres ŏf | thĭs fāll-|ĕn nā-(ture);

but he does not tell us how rhythm is preserved when pyrrhics alternate with spondees (p. 13, *note*). Syncope, synaeresis, and the rest are freely invoked (p. 6, *cf.* Preface, p. xv); in "Full many a bard" the *y* is held to be elided. While opposed to trisyllabic feet in heroic verse, however, he admits that they sometimes occur;

nor does he object to Milton's intermingling of iambic and trochaic, for which he quotes precedent from Greek comedians (p. 27, *note*). He hints at a reason for the initial trochee (p. 42), and defends variety of caesura (p. 57 *seq.*). The amphibrach he rejects utterly, affirming that English versification requires an accent on either the first or last syllable of a foot (p. 52, *note*). On the whole, popular ideas are put not amiss in this short sketch of sixty-two pages, but it is amazing that any competent critic should believe its main position tenable. How a line composed of heterogeneous feet, restricted indeed in number but not in kind, could possibly produce an impression of uniformity, one despairs to conceive; yet surely our verse does produce that impression. Critics of Carey's school neglect half the problem; they perceive syllabic diversity, but fail to reconcile this with temporal uniformity.

In 1817 Coleridge published both *Sibylline Leaves* (the first collected edition of his shorter poems) and *Biographia Literaria*, which contains much analysis and criticism of poetry. Here, if anywhere, we might have looked to find a philosophy of metre; but we look in vain. In its Chap. XIV, metre seems to be defined as "an exact correspondent recurrence of accent and sound"; which does not take us very far. Chap. XVIII discusses the origin and function of metre, but not its nature. And in "Satyrane's Letters" Wordsworth and Coleridge discourse with Klopstock about the blank verse of Milton and Glover [!], Wordsworth asserting that the merit of good blank verse lies in "apt arrangement of pauses and cadences, and the sweep of whole paragraphs," rather than in the even flow of single lines. What constitutes that "even flow" we never hear. In the "Table-talk" of Coleridge, it may be here added, there are *obiter dicta* about prose being "words in their best order", poetry "the best words in the best order"—complaints that the metre of some modern poems is to true metre as dumb-bells are to music—much praise of Shakespeare's and Milton's rhythm, with strictures on Byron's and on

Tennyson's versification; he sometimes "can scarcely scan" the latter—and frequent mention of iambics, hendecasyllabics, and the like. But any real discussion of verse-structure I have not found. He is familiar with technical prosody, and discusses the nature of Greek accent; but he never philosophizes about rhythm in itself, or mentions Steele's doctrines. It is equally difficult to believe that he did not discuss these with Thelwall, or that they failed to interest him. Some time might have been spared from ontological discussion to these humbler themes. His pseudo-Classic verse, printed in the *Leaves*, is no better than other people's; "Metrical feet: a lesson for a boy" is not particularly happy. A false stress must be laid on the first syllable of each line in the couplet translated from Schiller, and so often quoted—

In the hexameter rises the fountain's silvery column;
In the pentameter aye falling in melody back.

And these things, at best, are mere toys. No man, surely, was better fitted than Coleridge to have given us a real analysis of metre, to have unravelled the harmonies that blend in such verse as his own. But he left the task unattempted, left it to writers such as the one who next meets us.

Rev. James Chapman, a teacher in Edinburgh, published there in 1818 *The Music, or Melody and Rhythmus, of Language*, and in 1821 *The Original Rhythmical Grammar of the English Language*. Both books may be considered together; I have given the first words only of their somewhat voluminous titles. A follower of Steele and admirer of Thelwall, he draws largely on both. Not only is his "system" avowedly "taken from" Steele, but whole sentences and paragraphs are reproduced (without notice given), phrases like "I believe" and "I think" being transferred without alteration. The large print of the *Rhythmical Grammar*, indeed, is almost all Steele. The same is true, in less degree, as regards other writers; sentences from Thelwall reappear, with the phrase "clausular divisions"; Webb and others are similarly honoured. I do not suggest that there was any thing underhand in this wholesale plagiarism; but it should surely have been acknowledged in his Prefaces. That to the *Rhythmical Grammar* gives a list of books which he has "consulted" (p. xiv); but it also boasts that he has "ventured to think for himself" (p. viii). As concerns theory, at any rate, the books unreservedly repeat Steele. His eight degrees of quantity, his six normal cadences of heroic verse, his readiness to let pauses increase the number of cadences, all are accepted unhesitatingly. No position taken by Steele, so far as I have seen, is challenged by Chapman. On the other hand, the pupil supplies orderly arrangement, copious examples, a lively style of controversy. He is amusingly contemptuous of all other systems of prosody, and amusingly confident in his own. It seems unnecessary to go through the volumes in detail, but of the *Music of Language* Chapters I to XII state his [*i.e.* Steele's] theory, the remaining nine are mostly occupied by illustrations, scansions, and pieces for recitation. (Chap. XIX deals with prose, Chap. XX with Biblical passages.) In the *Rhythmical Grammar*, which is the fuller and larger of the two books, but abounds in misprints, the Chapters on Quantity, Emphasis, Cadence, Meter [*sic*], and Rhythm are perhaps the most important; and the end of Chap. XIII, on "Errors of English Prosodians", should not be missed. Both books, indeed, are eminently readable throughout; borrowed ideas are handled and explained with vigour if not with discretion.

How boldly Chapman adopts his teachers' doctrines is shown by his actually asserting (*Music of Language*, p. 75; *cf.* a similar instance on p. 20, and *Rhythmical Grammar*, p. 203) that Milton's line—

Rocks, caves, lakes, fens, bogs, dens, and shades of death—

is read precisely as if an *and* intervened after each of the first five words! This is Thelwall's view of single-syllable feet pushed to an absurdity. This line would thus contain eight feet or "cadences". Similarly, for Milton's "I 'sdained subjection" he bids us read "I dis-|dained sub-|jection" (*Rhythm. Gramm.* p. 215). Nor does he ever stick at mere number of cadences, but writes (*ibid.*, p. 124)—

    Great ʌ | source of | day! ʌ | best ʌ | image | here be-|low,

and

(The) | thunder | rolls ʌ | — | ʌ Be | hush'd the | prostrate | world

[my *carets* stand for "rests" of various length]; or, in Alexandrine metre (*ibid.*, p. 192)—

Flies ʌ | o'er the un-|bending | corn, ʌ | ʌ and | skims a-|long the | main.

Individual lines, as will appear from these instances, are often tortuously divided. On the other hand, it must be understood that these are the exceptions, not the rule. The bulk of his scansions are reasonable, if not certain. But for his tendency to make 'anacrusis' a separate foot, line after line would pass muster to-day. His full recognition of the pause-element in verse is admirable. Most exposition in either book, his own as well as that of others, is clear and cogent. With his strictures on our "Classical" prosodists I have naturally no quarrel, though his condemnation of Carey's and Lindley Murray's scansions lately quoted only leads to this no more credible one (*ibid.*, p. 219)—

    ʌ | From the | low ʌ | pleasures | of this | fallen | nature,

which may give the prose value of the syllables, but surely not the prosodial. His remarks on Greek metre may be safely neglected. In one respect Chapman follows Thelwall rather than Steele, *viz.* in making the bulk of our 'iambic' metre move to common instead of triple time. It is remarkable how persistent, in one form or other, is the idea that our commonest form of verse moves to "even measure", though for three Centuries most of our grammarians have sought to identify it with triple rhythm.

In 1819 Thomas Campbell, the poet, published his *Specimens of English Poets*, in two volumes [second edition in one volume, edited by Peter Cunningham, 1841], to which is prefixed an "Essay on English Poetry". I omitted this from my Bibliography because, like Warton, he deals entirely with the history of English verse, not at all with its structure. I also omitted, but inadvertently, a paper which interests as being the first from across the Atlantic. In the *North American Review* for September, 1819, appeared an article "On trisyllabic feet in iambic measure", which may now be read, altered and enlarged, in the Works of William Cullen Bryant [*Life and Works*, New York, 1883-4, Vol. V, pp. 57-67]. The writer contends that such feet should be allowed, but does not say *why*. He notes that they are frequent in Shakespeare and Milton, rare in Denham and Waller, "rigidly excluded" by Dryden and his successors [yet Pope has not a few]. "I find no traces of them in Thomson or Dyer." Akenside, after eschewing them in the first edition of his *Pleasures of Imagination*, introduced them into the second; Cowley used them "without scruple". If the paper contain no theory, it at least protests against effete pedantry, and vindicates for the author of "Thanatopsis" [did any work of his later years equal in merit that youthful poem?] his place as *doyen* of American prosody as well as poetry.

[1] In 1820 Southey wrote, in 1821 published, his *Vision of Judgment*, a poem in "English hexameters". This practically introduced that metre to the British public, and inaugurated a tremendous controversy. Henceforward, the "Classic" problem assumes new shape, and becomes mainly a question touching the *raison d'être* of this metre. I have discussed this question elsewhere,[2]

[1] A paper in *Blackwood's Magazine* for September, 1820, on "Sweetness of versification", which does not call for comment here, is noted in Appendix B.
[2] In a pamphlet, now out of print, and in the Appendix to my *Study of Metre*.

and need only summarize my view here. The metre has no claim whatever to represent Classic hexameter. Apart from all other differences—want of spondees, want of true caesura, *etc.*, *etc.*—it differs fundamentally in respect of time. It moves to triple rhythm, Classic to quadruple. This has been overlooked, simply because so few people read Classic verse according to quantity. They do not really give double duration to each long syllable, to the second syllable of a spondee as well as the first. What they do is to place a strong accent on the first syllable of each foot, and imagine that this represents quantity. The main difference between the metres thus disappears, since most people read

Arma virumque cano, Troiae qui primus ab oris...

to the very same time as

This is the forest immense, where oaks and beeches assemble.

To realize what ought to be the difference, we need only try to make the latter line move to quadruple rhythm, giving two full beats wherever two are marked—

$$\overset{1\ 2}{\text{This}}\ \overset{3}{\text{is}}\ \overset{4}{\text{the}}\ |\ \overset{1\ 2}{\text{fo-rest}}\ \overset{3}{\text{im-}}|\overset{4}{\text{mense,}}\ \overset{1\ 2}{\text{where}}\ |\ \overset{3\ 4}{etc.}$$

It is obvious that this is not the rhythm to which these words are intended to be set; but it is, beyond question, the rhythm to which the Latin words were, and ought to be, set.

While, however, Southey's metre has no claim to represent Classic hexameter, it is perfectly admissible as an English form of verse. It is simply a triple-time six-cadence line, with falling accent, and without rhyme. It should be written like any other English measure, with the usual latitude as to syllables, and the usual reliance on time instead of finger-counting. This the public, with its irresistible common sense, has long since recognised. Whatever critics may say, this metre is accepted and enjoyed by English readers; from their verdict there is no appeal. What future is in store for this metre depends on poets, not on critics. By trial alone can its possibilities be discovered, whether for good or evil, success or failure. Hints in this direction can, in my opinion, be derived from poems like Mr. Swinburne's "Hesperia" and "Evening on the Broads". No good will be done by relying on rules of an alien prosody; English verse must be ruled by English speech-law. The above remarks will, at any rate, relieve us from needing to follow with any minuteness the often irrelevant arguments so copiously poured forth against the "pestilent heresy" of Southeyan hexameters.[1]

Southey's poem was accompanied by an interesting Preface. He claims priority as an experimenter, yet refers to two or three (only) of his many predecessors.[2] In a footnote he asserts that the word *Egypt* is the only pure spondee in our language; twenty better ones could easily be produced. On the other hand, he justly points out that words which seem spondees when pronounced singly become accentual trochees or iambs in verse. But the capital blunder in both Preface and poem is that he makes syllabic feet the sole basis of verse, and dispenses with "regular recurrence of emphasis". Nay more, he claims to use "any foot of two or three syllables" in any of the "four first" feet, and most frequently in the first of these—which is destructive of true rhythm. Constantly we come on lines which can only with an effort be read to the required tune. As a friendly critic [understood to be Wordsworth] told him, the first part of his lines is apt to be not metrical enough in its effect, the last part too much so. This is directly due to false theory. Striving to avoid the exotic character of lines leading off always with a strong syllable, the poet begins with a 'pyrrhic'

---

[1] Etymologically, 'hexameter' means any line of six feet, but practice has restricted it to one particular form of these. It is therefore very undesirable to use the word in its general meaning; and the same applies to 'pentameter', 'tetrameter,' and ' trimeter'. Why use Greek terms at all? *Six-foot* or *six-cadence* is just as good, and free from ambiguity.

[2] *Cf.* the "Specimens" subjoined to the *Notes* which follow the poem.

in place of a 'dactyl', and so ruins the structure of his line.

We have nothing to do with the theme of the poem, which roused Byron to killing satire. But it may be noted that the matter did little to help the metre. It is a fact —used as an argument sometimes for, sometimes against, their adoption—that accentual hexameters occur freely in ordinary prose. Lines like

> Nay, it is better thus, the Monarch piously answered—

show how natural is the swing of this measure, but also to what danger it is liable. Except in strong hands, it quickly degenerates into prose. Southey's subject should have prevented this happening, but his handling gave every chance to it. The mixture of George III and heavenly mysteries dispels poetry; tumbling back into prose, we find the metre insufficient to stay our fall, while some lines are positively and unintentionally comic. Even in the admired opening passage there is hardly a line which might not be bettered. There is no victory in the march of its verses. At best we can read them, admiring ideas rather than execution, and taking pleasure in pictures of scenery—

> Derwent retaining yet from eve a glassy reflection
> Where his expanded breast, then still and smooth as a mirror,
> Under the woods reposed.

Such words—and they furnish a favourable sample—have no magic in them, no "inevitableness". This, indeed, is only to say what we all know, that Southey was not a poet of first rank. Enough, then, to realize that a poem of considerable size, by the Laureate of that day, was bound to attract attention; and that its faults as well as its merits secured special consideration of its metre.

The critics soon opened fire. First came the *Edinburgh Review* (for July, 1821),[1] not averse to let Tory dogs taste the lash. Metre is dealt with from a standpoint of

---

[1] Vol. 35, No. 70, Art. IX, pp. 422-36. The page-reference in my Bibliography is erroneous.

pedantic orthodoxy, ours being made a mere succession of accented and unaccented syllables. "Versification consists in the recurrence of certain marked or conspicuous sounds, at regular and fixed intervals" (p. 424); any "regular series of marked syllables" would gratify the ear as much (p. 428). Yet time belongs to Classic verse only, and ours depends on mere number of syllables (p. 425). "No legitimate English measure admits of any change in *the number* of syllables that make up the line" (p. 426). When words like *heavenly, watery, etc.*, occur in heroic verse they are "used as dissyllables, . . . the middle syllable suffering a substantial elision" (p. 427). A trochee can never replace a dactyl, for one unaccented syllable can never be equal to two of the same description (p. 432); nor can one or more unaccented syllables replace an accented (p. 427). The reviewer's strictures on Southey's poem, first as to its form and in the last few pages as to its matter, may be right in the main, despite their *animus*; his own positions are no less vulnerable. To say that "wherever the structure of the verse requires an accented syllable, *nothing but an accented syllable* can be admitted" [the italics in these quotations are the *Review*'s] (*ibid.*) is, as we have seen, simply to condemn the practice of all our best writers. On p. 430 it is truly remarked that spondees are frequent in our prose speech (in phrases like *vile slave, fair play, etc.*), and not unknown in our verse, *e.g.*

Thou First | *great Cause,* | least un-|derstood;

while a *note* to p. 428 shows how the then current pronunciation of Latin mangled the cadence of its verse. But, as regards general principles, the dogmatic assertions of Southey's critic are mere echoes of Johnsonian narrowness, and will not bear testing by fact.[1]

Better in tone and scholarship are the *Remarks* of

---

[1] The objections to "double endings" and to the " singing and dancing cadence " of triple time (p. 433) were natural at this date, but have now become antiquated. Critics are seldom quick to appreciate novel music.

Rev. Samuel Tillbrook, B.D., Fellow of Peterhouse, Cambridge (1822), the first of many similar treatises devoted to the hexameter question. Without undue violence, and with far greater historical knowledge than Southey, he sketches the history of previous attempts, and sums up against the innovation. Italian Trissino is mentioned, our chief Elizabethan and later experiments described, and German models briefly referred to. He does not, however, explicitly distinguish between earlier quantitative and later accentual bases. Rather he assumes that the basis must be quantity in some shape, not necessarily as formulated by Classic rules, and asks Southey to state on what principles of quantity his verse is framed. The book being confined to this one question, its contents will appeal only to those who are interested in this particular branch of prosody; but to them it may be commended as an informing piece of work, both in its history and its criticism, though the latter hardly takes quite wide enough views of its subject-matter.

In passing may be mentioned a translation of the first canto of an Italian poem called *Ricciardetto* by Sylvester Douglas, Lord Glenbervie (1822; privately printed the year before), merely because the last of its explanatory Notes (No. 95) is said to be "an extract from an Essay I have in part composed on the different modes of versification in several of the modern languages" (p. 185). This Essay does not seem to have been published. Judging from the sample, it dealt with rules of versification, not with the nature of verse.

From these minor matters we turn to the latest and most systematic work of the Steele school. Comparatively little is known about Rev. Richard [Baillie] Roe, author of *Principles of Rhythm* (1823); he seems to have been confused (*e.g.* in *Bibliotheca Britannica*) with another Richard Roe, a surveyor, who died in 1814. But, according to the *Dictionary of National Biography*, our Roe was a B.A. of Trinity College, Dublin, who later in life took orders, wrote on theology as well as a treatise on shorthand, was also a popular singer, and gave concerts in London, where he died in 1852. His first book on rhythm has disappeared, as previously mentioned; that of 1823 is a goodly quarto volume, published in Dublin, and dedicated to the President and members of the Royal Irish Academy. The copy now in the British Museum was presented by the author. It contains preface, an elaborate table of contents, 189 pages of text, and some 30 of notes—controversial matter being mostly relegated to these last. Music is constantly referred to, and musical signs employed. Print and binding are both good, contrasting markedly with those of his three fellow-disciples. Seven out of eight Chapters deal with rhythm in speech, the eighth and last with music proper. Thelwall read the whole in proof (Note 19, p. 128).

Distinguishing tone from time, the Preface states that Steele and Odell sufficiently dealt with the former, theirs being "the only works extant in which it is clearly investigated" [*cf.* Note 2, which reproves Walker for disparaging Steele, while "actually purloining his explanation of the nature of accent"]. The present work, therefore, is confined to time or rhythm, in expounding which it is perhaps implied that these writers were less successful. Yet, by his own account [Note 35], there are only two points where Roe differs from Steele, *viz.* in making an essential difference between prose and verse, and *in* not making grammatical pauses constituents of verse-structure. However this be, Steele's doctrines are at any rate recast in Roe's mind, and set forth in Roe's words; and the practical results differ considerably when verse is scanned into feet.

Chap. I deals with "principles of rhythm in general", points out that rhythm may be marked by "degrees of pulsation, of tone or of quantity" (p. 7), and praises Young's treatment of the subject [*ante*, 1786]. Chap. II, on "Elements of speech", makes pulsation inseparable from quantity, and predicable of every portion of utterance (pp. 34–5, *cf.* 42). This double factor has two effects, elementary and rhythmical; Sheridan noticed only the latter, but was right concerning it, since "a pulsated consonant is longer than the vowel which precedes it" (pp. 34, 39–40). So we come in Chap. III to "English feet", which are "simple or compound integers", but in either case "all relatively equal" (p. 41). Dissyllabic intervals usually carry one pulsation, trissyllabic[1] two, the subordinate pulsation in the latter case not affecting rhythm (p. 42). Pulsations differ indefinitely in strength, but may generally be classed as *primary* or *secondary*; the weakest "scarcely distinguish a pulsated from a remiss syllable" (*ibid.*). Of quantity there are three grades, long and short and *mean*, the last occupying either one half or one third of the ratio, while the others are respectively one-half longer and one-half shorter (pp. 43–4, *cf.* Note 24). "Entire intervals" are even or uneven, according as the syllables are or are not of a mean quantity (p. 44). These statements are illustrated by examples, not always very convincing, but clear and precise. Quantity is shown to be in one sense fixed, in another variable (pp. 49–51, *cf.* Notes 29, 30). "Length by position" is well explained on p. 48 (*cf.* Note 27), Mitford's view being fully endorsed.

There are said to be four modifications of feet as time-beaters (pp. 52–3). And feet are either perfect or imperfect; in the latter, "rests, or measured portions of silence, supply the place of absent syllables" (p. 53). Five sorts of feet are enumerated, amphibrachs being added to iamb, trochee, dactyl, and anapaest (*cf.* Note 31). "The misconceptions of the Ancients on the subject of quantity have led most writers to suppose dissyllabic feet to be in triple time, and trissyllabic feet to be in duple time, whereas the very reverse is the truth" (Note 31). All the foregoing applies to prose as well as verse. In prose, imperfect feet "are *negatively* determined to the most simple, that is, to the duple species"; in verse, they are *positively* determined to whatever species predominates,

---

[1] In this and the next two paragraphs, Roe's spelling of *trissyllable* is adopted. The only objection to it is possible confusion of sound with *dissyllable*.

duple or triple, for "no species of verse is wholly formed of feet exceeding three syllables" (pp. 57–8). Prose feet are numberless, including all words of but one primary pulsation (on p. 42 he had claimed that no word naturally occupies more than one foot). Imperfect dissyllabics are common to prose and verse, imperfect trissyllabics are peculiar to trissyllabic verse (p. 59). Finally, verse contains "irregular feet", formed by inadequate or super-adequate syllables; this is due to unavoidable defects of language (*ibid.*). A similar effect may be observed in music (p. 65).

This elaborate analysis, open to doubt in parts—a foot of *nine syllables* (p. 52) seems absurd; and the doctrine of "irregular feet" is surely a confession of inadequacy in theorizing—leads to a discussion of "English lines" in Chap. IV. This may be more briefly dealt with. It is here, however, that he states his divergence from Steele, and makes "incidental pauses" no part of rhythm (p. 74, *cf.* Note 35). Lines are either pure or mixed, and are determined either by sense or by modification of feet (p. 75 *seq.*). Trissyllabic lines run on continuously (p. 83). Strangely, he makes lines of three and five feet "possess a character of stability and firmness" (p. 84). Caesuras with us are merely "greater or less internal pauses", not analogous to those of Classic verse (pp. 86-7, *cf.* Note 36). The initial trochee is declared always to form part of a trissyllabic foot (p. 89). Copious examples are given, but in "mixed lines" he seems guided too much by the airs to which verse has been set. Milton and Pope are compared, the latter being "for blunt ears", the former for delicate (p. 103); yet some of the former's lines strike him as hardly metrical in "just pronunciation". Cowper too is mentioned, and Southey's irregular verse, "imitated from Percy's *Reliques.*" "The intermixture of different feet," in our verse, "is more used in dissyllabics than in trissyllabics, more in iambics than in trochaics, and most of all in heroics" (p. 107). The first part alone of this Chapter contains much that is of importance, the residue travelling mainly along accepted lines.

What remains can be shortly summarized. Chap. V, "Of English clauses," treats mainly of unrhymed stanzas, to which he is evidently partial (Southey's *Thalaba* is mentioned). Chap. VI deals with Classic verse, not helpfully, for he replaces quantity by pulsation, and sees no difference between *turris* and *turret, annual* and *annuus*; pp. 142-3, however, show that this view does not wholly satisfy him. Chap. VII compares prose with verse, their differences being summed up on pp. 151-2; the same words are sometimes set to one time in prose and another in verse (pp. 149-51). In Chap. VIII he takes up the "second part of his subject", Musical Rhythm, but handles it concisely, principles having been already determined. Musical tones can be detached and combined with a freedom which is impossible with spoken syllables, since the poet finds these latter already formed into words (pp. 164-5). Into purely musical questions we need not follow him. Of the "Notes" which succeed the text those chiefly important have been already cited; in one (Note 50) he suggests a "mixed Alexandrine" to imitate the *style* rather than the *form* of ancient hexameter.[1] Many excellent remarks might be quoted from these pages, and the whole book well deserves reading; but the most notable part of it from a prosodian's point of view is certainly the Chapter on "feet".

Of Steele's professed followers, Roe is the clearest and most methodical; his master's teaching loses nothing at his hands, and wears a garb of scientific exactness. Some pitfalls into which Steele fell are avoided by his pupil; the difference between prosaic and prosodial value of syllables is duly recognised. If it were possible to attach a definite relative length to every fraction of speech, Roe has shown how to record it. The fault of his book, to my mind, is that it attempts the impossible. Such precision as he seeks to find between long, short, and "mean" syllables is a fond imagination; syllables

[1] He mentions Taylor and Odell in this connection, and praises the latter's verse (p. 147), but doubts the possibility of reproducing Classic measures.

do not in themselves express time thus precisely, though they may be so manipulated as to suggest more than they express. Even to fail in such an essay, however, is honourable, far more so than to linger amid vague generalities. Roe's strenuous attempt to analyse the actual facts of verse deserved a recognition which it never received. Hardly ever is his book quoted, even by "musical scansionists"; yet their view of verse, now becoming so popular, was efficiently stated by him. Not till we come to Sidney Lanier [1880] shall we find it adopted so fully and unreservedly. If Steele first claimed a musical basis for verse, Roe first wove his ideas into a connected and only too elaborate system.

John Hookham Frere, friend of Canning and joint-author of the *Anti-Jacobin* [*ante*, 1797], professed himself a metrist and was a brilliant writer of verse, original and translated. His volume of *Poems*, published in 1824, contains one piece of so-called hexameters on "Malta", a Note to which declares it to be "without false quantities"; but it is difficult to know what rules of quantity sanction making *chivalry* a dactyl, or lengthening the first syllable of *honour*, the second of *precipitate*, and others. The second line begins with a redundant syllable ("Of chivalry, honour, and arms"), and in a Postscript to his version of the *Frogs* of Aristophanes (published 1830) he claims this as an allowable licence, and asserts that a Classic hexameter was somewhat longer, "or at least slower in enunciation," than an English heroic couplet, since it contained six bars of quadruple time, while each English line contains but two and a half. Beyond these statements (easily found in his *Works*, edited by Sir Bartle Frere) I have not found any utterance bearing on prosody in the writings of one who was scholar as well as poet, but whose just-quoted *dictum* about heroic verse seems to me doubtful in the extreme.

The *Treatise on English Versification* (1827), by William Crowe, D.D., Public Orator at Oxford, is the work of an old man (dedicated to a "friend of seventy years' standing") who thinks that all experiments have been already made, and there is no room for further discovery (pp. 35–9). Not here need we look for fresh ideas; the "new verse" of Scott and Southey he thinks unfit for epic strains (p. 3). A good historical Introduction (pp. 1–34) enumerates our chief prosodists; then in twenty-one Chapters he reviews orthodox verse on Eighteenth Century lines. Elision explains superfluous syllables, except in dramatic verse, where trisyllabic feet are admitted; Classic rules of quantity are adopted without question, length by position being rightly explained (p. 53); Greek [printed without accent-marks, but with breathings] is read by accent instead of quantity. Letters, instead of sounds, are taken as units. The first four Chapters deal with elemental questions, after which rhyme is discussed through several more; Chap. XI is on caesura, XIV on elision, XX on dramatic verse, XXI on Milton's versification. The style is pleasant, the criticism apt if not novel, but beyond dividing verse into feet there is no discussion of structure. Of feet he recognises the usual four, iamb and trochee, dactyl and anapaest; amphibrachic verse is not acknowledged, because this foot never predominates (p. 62). Accent is identified with force,[1] but quantity is held to play its part in our verse; instances, not very satisfying, are given of its effect (p. 57). He praises Milton's verse for its "variety", but doubts whether this is not carried too far. If there is nothing novel in Crowe's exposition, there is much that is interesting and attractive; old-fashioned ideas are handled with skill, and the diction is that of the Nineteenth Century. But the book shows how little even a capable critic can foresee what is coming, or rightly estimate new departures.

[1] Accent he makes "closely akin to emphasis", which may be defined as "a certain grandeur" given to syllables, it being so described by Holder (*Elements of Speech*, 1669). But Holder explains (*op. cit.* p. 99) that this "grandeur" or largeness is given by "a more vigorous pronunciation, and a longer stay upon it". The phrase is not metaphorical, and Holder distinguishes between accent and emphasis, reserving the former word for *tone*.

In *Blackwood's Magazine* for November, 1828 [not in old list], "Noctes Ambrosianae" No. 39, Prof. John Wilson, as Christopher North, prelects on the difference between prose and verse (pp. 642–52). He thinks that metrical phrases first occurred accidentally in speech, attracted notice, and were intentionally imitated (p. 642). Versification, he remarks, often proceeds historically from more complex to more simple structure. There is little else to our purpose in his disquisition, which toward the end becomes very 'flamboyant' indeed.

The Music of Nature, by one William Gardiner (1832), is "an attempt to prove that what is passionate and pleasing in the art of singing, speaking, and performing upon musical instruments, is derived from the sounds of the Animated World". The bulk of its fifty-one Chapters deals with music, but the last four belong to our subject, particularly Chap. 50 "on rhythm in language". Here the handling is wholly musical. Though the work of Steele and his followers is not mentioned, the writer is in substantial accord with it. To scan by feet alone is "mere visionary theory"; "syllables are as various in their duration as the notes in music," and a classification into long and short is "much too rude for a musician's ear" (pp. 500, 520). Instead, he scans by bars, claiming that "the words which convey the sense invariably fall upon the bar" (p. 510),[1] and that every verse must divide into an *even* number of bars (p. 501). Our heroic verse he makes always consist of four bars, *e.g.*—

    All are but | parts of | one stupendous | whole,

the second and third bars containing rests and 'dotted notes'; while the apparent three units in

    I have found out a gift for my fair

become four through the addition of a silent bar. This seems arbitrary, as does the setting of Pope's couplets now to triple time, now to common (*cf.* pp. 501, 505, *etc.*);

---

[1] For explanation of this phrase see p. 503.

and one fails to see why the demand for "equal times" precludes a strain of five "measures" in verse or in music (p. 504). But the importance of "rests" is duly felt (p. 502), and the distinction between prose and verse referred to (p. 512); examples of prose follow the latter reference, some being in common time, some in triple. The final Chapter on "Quantity" gives representative words with musical equivalents, as well as sometimes with such phonetic transliterations as "pik-cher" for *picture*. The whole treatment of speech, however, is far too short and superficial to carry weight, and is interesting mainly as recording a musician's hasty view. As such, it may profitably be compared with those of more erudite and equally dogmatic analysers.

America now began to send us important treatises on speech and grammar, notably those of James Rush and Goold Brown [the latter I have but lately discovered]. The first edition of Rush's *Philosophy of the Human Voice* appeared, I believe, in 1827; the second came out in 1833, the third and fullest (which I quote) in 1845. It does not deal directly with prosody, but examines the material with which prosody is concerned, and as a study of intonation won the praise of no less a critic than the late A. J. Ellis [*infra*, 1873-4]. A practising physician, Rush first studied vocal physiology for himself, then read "all accessible treatises", finding none satisfactory, but those of Steele, Sheridan, and Walker valuable in parts (*Introduction*, especially p. xxvi *seq.*).[1] His own analysis distinguishes five features of sound, *viz.* Quality, Force, Time, Abruptness, and Pitch (text, p. 1). Into his elaborate discussion of these we need not enter. Perhaps Sections [*i.e.* Chapters] 4 on syllabification, 44 on accent, and 45 on quantity, contain most that is

---

[1] He thinks that Steele's "belief in certain fancied analogies between the system of music and the melody of speech... rendered his account of intonation meagre, indefinite, and erroneous" (p. xxvi). Sheridan neglected tone entirely, and Walker's view is less novel than he claims (pp. xxvii-viii). Accent on consonants is a ridiculous idea (pp. 323-4).

apposite. Accent he separates from emphasis, and makes depend on time as well as force; while there are "six modes in which the force called Accent can be laid on the concrete" (p. 93). "Other audible means than force" can be employed to bring a syllable "under the special notice of the ear" (p. 318); the "accents of stress and quantity" readily give way to each other, but in English speech "the accented syllable is generally the longest" (p. 322). In an Appendix he states the difference between song and speech (p. 490 *seq.*), and incidentally makes some rather futile remarks about Greek accent (p. 488, *note*). Rush's phonetics are now naturally out of date, but were certainly remarkable at the time. Amid vague talk, or heedless dogmatism, he took nothing for granted, and tried to leave nothing undefined; American prosodical study must have benefited by his investigations.

Goold Brown's *Grammar of English Grammars*, first published in 1836, was greatly enlarged in later editions; the tenth (1875), which I quote, contains over eleven hundred closely printed pages. "Observations," in small type, following each paragraph, discuss other writers' opinions. An alphabetical list of Grammars (pp. xi-xx) is followed by a long Introduction (pp. 21-143), and this by the body of the work under the four usual heads of Orthography, Etymology, Syntax, Prosody. The last of these includes punctuation, utterance, figures, and versification, so that to Part IV, Chapter IV, our attention may be restricted.[1] The teaching of this Chapter, I imagine, has sustained little modification. It is highly dogmatic, and most questionable. Quantity is made to depend upon loudness. "A syllable fully accented cannot be reckoned short." "A syllable accented will always be found longer as well as louder than any unaccented one immediately before or after it." "The first syllables of *habit*, *borrow*, and *battle*, are twice as long as the last" (pp. 834, 835). This is the old

[1] Part IV, Chapter II, on "Utterance", contains some brief remarks about accent and quantity; but the sentences which I am about to quote will show that on this subject Brown is no safe guide.

fallacy of Eighteenth Century critics revived, and one is not surprised to find that he scans everything by syllabic feet (Section 3), and postulates absolute regularity in these (Section 4). Practically, the principles inculcated are those of Lindley Murray, so far as verse-structure goes, though with that writer Brown picked many bones of contention. However inadequate its theory, the fourth section of this Chapter is (in the said tenth edition) a perfect storehouse of examples, illustrating varieties of English metre. The "Exercises" with which it concludes, and the subsequent "Key" to these, belong to an elementary stage of study; but in no book have I found so copious a collection of extracts. "Monosyllabic feet," it should be mentioned, are fully recognised (p. 841), some of the examples quoted having clearly accrued since the original edition was published.

Hallam's *Introduction to the Literature of Europe in the Fifteenth, Sixteenth, and Seventeenth Centuries* (1837-9) is too well known a book to need description. Questions of structure are scarcely mentioned. Yet, in Part I, Chap. I, the thirty-fourth paragraph summarizes the change from quantitative to accentual metre, and justly (as against writers like Goold Brown) remarks that "no want of emphasis or lowness of tone can render a syllable of many letters short". In Part II, Chap. V, paragraphs *seventeen* and *seventy-five* note attempts to introduce Classic metres into Italy and England respectively, and leave us in no doubt as to his opinion concerning the wisdom of such attempts.[1] Beyond these incidental references, I do not find any thing which bears on our subject.

Among our older magazines the *Eclectic Review* held no undistinguished place. Its number for April, 1838 (Vol. III of a "new series", Art. 3, pp. 395-414), contained a paper which I surmise to have been written by the late

---

[1] "A folly with which every nation has been inoculated in its turn" (par. 17); "an injudicious endeavour... met with no more success than it deserved." Our language, "abounding in harsh terminations, cannot long observe the law of position" (par. 75).

Prof. Blackie [*cf.* 1866]. Nominally a review of Foster's book on Accent [seventy-five years after publication!], it deals mainly with the question of Greek accent, but has some interesting allusions to English prosody. Three kinds of metre are recognised, dissyllabic, trisyllabic, and "mixed"; the last, brought back by Coleridge and others, is "irregular style", reserved for "wild passages" (p. 399). He notes "separation of accent from quantity" in the line

Say, rush'd the bold eagle exultingly forth,

where *bold* must be lightly stressed (p. 400), as earlier he had pointed out that words like *balance, honors* [*sic*], *shadow* are accentual trochees but quantitative iambs. The same word may be now accented, now unaccented, in the same line, *e.g.*—

Wild rushes the torrent, the boat rushes wild;

especially in trisyllabic metre, which as compared with dissyllabic is "more removed from speaking and nearer to song", and has more liberty of accommodating words to metre (p. 405). Accent rules our verse, yet quantity gives "expression, harmony, variety" (p. 401). Ordinary word-accents are often altered in verse, as when *wíld hòrse* becomes either *wíld hórse* or *wìld hórse* (p. 404). A "trochee" usually comes after a pause, Milton's double trochees being therefore questionable, and it is even suggested that in one case the line would have read better as "*All* in their triple degrees" (p. 402). Southey's hexameters come in for censure toward the end of the article (pp. 412–13) as too careless of quantity, and for other reasons the metre is pronounced not likely to succeed. From papers like this one can often gather hints of more value than can be got from professed treatises on metre, and such studies become more plentiful as the Century advances. On the other hand, books and papers with attractive titles sometimes turn out useless for the purpose of our quest.

Hexametrical Experiments, published anonymously in 1838, and understood to be by James Blundell, M.D., an eminent physician, translate four of Virgil's Eclogues into lines professing to regard both accent and quantity. The Introduction boldly tries to make quantitative rules for English verse, recognising that these must differ from the familiar rules of Classic prosody, and must not run counter to accent. Syllables it divides (p. 11) into long, short, double-short, and "common" or doubtful, claiming the right to use an extra short or double-short syllable in any foot (as in the phrase " | glory of the | earth "), as well as to prefix redundant syllables to the initial beat. Both these licences, I need hardly say, accord thoroughly with the practice of our chief poets in ordinary verse. Accented syllables are to be accounted long, and are so marked, others being left unmarked, while redundant syllables have a dot under them, *e.g.* *radi̯ant* (a further distinction of "redundant feet" by two dots seems uncalled for and unnecessary). The last line of the First Eclogue will sufficiently illustrate his method—

A̯nd, lēngthe̯ning apāce, from the tōwery Ālps sēe
shādows descēnding.

Sticklers for quantity must rebel at such a dactyl as "shadows de-", and certainly accentuation there entirely replaces length. Yet, to my mind, Blundell's lines read more happily than most, because less at variance with real English prosody; despite many eccentricities of diction, such as *godden* for *gods*, which are duly preannounced in the introductory remarks. At all events, the experiment interests as coming at a time when the current set in favour of loose and shapeless 'accentual' structure.

A landmark of great importance is reached with Guest's *History of English Rhythms* (2 vols., 1838; revised edition, with Notes *etc.* by Prof. Skeat, in one volume, 1882; my references are to this latter edition). Till lately, this book, by a Cambridge scholar and philologist of high rank, was our chief—indeed, our only—masterful and exhaustive treatise on English metre. If we exclude the work of foreign scholars, which in the present survey is deliberately left out of account, it remains our standard textbook, to be finally superseded in all probability by Prof. Saintsbury's forthcoming *History of Prosody*, which on the narrative side at least will re-traverse the same ground with ampler because later knowledge. Guest's views have profoundly influenced all students of his subject. It is unfortunate, therefore, that they were based on a theory which must be pronounced defective and misleading.

In one sense Guest was the last of an old school, in another the pioneer of a new. His rooted objection to trisyllabic feet in dissyllabic verse linked him with Eighteenth Century critics. He began, as Prof. Skeat points out, by totally denying the existence of such feet. He maintained that Shakespeare pronounced a word like *delicate* in two syllables, and asked Wordsworth and Coleridge whether they did the same, implying that otherwise they should not use it in place of a dissyllable (p. 176, *cf. note*). From this view he was gradually driven, and it is significant that his book was not republished during his lifetime,[1] though offers to do so were not wanting. With him one had thought this view died, but it has been resuscitated in our day. To me it seems clear that any word may be used which can be readily pronounced in the normal time of dissyllabic feet, even quadrisyllables like *ministering* or *spiritual*, and that there is not the slightest reason to suppose that such words were ever pronounced by readers of our verse *m'nist'ring* or *sp'ritval*. A contrary opinion verges on paradox.

In another direction, however, Guest was revolutionary. For the traditional scansion by feet he substituted division into versicles or "sections". Enthusiastic in the study of "Old English" verse, he found there a loose syllabic structure punctuated by alliteration and strongly marked by a midway pause; this structure he sought to

[1] He lived till 1880.

find in all English lines. So far as this conception encouraged syllabic elasticity, it did good; but as a theory it will not hold water. A great change admittedly came on our verse between (say) 1100 and 1400 A.D. What is called Old English verse is not what we now know as English verse, though related as sire to son. Modern long lines tend, like all long lines, to have optional breaks; but these are not essential, and often a poet's whole art is given to avoiding them.[1] Our verse is made up, not merely of sections, but of smaller units recurring with regularity, whether these units be primarily syllabic or temporal. The causes of this change historians must declare, but the fact is evident. Even if the influence of Anglo-Saxon verse (to use a name which at any rate emphasizes racial and linguistic change) survive in the tendency to weaken the medial accent, to write lines like.

The glass of fashion and the mould of form—

even so that is not the whole story. The five feet are there, though one be not signalized by accent; are there, though some critics recognise only four, others claim to find six. Our verse is not merely rhythmical prose; it differs from such by its metrical structure. The verse of *Piers Plowman* may represent an ancestor of the verse of *Paradise Lost*; but it is absurd to suppose ancestor and descendant one and the same person.

Guest's exposition should therefore be studied, not taken for gospel. And it makes delightful reading. The four "Books" into which it is divided are arranged on a scale of descending importance from our point of view. Book I deals with general questions and the factors of rhythm. In Book II his doctrine of "sections" is formulated and expounded, while treating of "origins". Book III discusses different metres, beginning with the

[1] *Cf.*, *e.g.*, the metre of Tennyson's poems "To Virgil" and "God and the universe", or Mr. Swinburne's "March, an Ode", and parts of "The Armada", "The Garden of Cymodoce," *etc.*

shortest; its seventh chapter is concerned with heroic verse ("metres of five accents"), its tenth and last with "metrical experiments". Book IV explains old forms of verse, rondels and virelays and the rest. In all there is interesting matter, and lavish quotations add to enjoyment. The first half of the work (the first volume of the old edition) contains most that is of interest to us. Even there, it will be found that fully half the space is occupied with discussion of verse that preceded English verse proper. For Guest was primarily a philologer and only secondarily a prosodist; and his book is a "history of rhythms", not a study of rhythm.

Yet he begins with a definition. "Rhythm in its widest sense may be defined as the law of succession." Applied to motion, it gives us the dance; to matter, sculpture and architecture; to sound, music; to articulate sound, prose and verse. In verse, the rhythm is so definite that its succession can be anticipated; in prose, so wide that this rarely happens. "Rhythm may be marked either by the time or the accent;" Sanscrit, Greek, and Latin used the former, all other languages the latter. Its parts are "proportional", not necessarily equal (pp. 1–2). Introductory remarks of this kind occupy Chap. I in the First Book, while Chap. II deals with letters, Chap. III with syllables. The last takes up "elision", which to him is absolute contraction, as when Burns shortens *Edinburgh* to *Embro'*. Similarly, the *i* in *Niobe, lion, riot*, even *having*, and the *e* in *heaven* and *given*, are left out by poets, the first being made a dissyllable and the rest monosyllables (pp. 40–51). Chap. IV discusses accent, Chap. V quantity. Accent, in our "prevailing dialect", he considers to be essentially loudness, though sharpness of tone usually accompanies it, and though the muscular action it involves tends to make us dwell on sounds so marked, whence the "vulgar notion" that accent always lengthens a syllable (pp. 74–75).[1] "Our earliest writers, almost to a man, confound

---

[1] Note his remark (p. 22)—"I am far from sure that our English accent pervades the syllable."

accent with quantity" (p. 75, *cf.* 284). He, on the contrary, distinguishes these, tries to differentiate accent from emphasis (p. 79), and also (like Greek and Roman writers) distinguishes actual from metrical quantity, denying the latter to our verse while admitting the former. "We have most certainly both long and short vowels" (p. 103). Our treatment of consonants differs from that of the Ancients; Mitford is right about the doubled consonant. The first syllable of *hilly* cannot be long. But rules depend on usage, and ours has laid down none (p. 107). Accent is therefore "the sole principle that regulates English verse" (p. 108), though a skilful use of quantity "embellishes" it (p. 111). Apropos of this, he quotes the attempt made "in one of our leading Reviews" [*cf. ante*, 1805] to prove quantity vital to English verse, and totally rejects its illustration by the line "O liquid streamlets, *etc.*" (pp. 109–10). Of the two remaining Chapters in Book I, Chap. VI deals with rhyme and alliteration, Chap. VII with pauses. The last he considers merely as caesural, and finds fault with latitudinarian views. "When we see how nearly the freedom of our elder poets approached to licence, we may appreciate ... the obligations we are under to the school of Dryden and Pope" (p. 157).

Having thus laid his foundation, he proceeds in Book II to show how English verse uses rhythm. It does so by dividing lines into definite "sections", indicated by accent. From this follows, one would think, that exact number of syllables is immaterial, and that three syllables may easily be 'equivalent' to two. But Guest draws no such deduction. He lays down precise rules as to both number and relation of syllables. "Two accented syllables may come together, if they have a pause between them.... Adjacent accents must be separated by ... not more than two syllables which are unaccented" (p. 159; *cf.* pp. 78, 86, 284). Apparent exceptions in Spenser and Shakespeare, Milton, Burns, and Moore are sought to be explained away. The whole of this exposition, like his system of scansion in general, I consider

K

unsatisfactory,[1] so will not redact, merely noting salient points. His use of the bar-mark in scanning is peculiar but intelligible; compare Prof. Skeat's remarks in Preface, pp. x–xi. He rejects Mitford's view of common and triple measure as unhistorical (p. 161, *cf.* 550), yet himself often uses both terms. Substitution of trochee for iamb is considered on p. 165. Elision is again taken up (p. 172 *seq.*), such contractions as *om'nous* (for *ominous*), *pill'r* (for *pillar*), *sp'rit*, *etc.* being insisted on, and a sneering reference made to "Thelwall's fashionable *appogiatura* [*sic*] syllable".[2] Book II, Chaps. IV and V, treat of "verse of five accents", according as the section containing two accents precedes or follows that containing three; while Book III, Chap. VII, discusses "the metres of five accents"—an arrangement which involves much repetition. Both deal with heroic verse, which is elsewhere said (pp. 160, 561) to contain 1296 possible variations or varieties. Milton is frequently praised, and defended against Dr. Johnson's strictures. But, as the book advances, he is more and more excepted against. For, indeed, Milton's verse collides with Guest's doctrine, being often devoid of regular sections and medial pauses, and is condemned accordingly.[3] In Book II (p. 230) it is admitted that "our heroic metre was from the first a mixed one, . . . though . . . it has approached nearer and nearer to the common measure". But in Book III,

---

[1] He ridicules (p. 75) the idea that Milton's words "both turned, both stood" carry equal accents. So far as certainty is attainable in such matters, I deem it certain that Milton intended them to do so.

[2] With this compare two later passages, where he evidently refers (without naming names) to the Steele school. "With them rhythm is rhythmus, and an elided syllable an apogiatura [*sic*] . . . Much which they advance, I do not understand, and much that I do understand I cannot approve of" (p. 299, end of Book II). "Some of these theories I have vainly tried to comprehend, and others I have found wholly inapplicable" (p. 532, in Book III, chap. VII). This shows how entirely unfamiliar, even to a critic like Guest, was the whole notion of temporal periods.

[3] *E.g.* (p. 445) he reprobates the absence of caesural pause in those otherwise "exquisite" poems, *L'Allegro* and *Il Penseroso*.

Chap. VII, Milton is said to have carried this mixture beyond all bounds in his "passion for variety" (p. 531). And toward the end of the same Book his "fatal example" is made a warning, his violation of metrical orthodoxy asserted. "He split the sections, and overlaid the pauses, and the law of his metre was broken, the *science* of his versification gone. The giant put on the habiliments of the dwarf—what could he do but rend them?" (p. 560).

A view of metre which ends by condemning the work of one of our greatest and most 'musical' poets cannot deserve respect. Where it fails, I must maintain, is in ignoring *time*. This he leaves entirely out of reckoning. Even when he says (p. 109) that "the time is occasionally of great importance to the beauty of a verse, but never an index of its rhythm", he refers merely to syllabic quantity. Similarly, when (p. 169) he denies that any "temporal rhythms" are to be found in our literature, he is thinking merely of quantitative feet, and probably feels that pseudo-Classic attempts lie outside of our real "literature". But of time in the musician's sense, time as the real basis of verse, he has no conception; Mitford's partial acceptance of it, we have seen, he denounces. For want of this, he can see no difference between a line devoid of his sections and a prose sentence;

Such verse we make when we are writing prose (p. 560).

That the book is full of information goes without saying. I would fain quote many passages, as on "tumbling verse" (Book III, Chap. VIII), "triple [*i. e.* trisyllabic] verse" (*ibid.*), "riding rhyme" (p. 526), *etc.* His strictures on pseudo-Classic verse (Book III, Chap. X) are much to the point[1]; an experiment by himself will be found on p. 553. (A page earlier he says, "I have seen few German

---

[1] Of modern "hexameters" he says (*ibid.*, near beginning) that they move to triple rather than common time, but this is so because syllables lack length; because, as he puts it, accent is in them taken as equivalent to quantity, whereas it is really equivalent only to *ictus* or sharp tone. [For his own experiment see Appendix A.]

hexameters which, to my ear, were satisfactory.") On all historical matters his verdict carries weight, except when biassed by his theory. But on the main question of prosody, the question of the absolute basic foundation of verse, his view seems to me altogether at fault; and this has been a great misfortune for English metrical science.

It would be difficult to fix limits to the extent of this misfortune. For two generations Guest has been the chief ruler of our prosody. Students of verse, as distinct from mere general readers, have gone to him for authoritative doctrine. The great merits of his book, its philological and historical excellence, its bold theorizing, its catholicity of quotation, secured for it general acceptance, the more so because its seed fell on prepared ground. The tendency of the time was to exalt accent to exclusive supremacy. Those who make 'beats' the sole reality in metre—those who talk of "stress-rhythms", usually meaning thereby a verse which has stresses but no rhythm—shelter behind Guest's shield. His rigid views about syllables have been discarded, but his theories of accentual basis pass for absolute truth. We shall see, as we go on, how widespread has been their domination. Yet theories which leave out the one fundamental factor of English verse, and which can find in Milton's harmonies only a violation of prosodic law, should not have been received without challenge, nor have coloured our whole notions of prosody as they have done. To Guest every student of our poetry owes much; his learning and labour must be gratefully acknowledged; but his whole view of metrical structure rests on unwarranted assumptions, and presents neither a true nor a complete account of the phenomena of English verse.

With the Forties of last Century we seem brought nearer our own time. Latham's *English Language*[1] is

[1] This should be distinguished from his *Handbook to the English Language* (first published in 1851), a separate book, which also went through numerous editions. Prosodical teaching is the same in both.

still an accepted class-book, yet its first edition appeared in 1841. Succeeding editions greatly modified and enlarged it, without however altering its method of prosody. Adopting the crude popular dichotomy of syllables into accented and unaccented, Latham calls the former *a*, the latter *x*, then resolves verse into such feet as *a x, x a, x x a, etc.* And, certainly, such a line as

The weight of all the hopes of half the world

may fairly enough be described as "5 *x a*", that is, a line containing five pairs of syllables thus related. But English verse does not long preserve such ideal regularity —very insipid it would be if it did. Already in a line like

Now trebly thunder'd on the gale

we find the third foot escaping his category; and the vital fact in English verse seems to be less its compliance with these categories than its habitual and persistent departure from them. Nor does Latham explain in virtue of what principle *a x* and *x a* alternate in the same line, much less how *a x a* is possible along with *a x x* or *x x a*. This "innocent" theory, with its unquestionably convenient if otherwise permissible nomenclature, seems to confound verbal accent with metrical stress; a confusion which existed before Latham, and has had only too many exponents since.

In Latham's first edition the Section on Prosody ("Part V") is extremely meagre. By 1855, when the fourth edition appeared, this Section had become "Part VI", and had received many additions, including a Chapter on imitations of Classic metre, said to be reproduced from the *Transactions* of the Philological Society (1843) [but the reference is incorrect as regards date]. The analysis of "caesura" there contained, with his deductions as to its place in English verse, may be left for scholars to study. As to English metre generally, his conception is wholly limited to syllables, and postulates an artificial regularity among these. "No English measure [*i.e.* foot] can have either more or less than one accented syllable"

(p. 701[1]). "On every even syllable," in heroic verse, "there shall be an accent"; and "the end of lines should coincide" with "the breaks in the sense" (pp. 706-7). He recognises no quantity in English except that of vowels (Prosody, Chap. II), and rejects the whole idea of division into feet. "The classical names are never used with impunity" (p. 669). In his Seventh Chapter there is much talk of "convertible metres" and "metrical combinations", by which are apparently meant lines that violate his imaginary rules. Deservedly esteemed as the book is otherwise, its view of prosody seems to me wholly insufficient; I cannot even see that it furnishes a criterion to distinguish verse from prose.

This closing decade of the Half-Century brought a considerable epidemic of 'hexameters'. Longfellow in America did much to popularize them, and many writers in our country worked at them. I do not propose to follow in detail either these attempts or the criticisms of them which appeared in magazines; the chief ones are enumerated in my Bibliography. Among writers, Shadwell and perhaps Lockhart[2] deserve note as trying to maintain some regard for quantity, when most writers rejoiced to

> Flounder at will over consonant, vowel, and liquid,

relying on accent to cover all deficiencies. The verses of Whewell, Herschell, and others who worked under German inspiration (conveniently sampled in the volume published by Murray in 1847) show all the faults of their Teutonic prototypes, and rarely give us a smooth or memorable line. Dr. Hawtrey's short specimen from the *Iliad*, often held up as a pattern, seems to me only a degree better than the others. In contrast with this "mob of gentlemen", Clough stands forth as a true

---

[1] My references are to the fifth edition (1862).

[2] Clough may have taken a hint from such lines of Lockhart's as

This was her answer from Priam, the old man godlike in presence.

Lockhart's basis is accentual. For Shadwell's, see Appendix A [1844].

though not great poet and an independent investigator and experimenter; but his experiments were too often forced, being out of accord with natural English prosody.[1] The charm of his *Bothie* is perennial; his later quantitative verses will be referred to in next Chapter. Charles Kingsley (to overstep for a moment the Half-Century) in his *Andromeda* achieved perhaps as great a success as is possible to any one starting with Classic verse as his ideal; sundry Letters, given in his *Life*, show real and remarkable thinking. But, on the whole, verse of the *Evangeline* type represents what most writers at this time aimed at, and what most critics either decried or exalted. Its facile, sugary, somewhat nerveless and monotonous lines were well adapted to become popular, having that singing cadence which Longfellow seldom lacks. And they certainly did more than any other verse to commend so-called hexameters to the million.

The magazine articles of this decade are often most interesting. Around verse of Longfellow's type the battle of prosody raged keenly. Whewell with his breezy dogmatism scouted the notion of relying on aught but accent; others pointed back to Classic perfection, and scoffed at the modern bard with his

        . . . Mamma has forgotten her tea-spoons,

or

Softly, Louisa, be careful, and mind you don't trip in the bushes!

The contention of Whewell's school was that English hexameters should "read themselves"; his opponents

---

[1] Much criticism has been passed on one line of Clough's—

    With a mathematical score hangs out at Inveraray.

The only remarkable feature in this line is that the normal strong initial syllable is replaced by two weak ones. Substitute such a word as *His* for *With a*, and the line becomes ordinary; the second half is frankly trochaic. A more natural prosody would have simply prefixed the word *With* to the first beat, as is so commonly done by our poets in 'trochaic' and 'dactylic' verse. But I doubt if a single instance of such prefixing can be found amid all the wild metrical libertinage of the *Bothie*.

urged that this did not differentiate verse from prose. Glimpses of prosodic theory emerge in these disputes, but no complete survey of facts. Meantime Lowell impartially satirised both sides, and Longfellow himself confessed, in the Notes to his "Children of the Lord's Supper", that in verse like his "the motions of the English Muse are not unlike those of a prisoner dancing to the music of his chains". Not from such fetter-dances can natural verse or sound criticism arise; for these we must look elsewhere.

Few general treatises on metre appeared during these years. In his "Introduction" to *Poems of Chaucer, modernised* (1841) [not in my Bibliography; *cf.* especially pp. xxxvii–xci; I shall substitute Arabic numerals] "Orion" Horne discourses lengthily on trisyllabic feet, speaking of "appoggiatura" (pp. 45, 83) and "musical time" (p. 68), and obviously recognising temporal periods, yet without definitely saying so. One pregnant sentence may be quoted. "It would be far nearer the truth were we to call our scanning gear by such terms as systole and diastole,—metre being understood as muscle, and pulsation as rhythm,—varying with every emotion" (p. 84, *note*). That suggests much, but it is not followed up, and Horne's ideal of structure is loose; he praises the "new metre" of Leigh Hunt's *Legend of Florence*, and desires a theory of prosody from its author, as from "the hand most competent to instruct us" (pp. 86, 89). I know of no response to this request, though in an Essay of seventy pages on "What is poetry?" published in his *Imagination and Fancy* (1844) Hunt refers slightly to metre, remarks that "the whole real secret of versification is a musical secret" (p. 49), and credits Coleridge with "dividing by time instead of syllables" (p. 55). These sayings are not explained, but writers of this group—among whom may be included Elizabeth Barrett[1]—evidently held advanced views about the *technique* of verse.

[1] Both the theory and practice of this lady (afterwards Mrs. Browning) show a tendency to experiment in prosody, witness her defence of imperfect rhymes as forming a species of "assonance".

O'Brien's *Ancient Rhythmical Art Recovered* (Dublin, 1843), though concerned with Classic verse, of which he sought to demonstrate the rhythmic as opposed to the metric structure, refers several times to English. Isochronism of bars is generally held essential (*cf.* Editor's Preface, pp. xiv, xix)[1]; a completed cadence must always contain two parts, just as a soldier halting first advances one foot, then brings the other up to it (text, pp. 13, 16). On p. 19 *seq.* the writer discusses our heroic verse, refuses to call its structure iambic, and claims that its beats are separated by equal intervals. These, however, are but *obiter dicta*, and his scansions are not very conclusive. In the recently started Philological Society's *Transactions* for May, 1847 (Vol. III, p. 95), is a paper by Prof. Malden on "Greek and English versification", of little interest save to Classical scholars; time is made synonymous with syllabic quantity. A small book called *Essentials of Phonetics* (1848), by A. J. Ellis, on the other hand, would repay examination, but I reserve it for mention under date 1873-4, when its author's matured views on prosody received their fullest expression.

America contributed independently to discussion at this time, notably by one remarkable paper (see next paragraph), also by other writings of which I have but lately become aware. *English Prosody*, by Asa Humphrey (1847), I have failed to see, but *A System of English Versification*, with rules and examples, by Erastus Everett (New York, 1848) does not seem to go much beyond Lindley Murray. The Preface complains of our having no system of quantity, but on the first page of text comes the fatal assertion that "the quantity of each word depends on its accent", and his very first example runs—

Whĕre slāves ŏnce mōre . . ., *etc.*

Far more interesting is a short article in the *American Review* for May, 1848 (pp. 484-92), signed with the initials of the editor, James D. Whelpley, and entitled

---

[1] The reference to "p. 39" in my Bibliography is erroneous.

"The art of measuring verse". Nominally a review of Everett, it really gives its author's own ideas about English verse-structure, which he asserts to be wholly based on quantity, that word, however, comprising both time and accent, "the two elements of musical metre" (pp. 488-9). Words he divides by their sounds, which in verse are continuous, so that in the above quotation the first syllable is unquestionably long. These sounds create musical impressions, apart altogether from their meaning; and it is by no means right or necessary that feet should coincide with complete words, in English any more than in Latin. There is much that is suggestive in this short paper, though its ideas seem hardly worked out. It concludes with the remark "We propose to revert again to the subject", but so far as I can ascertain this promise was never fulfilled.

But incomparably the most noteworthy contribution to prosodic study at this time was the "remarkable paper" referred to in last paragraph, by Edgar Allan Poe. Handy English editions of his "Poems and Essays", unluckily, rarely or never include this paper on "The rationale of English verse", even when they profess to contain his "Complete Poetical Works and Essays on Poetry", contenting themselves with including three other papers of less consequence, these being indeed only notes for popular lectures. The "Rationale" must therefore be sought in one of the really complete editions of Poe's *Works*, such as Ingram's in four volumes (1875), or some later and still more exhaustive collection; or it may be procured from America in the single-volume edition of Poe's *Best Poems and Essays* by Sherwin Cody (Chicago, 1903), which contains critical remarks by the editor on this as on other articles. The date of its first publication I have, since printing my former pamphlet, ascertained to be 1848 [*cf.* Appendix B]; with its examination we may close our record for the first half of the Nineteenth Century.

This rather discursively written paper, occupying some fifty pages (331-82) in Mr. Cody's edition, to which my references are made, attempts to dissect the actual structure of our verse. The work of a brilliant analytic genius, famous in other fields as in poetry, it abounds in striking passages, but has equally striking defects. To begin with, its author attends only to syllables, neglecting the pauses which form equally essential parts of a line. Thus (p. 361 *seq.*), while rightly scanning as a continuous measure Byron's lines—

> Know ye the land where the cypress and myrtle
> Are emblems of deeds that are done in their clime?
> * * *
> Where the virgins are soft as the roses they twine,
> And all save the spirit of man is divine—

he objects to the foot "twine, And" as too short, whereas it is obviously filled out by silence to equal time with its neighbours. This preoccupation with bare syllables vitiates his whole analysis, prompting him for example (p. 361) to find inequality of time in this couplet—

> The water-lily sleeps in pride
> Down in the depths of the azure lake—

where I venture to say every untutored reader is conscious of perfect equality. Still more serious is his failure to distinguish between quantity and accentuation. Here his self-reliance and contempt for traditional teaching lead him far astray. Like many others, he cannot conceive any verse-scheme save our own. He evidently read Latin verse wholly by accent; for proof, he thus misquotes (p. 376) a familiar line—

> Parturiunt montes, et nascitur ridiculus mus.

We must not follow him through this argument, but when he assures us (p. 375) that Horace wrote "Sunt quos curr-" as a dactyl, and would have made "great eyes" if told otherwise, it is clear that the essayist fails to perceive the initial difference between English and Classic verse-rhythm.[1] So failing, while rightly con-

[1] "To melody and to harmony the Greeks hearkened with ears precisely similar to those which we employ for similar purposes at

temning the wooden scansion of the schools, he substitutes for it one which ignores the whole structure of Classic speech. And this, in turn, reacts fatally on his conception of English verse.

It is with this conception that we are concerned. As will be seen, it borrows nothing from music or from Classic prosody, and deals wholly with syllabic value. It makes such value depend almost entirely on accent. He does, indeed, recognise (p. 341) that a syllable clogged by many consonants must take longer to pronounce than one composed of fewer; to the other element of natural quantity, which makes *far* a perceptibly longer syllable than *fat*, he remains wilfully deaf.[1] But the main element of length, to him, is accentuation. "Accented syllables are of course always long" (p. 343), *naturally* if their structure so permit, *unnaturally* if it do not. Such a long syllable is accounted exactly equal to two short, being made so by any just reciter; and verse depends for its effect wholly upon this contrast between long and short syllables (*ibid.*, and *passim*).

So far there is nothing novel in this view. He proclaims the nullity of all previous investigations into our verse (p. 332), yet himself repeats their fallacies, nor do we know how far his reading went—Steele and his school are never mentioned. It is in working out his view that originality appears. Passing by criticism of others, we find him (p. 339) make verse originate in enjoyment of *equality*, under which term he includes "similarity, proportion, identity, repetition, and adaptation or fitness". This enjoyment it shares (p. 340) with the simpler forms of music—"scientific music has no claim to intrinsic excellence"—and verse "cannot be better designated than as an inferior or less capable music". [This solitary reference to music is, unfortunately, not followed up.] The rudiment of verse, it is suggested (p. 341), may have been the

---

present" (p. 339). But this does not prove that their mode of utterance was identical with ours.

[1] He grasps, however, the fact that in 'length by position' it is the syllable, not the vowel, which is long (p. 342).

spondee, and the next step the collation of "two syllables differently accented (that is to say, short and long)". Thus came iambs and trochees, from which the transition was easy to anapaests and dactyls; and these five feet—with one previously mentioned (p. 337), the "caesura" or foot of a single syllable—exhaust the real feet, others being combinations of them. These feet had next to be divided into lines, which (p. 344), in defiance of history, Poe assumes to have been done by *rhyme*. He protests, indeed (*ibid.*; *cf.* pp. 349-50), that dates are immaterial, and that even if rhyme be modern his "positions remain untouched"; but he does not explain how. Lines thus secured, progress was easy to couplets, quatrains, stanzas; and the rest of this imaginative history of verse is occupied mainly with explanations of what are called "bastard feet", where three or even four syllables replace two, and *vice versa*. Such replacement, I need hardly say, is possible only in virtue of a higher law, that of temporal equality; but, conscious though Poe the poet must surely have been of this as a guiding principle, it is never explicitly stated by Poe the prosodian.

Summarized thus baldly, Poe's view appears crude and narrow; but it is expounded with spirit and ingenuity, as well as flashes of true insight. Absurdities, indeed, are not wanting. His notion that dactyl and anapaest may meet in a line is as monstrous as his illustration of it (p. 337) by the example—

Sĭng tŏ mĕ | Ĭsăbĕlle,

which I do not believe would be so rendered by any reader. His contention (p. 360) that length in a syllable is perceived absolutely, shortness only by contrast with length, would have been ridiculed had he found it in another writer. That the "sum of the syllabic times" in *whether* is equal to that in *thou choose* (p. 354) cannot be admitted; while the suggestion (*ibid.*) of his being the first to use two initial inversions shows extraordinary ignorance of Milton, to go no farther. On the other hand, his recognition of single-syllable feet is throughout excellent, though his term "caesura" is misleading, and though he ascribes varying length to the syllable (p. 337), instead of to the foot containing it. His vindication of trisyllabic feet (p. 350 *seq.*), where the syllable is not elided but adjusted to time by rapid pronunciation, shows clear perception of temporal law in this case, as does a later statement (p. 358) that feet must be "*made* to occupy the same time".[1] Wherever Poe trusts his ear he goes right, as in his scansion (*ibid.*) of the line—

Many are the | thoughts that | come to | me.

But his theory makes scansion depend on fictitious syllabic values (*e.g.* "the sixth of long ", p. 359) instead of on overruling rhythm. He quotes (p. 358) the immortal

Pease porridge hot—pease porridge cold,

actually without making a silent interval follow any word. How little Poe's notion of scanning really differs from the traditional may be seen by comparing the samples of each on p. 369. His merely refines on the orthodox view by denoting sub-varieties of accentuation. In all other respects the two methods are absolutely identical.

Some extravagances of criticism need but bare mention. "The nicety of Byron's ear" (p. 364) contrasts with the "roughness" of *Christabel* (p. 356), and Coleridge's system of scanning by accents is roundly pronounced "nonsensical" (*ibid.*). Horne's *Orion* is "the most happily versified long poem in existence" (p. 353). The French "have no verse worth the name" (p. 378). Such utterances, like the reference to "German Greek prosodies" (p. 338), must be taken with a large grain of salt; nor do I see why Leigh Hunt is censured (p. 341) for speaking of "the *principle* of variety in uniformity". More to the point are his strictures on the "Longfellownian hexameter" (p. 381), but his own attempt in that metre

---

[1] *Cf.* the phrase (used once only, p. 366) "equality between two or more pulsations". That Poe had a true sense of metrical rhythm I do not doubt, but his theorizing all but ignores it, as witness his definition (p. 339) that rhythm concerns merely the "character of feet, that is, the arrangement of syllables".

(p. 382) is singularly weak. Well may he say that "some of the dactyls are not so good as I could wish", for *hope to make* and *men of sense* are as little like dactyls (in any sense of the term) as can well be imagined. A critic like Poe should have realized that the measure of his lines is derived, not from their syllables, but from a preconcerted rhythm with which these syllables are somewhat violently forced to keep time.

My citations have done scant justice to the *verve* and brilliance of Poe's Essay. But these cannot hide the fundamental weakness of his position. It is weak, *first*, through omitting all notice of silent spaces—as though one should read a page of music by its 'notes' alone, neglecting 'rests'. It is weak, *secondly*, in its analysis of syllabic quantity. In English verse, accentuation usually reinforces metrical *ictus*; Poe assumes that this implies temporal protraction of the accented syllable. In other words, he mistakes conspicuousness for length. The first weakness could be easily remedied; not so the second. It constantly affects his judgement, and sets him to the impossible task of "expressing to the eye the exact relative value of every syllable employed in verse" (p. 367)—impossible, because such value fluctuates with each reader, and with the same reader at different times. Indeed, Poe's whole view of verse is made artificial by it. He begins by saying (p. 331) that nine-tenths of prosody "appertain to the mathematics", and follows this up by a demand that long and short syllables shall be mathematically proportioned (p. 342), and by the assertion that in perfect verse there would never be any disagreement between "the rhythmical" and "the reading flow" (p. 360). Is this, perhaps, why he seems to prefer the melody of "Mr. Cranch" and "Miss Mary A. S. Aldrich" to that of Coleridge? In Poe's own verse, is there not sometimes too obvious an effort to provide luscious syllables, too apparent joiner-work in the carpentry of his lines? So does theory influence practice; so important are just views of prosody. The greatest singers may not need them, but they certainly help others. How wedded

Poe is to his theory, how fearless in following it, is shown by his complaint (p. 355) that "many even of our best poets do not scruple to begin an iambic rhythm with a trochee", a dactylic with an anapaest, and so forth. The common practice of our best poets is more likely to be right than the criticism of even a Poe; sounder views of metrical structure easily justify such apparent licences as are found (for example) in the opening lines of Mr. Swinburne's "Hesperia".

I have thought it needless to give a *précis* of this paper, or recount its many amusing divagations and incidental felicities. These no student will fail to enjoy, as he will profit by what is said about "quick trochees", "bastard dactyls," and the like. By his main issue Poe must be judged. He aimed at nothing less than a complete analysis, making "the scansion and the reading flow go hand in hand" (p. 371). No English writer for at least twenty years had made such an attempt; those who earlier had done so he does not seem to know. All credit, therefore, must be given him for originality, and his paper marks a stage in our enquiry. It shows men ready to enquire, aware that there is a problem to solve, casting aside conventional explanations. If the problem is not solved by Poe, at least he shows how to attack it. And no contemporary of Poe's known to me made so bold and thoroughgoing an attempt to lay bare the heart of English verse.

So ends the Half-Century, its "new verse" having as yet found no trustworthy analyst. The most familiar phenomena of English metre are still ignored by the prosodist, even by one so able and iconoclastic as Poe. It remains to see what may reward our search in the fourth and last Half-Century included in this survey.

CHAPTER IV

THE NEW PROSODY

1850-1900

During the second half of the Nineteenth Century a more adequate conception of metre gradually emerged. It appeared neither suddenly nor from the first full-grown. Following, as hitherto, an order mainly chronological, we shall still find ancient ineptitudes furbished up anew. But, with and among them, more rational and real methods of scansion slowly assert themselves; critics are less apt to assume beforehand how English verse ought to be written, more ready to discover for themselves how it actually has been written by our chief poets.

A Treatise on Versification, by Rev. R. W. Evans (1852), illustrates these assertions. Verse is to him still merely an affair of syllables, the "regulated recurrence of a syllable" constitutes metre (p. 3), and "the stress on a single vowel necessarily prolongs its time" (p. 20). "Our literature has long ago reached its maturity" (p. 169), and its rules are fixed. He sees how we habitually neglect quantity (Chap. II) and exalt stress (Chap. III, *cf*. Chap. XIV), the latter alone guiding our prosody. There are some singular remarks on "the modern hexameter" (Chaps. XV, XVI), accentual succession being taken as the sole regulative principle. It is needless to recapitulate familiar views, or quote just criticism on particular points. Shortcomings of theory are best seen in the concluding Chapter, "Of lyric poetry." Ignoring temporal structure, he finds no room for such verse in English. "Our truly lyric poetry must ever be almost a blank" (p. 169). "An evil genius" presided over its birth (p. 165). The choruses of *Samson Agonistes* are not verse at all (p. 166). To such conclusions can false theory force a man brought up on Shakespeare and Milton, and in whose ears Tennyson's youthful melodies had for a decade been sounding. The only possible reply to them is—there are none so deaf as those who will not hear.

Poetics, by E. S. Dallas (1852), on the other hand, leaves old lines entirely, but not always advantageously. Book III, Part II, Chap. II, on *Verse*, contains some striking remarks, such as that metre, in its simplest form, is "*time heard*" (p. 164)—a definition to be pondered by those who ignore temporal relations in their analysis of verse— and much excellent discussion as to why poets use metre at all ; but such speculation leads him away from the practical question, What exactly is this same metre? When he does touch on actual structure, his views are apt to be wild, as when he contends (p. 185) that blank verse should be written in lines of irregular length, and should never contain a pause ; that dramatic verse alone has *feet*, while epic has *bars*, and lyric has *stanzas* (p. 176) ; that Shakespeare's dramatic verse, even when most melodious, is merely "metrical prose" (p. 179). We get from Dallas little help regarding actual verse,[1] but many suggestive hints about principles of poetry—which, after all, form his subject. With his book should be read Prof. Masson's enlightening criticism in *Essays Biographical and Critical* (1856) ; the last three or four pages deal with metre. And the student should go on to the next paper in this volume, on "prose and verse", which well vindicates the naturalness and appropriateness of metre in moments of emotion. The Essay on "Milton's versification and his place in the history of English verse", in Prof. Masson's edition of that poet, though published

---

[1] He combats Guest's view that rhythm is equally real in whispers, and with regard to accent lengthening syllables says "an acute sound is naturally louder than a grave one; a grave one is longer lived" (p. 164). With less justification he blames "the absurd practice of letting one line run over into the next" (p. 175), and asserts that Milton's "bars" are not of equal length (p. 179). These "bars", however, are not what most people mean by that term, but represent "the dance or motion of verse between pause and pause" (p. 175).

much later, may be mentioned here. It is mainly practical and tabulative, but contains some remarks on Milton's "metrical management" (p. 212) and on the difference between accent and ictus (p. 219), and may profitably be read even after the yet more elaborate treatise of Mr. Robert Bridges on the same theme.[1]

Criticism of the variances in Shakespeare's versification at different periods of his life practically began in this decade, the works of William Sidney Walker and Charles Bathurst leading the way.[2] Though such criticism, since become so continuous and confident, bears directly on prosody, it rarely discusses structure, or at least principles as distinct from details of structure. "Weak endings" and "double endings" as characteristic, "end-stopt" lines giving place to "run-on lines", are matters interesting historically, but of small consequence from a theoretical point of view—hardly of more than the question whether a particular word is to be pronounced as monosyllable or dissyllable. Before we determine the value of such things for prosody, we must know what prosody is. I mention these enquiries here, that the reader may bear them in mind, but he need not expect

---

[1] I see no need to particularize other books on Milton, such as Thomas Keightley's *Account of the Life, Opinions, and Writings of John Milton* (1855), though this is specially mentioned by Prof. Mayor in his *Chapters of English Metre* (1886), and contains a few remarks on prosody (*e.g.* pp. 259-60). It is impossible to notice every critical edition of every English poet; nor is it necessary to do so, unless they throw fresh light on familiar questions. All students of Milton's metre should possess Canon Beeching's one-volume edition of the *Poems* (Clarendon Press, 1900), which reproduces typography supervised by the poet himself, often throwing light on matters of scansion.

[2] It is needless to quote titles of books which do not concern us. Craik's *English of Shakespeare* (1857), similarly, deals only with questions of articulation, *etc.*, as regards form. What has just been said of Milton applies far more to Shakespeare, works on whom form a separate literature. Unless incidentally, I do not intend referring to these, or to the discussions of his metre which they frequently contain. As a rule, these discussions are concerned with practice alone.

to find in such investigation what Poe called the "rationale" of our conception of metre.

In 1855 Walt Whitman published the first instalment of *Leaves of Grass*. Our survey cannot omit writings which raise in such acute form the question whether metre is essential to poetry. Whitman himself is credited with saying that the *Leaves* contain both prose and verse; his warmest admirer, therefore, need not contend that everything in them is poetical. And surely, it is beyond question that poetic feeling and rhythmic utterance, as a rule, go hand in hand throughout them. Neglecting some purely metric passages—such as "O Captain! my Captain!" and "Joy, shipmate, joy!"—the rhythmic pulse certainly beats strong in lines like—

When lilacs last in the dooryard bloom'd,
And the great star early droop'd in the western sky in the night,
I mourn'd, and yet shall mourn with ever-returning Spring;

or

Come, lovely and soothing Death,
Undulate round the world, serenely arriving, arriving.

To ignore the temporal structure of such lines is as absurd as to talk of shaking off the trammels of metre, form being a help not a hindrance to true singers. Whether irregular rhythms such as those favoured by Whitman will ultimately oust the more regular—whether, to go farther, recondite harmonies of prose, often nobly illustrated by Whitman, will finally supersede the more definite rhythms of verse—these are questions which no critic can answer. So long, however, as high emotion craves appropriate utterance, so long as in moments of excitement it is more natural to dance than to walk, rhythmic expression of some sort will assuredly continue. And as yet there is no sign of the old forms being effete. At the very moment when Whitman was trying to cast them from him, the author of *Atalanta in Calydon* was preluding a music soon to fill them with new life. Did verse answer to no instinct of our nature, it might well be abandoned as a thing outworn. Prophecy is the most futile of literary amusements, but we may at least be sure that fundamental instincts of our nature will demand satisfaction. The precise form which that satisfaction may or may not take cannot be foreseen; we can feel sure only that, in some shape or other, it will exist to gratify an ineradicable longing.

Imitations of Classic verse were less common in this decade. Kingsley's *Andromeda* has been already mentioned; two or three magazine articles, specified in my Bibliography, are readable but not important.[1] Scholars will like to consider two tracts by Lord Redesdale,[2] a nephew of the Mitford whose Essay on the harmony of language we discussed at length; they make measure depend on quantity, melody on accent, and refuse to word-accent the function of marking rhythm. Two poems by "Owen Meredith" may profitably be compared with each other in respect of structure. The paper by Barham, and still more the introduction and notes to his much earlier edition of Hephaestion, approach the subject of English verse from the Classic side, and are hardly suited to the general reader; but they handle both ancient and modern verse in a way quite other than the usual, insisting that both must be rhythmized to "isokhrony" [so spelt], even in such a couplet as—

>Come unto these yellow sands,
>And there join hands.

He apparently assumes that rules of Classic quantity apply unaltered to English speech, but the breadth of his general conceptions differentiates him entirely from the tribe of traditional prosodists.

By far the most remarkable contribution of this decade, however, was Coventry Patmore's *North British Review* Essay, now reprinted (with slight alteration)[3] as an

---

[1] Clough's "Letters of Parepidemus," published during his short American sojourn, can be read in his *Poems and Prose Remains*. The second Letter discusses quantitative verse, of which he afterwards attempted some examples (*cf. infra*, 1861; Appendix A, 1853).

[2] Bibliographical details, omitted here and elsewhere for brevity's sake, will be found in the list which has just been referred to above.

[3] Originally the paper reviewed Dallas's *Poetics*; some intro-

appendix to his collected poems (Vol. II, pp. 215-67),[1] with a Note in which, misdating the original publication as 1856 instead of 1857, he characteristically expresses pleasure at finding that, between then and 1886, "its main principles have been quietly adopted by most writers on the subject in periodicals and elsewhere." If this be true, the adoption is usually without acknowledgement, for the Essay is strangely seldom quoted by subsequent writers. I suspect, however, that the "adoption" was often merely coincidence of thought; Patmore voiced ideas that were in the air, and was sometimes less original than he fancied. However this be, his Essay is one of highest importance, and requires careful study. Its author was a poet, who some think has not yet reached his full measure of fame. He was also a learned critic, had read carefully the chief authorities, and does justice to Steele (p. 219) and O'Brien (p. 239). And he was a consecutive thinker, expressing his views clearly, if sometimes too dogmatically. Add that he observed and thought for himself, and we have a combination of qualities not easy to parallel. Accordingly, his Essay is a thing by itself. I regard it as inaugurating what I have called the "new prosody". Note, for example, his assertion that "the metrical expression of emotion is an instinct, not an artifice" (p. 223), and can be understood only after profound study, first of sounds in themselves,

ductory matter referring to this has been omitted. Two whole paragraphs at the end have been left out, making the Essay now close rather abruptly, also some sentences from the present last paragraph, while the parenthesis in it referring to Shakespeare is new. The entire paragraph on p. 244 beginning "The iambic ode" is new. On p. 246 a paragraph has been omitted which, among other things, remarked that "much modern writing, professing to be verse, is, in fact, no such thing". All these changes, I think, were made when the Essay was first reprinted as a preface to his poem *Amelia* (1878), where the introductory note is different. The Appendix in its present form dates from 1886, and has remained without further alteration since then.

[1] Alas, from the latest issue of these *Poems* (October, 1906) the Essay has been omitted. So much for appreciation of prosody in this country. [But cf. footnote at the end of above summary.]

then of "the philosophical grounds and primary laws of such expression" (p. 220). Here we are poles removed from the old idea of verse as a mere ingenious exercise, to be constructed as one puts together the pieces of a Chinese puzzle. A view of metre so serious as Patmore's postulates a thoughtful and thorough examination of all its constitutive elements. Such an examination is attempted in this Essay, and will be found carried out with increasing precision by writers who hold like views.

After brief tribute to precursors, Patmore develops his own view. This is, that "the co-ordination of life and law . . . determines the different degrees and kinds of metre" (p. 221). Primarily, metre is "a simple series of isochronous intervals, marked by accents" (p. 224). As such, it exists in all speech, when adequately rendered; time is as essential as tone, the two being inseparable. This brings him (p. 229 *seq*.) to consider accent, which he defines as that which marks, "*by whatever means*, certain isochronous intervals."[1] "Metre implies something measured;" "the thing measured is the time occupied in the delivery of a series of words;" and that which measures it, being itself unmeasured, is an "'ictus' or 'beat', actual or mental," which divides speech into "equal or proportionate spaces" (p. 230). But this is not all. Bare rhythm, mere succession of intervals, is not pleasing till distinguished by difference of tone. This, therefore, is an essential factor in metre. "The music of verse" is a truer phrase than "the rhythm of verse". "Rhythmical melody," not rhythm solely and by itself, is what makes verse agreeable (pp. 231–2).

Illuminative as this statement is, I must pause to express partial dissent. Patmore seems to me to attach undue importance to mere delivery, and not sufficiently to discriminate between word-accent and metrical beat or ictus. His "accent" is simply ictus. He himself identifies it with musical accent (p. 231), and this confusion leads

[1] "Those qualities which, singly, or in various combination, have hitherto been declared to *be* accent, are indeed only *the conditions of accent*" (p. 231).

him to say later (p. 238) that "the marking of the measure by the recurrent ictus may be occasionally remitted, the position of the ictus altered, or its place supplied by a pause"—remarks which are perfectly true of spoken word-accent, but surely not of that "mental beat" which, as he truly says (p. 231), most often "has no material and external existence at all". This confusion between mental and vocal punctuation leads him to think that metre is a matter wholly of elocution. Quoting two sample passages (p. 226), he opines that the sentence "Her ways are ways of pleasantness, and all her paths are peace" receives "entire metrical effect" from our ordinary reading; and that in a remarkable extract from "St. Jude" all accented syllables must, in proper reading, be separated by equal measures of time. Neither proposition seems to me certain or necessary. His identification of this "metrical accent or ictus" with change of tone also seems questionable, and still more his assertion that it always coincides with "long quantity" (p. 227). With much in these pages I entirely concur. The statements that in Greek verse "ictus, accent, quantity, and verbal caesura advanced... in parallel order" (*ibid.*); that our words have no fixed tones, these varying with sense (p. 229); that the time-beater of rhythm is mental; these and other points are admirably put. But the claim that prose and verse, when properly delivered, have the same temporal foundation (pp. 224–5) seems to me untrue to fact, and the scansion on p. 236 of

For one restraint, Lords of the world beside,

assumes that word-accent and metrical beat must coincide. On the other hand, Patmore sees clearly that the rhythm of our so-called dactyls and trochees is totally different from that produced by the Greek or Latin feet bearing these names, and rightly explains that difference as one of "time"; while he properly insists that the "very distinct character", in verse as in music, of iambic as against trochaic rhythm (and similarly in triple metre) requires us to find distinctive terms for each (pp. 236-7).

In considering how far the actual articulation of a syllable represents its metrical value (p. 237) Patmore makes the mistake of ignoring short 'rests', and is driven (p. 238) to hold that the equality of metrical intervals is "no more than general and approximate". Here, again, he seems to judge too much by spoken effect. And, though he professes to broach novel doctrines on the subject of pause, his consideration extends only to caesural and final pauses. He distinguishes, indeed, between metrical and grammatical pauses (p. 240), but by the former he means immensely protracted stops, often embracing a whole foot. That such do exist, as in 'poulters' measure' (p. 241), I fully believe. But his claim that every line containing an odd number of feet is followed by such a pause seems to me quite untenable. In advancing it (p. 242) he formulates with much complacency the thesis that English verse has for its unit a "dipode" or double foot, and must contain two, three, or four of these. It follows that every line of three, five, or seven feet comprises also a silent foot at the end, completing the "dipode". This I cannot for a moment accept. There is, doubtless, what Sheridan called a "suspensive pause" felt or expressed after every line of verse; but the expression may be, and in dramatic verse often is, infinitesimal in duration, and there is no reason whatever to hold that we feel it equivalent to an entire foot. Patmore's pompously announced "law" seems to me nonsense. It misreads a principle truly stated by O'Brien [*ante*, 1843], that a verse-unit must contain in itself two actions. But a single foot may be such a unit. It is absurd either to hold that our heroic line consists of two and a half units, or that it is supplemented always by a "silent foot". The only rational view regards each foot as complete in itself, containing action and reaction, systole and diastole; proof of this, if proof be wanted, is supplied by the fact that English poets have written pieces in which every line consists of one foot only, while the assertion that each of these is followed by an equal measure of silence must by the nature of things remain a mere assertion, incapable of demonstration.

With the rejection of this thesis some of Patmore's argument falls to the ground. His example of "six-syllable iambic" on p. 243 (taken from a poem of his own, Vol. II, p. 183) is hardly fair, since the seventh line is prolonged; if he means that pure six-syllable lines are necessarily mournful, facts are against him.[1] He was too fond of such rash generalizations. In the original essay, "jaunty choriambics" are pronounced totally unsuited for a dirge; this remark disappeared from the reprint, Mr. Swinburne having meantime utilised them for this very purpose. In a paragraph added to the reprint, on the other hand, it is actually maintained that a "catalectic pause" may cover the time of twelve syllables (p. 244); a contention which is surely theorizing run mad. The statement that "unmixed 'trochaics' or 'dactylics' have seldom been written by poets of fine musical feeling" (p. 245) I regard as equally disputable; practical difficulties have probably more to do with the matter than fineness of ear. And the immediately sequent scansion of lines by "sections" —as he there proposes to call his *dipodes*, possibly borrowing the term from Guest—attaches far too much importance to a poet's natural desire of avoiding monotonous agreement between word-accent and verse-beat. It would be a very 'wooden' verse where these always coincided, but a hardly less wooden which was bound by Patmore's sections. All such attempts to minimise liberty fail, and deserve to fail; our business is to discover the principle which justifies liberty, not to fetter it with bonds of our own devising.

The second and shorter half of the Essay (from p. 246

[1] In Cowper, for instance, this metre is not restricted to mournful subjects. Patmore's friend Tennyson ridiculed the idea of such limitation, and sent him some six-syllable lines of a very opposite character. See Tennyson's *Life* ("Alfred Lord Tennyson, a memoir, by his son"), single-volume edition, 1905, p. 395.

onward) deals with rhyme and alliteration, for the most part excellently. Mr. Swinburne may well have profited by Patmore's vindication of the true place of alliteration in our verse, while the account given of Anglo-Saxon structure, and the criticism of Rask's view of " anacrusis " (p. 252), seem unimpeachable. Dealing with Anglo-Saxon rhythm (p. 254), Patmore sides with Mitford against Guest, but speaks in a singular way of "'common' or 'iambic' time" (p. 255), whereas true iambic time is necessarily triple. I take this merely to mean, however, that (like other critics before noted) he recognised "equal measure" in our standard type of verse. For his remarks on four lines from Scott (*ibid.*), and his italicised statement that "an entire line may be in common or triple cadence, according to the cadence of the context" (p. 256), go to the root of the matter. On rhyme he is less entirely trustworthy, attempting to show that it constitutes as well as signalizes metre, and that octosyllabic couplets are non-metrical without rhyme, because they have no "catalectic pause" (p. 258, *cf.* 265); while he also commits himself to the view that "the verbal accent . . . gives length wherever it chances to fall" (p. 259). So, too, he contends that the true "Alexandrine" is a line of four sections, "having a middle and a final pause each equal to a foot" (p. 262). The scansion of triplets in common-time verse as "real anapaests" (p. 263) may confuse a reader who quite sees that the trisyllabic feet in triple-time verse are not either accentually or quantitatively anapaests (*ibid.*), because it seems to make syllables actually constitute rhythm; but the explanation that "two syllables are read into about the time of one" (p. 264) puts matters on their true basis. While these paragraphs, therefore, like their predecessors, must be read with caution, they yet contain much that is true, and much that is suggestive. The reference to Shakespeare in the Essay's final sentence, it should be noted, considerably qualifies previous confident assertions about "major and minor accent". The paper ends, as I have already said, somewhat abruptly, without anything like peroration or final summary of views.

However one may differ from particular conclusions of Patmore's, it is impossible not to admire the spirit and plan of his Essay. We have in it a real study of metre from an independent and intelligent critic. Its chief defect, in my judgement, is non-recognition of minute intervals of pause. The extraordinary assertion (p. 237) that " in music played *staccato* on the pianoforte, the actual duration of sound in a crotchet or quaver note may be the same ", shows this clearly. Not the duration of sound, but the interval between the beginning of one sound and the beginning of the next, is identical; and that interval is partly occupied by silence. So it is and must be in verse. Hearers are slow to admit the reality of such pauses. They will often deny the existence of any silent interval, even when phonetic considerations prove that such interval *must* occur. Recognition of these silent spaces is essential to just prosody, and often revolutionizes our ideas of a line's actual structure. It is therefore a mistake to concentrate attention on syllables so exclusively as Patmore did; and his peculiar view of accent tended farther to mislead him in this respect. But, after all deductions, his Essay remains a most important contribution to English prosody. Its importance was not at once recognised. So far as my reading shows, it was but seldom referred to, and only of late years has its value been properly appreciated. Those who now appreciate it are, perhaps, too much inclined to take all it says for gospel; I have therefore emphasized my dissent where its teaching seems to me erroneous. But I heartily agree in giving it a very high place among English studies of prosody, ranking it among the few papers of abiding value which the subject has elicited. By far the ablest contribution during the decade to which with it we bid adieu, it well deserves the permanent position now given it in the authorised edition of Patmore's poems.[1]

[1] *Cf.* a previous footnote! I am glad to learn, however, that the

The Sixties of last Century saw culminate the rage for pseudo-Classical forms of verse, and criticism of prosody was then mainly concerned with these. Here, again, I must decline to consider in detail the mass of 'hexameter' verse written by Cochrane, Dart, W. Simcox, and others, or the discussion of these in contemporary magazines. But it is necessary to point out that some of our chief poets at this time made experiments in this direction, while some very eminent critics entered into controversy on the subject. That controversy began with an assertion by a great Classical scholar, Munro of Cambridge, that modern speech had lost all sense of syllabic quantity. This theorem was assailed by James Spedding, in an article reprinted (with additions) in his collected *Reviews and Discussions*. Postscripts on either side continued the argument, which was taken up by Matthew Arnold in his *Lectures on translating Homer* (see especially the "Last words"), and by Prof. F. W. Newman in his vigorous reply to Arnold's criticisms. Of these, Spedding's paper has most relevancy for us. Munro's total denial of quantity in English syllables save as produced by accentuation (see his "Appendix") can only be called extraordinary. Arnold does little to elucidate this part of his subject, and his own model lines are singularly weak; he actually makes "To a" stand for the first foot of one line. Prof. Newman's reply deals mainly with ancient verse.[1] Spedding's modestly written plea for an interrelation of quantitative and accentual structure, however, interests both on its own

Essay will still be obtainable in the "collective edition" of Patmore's complete *Works*.

[1] I have but lately seen "Lectures on Poetry" [1869?], now reprinted in this author's *Miscellanies*, Vol. I. The second Lecture is on "forms of poetry", and contains some remarks on metre (pp. 82-4), distinguishing *duplicate* from *triplicate* forms. He contends that too uniform succession of accents is displeasing in verse, and that "equable times ... are to us an offence." [the latter statement is surely fallacious]. On the other hand he recognises that our English so-called dactylic and anapaestic measures move to "minuet or dancing time", therefore do not reproduce the Greek rhythms bearing these names.

account—however little one may accept his conclusions—and because of its influence on others, shown so recently as in the work of the late W. J. Stone [*infra*, 1898]. It was to this paper, and to similar efforts made by Clough,[1] that Tennyson referred in his well known lines; when he says these are

<blockquote>Hexameters no worse than daring Germany gave us,</blockquote>

I understand him to mean that the quantitative attempts of his two friends and others are as uncongenial to English verse as are the most lumbering 'accentual hexameters' perpetrated by German poets or their English pupils.

Tennyson's own "Experiments in Quantity" took a different line. Instead of contrasting accent and quantity, he sought to unite them on one syllable—a task in which he was later followed by Prof. Robinson Ellis in his complete translation of Catullus (1871). Certainly Tennyson's "Alcaics" have a majestic, his "Hendecasyllabics" a dainty swing, but one may doubt how far that is due to supposed structure, in which also flaws are perceptible;[2] poems like "The Daisy" and "To F. D. Maurice" appear more happily to unite Classic inspiration with native metre. "Boadicea," as the writer himself said,[3] is hardly intelligible without a key of some sort, teaching us for instance to say *célebráted* not *célebrated*. With these should be compared Mr. Meredith's "Phaethon", and some other poems in annotations to which that author plays the prosodist so far as to indicate accented syllables but not pauses. Mr. Swinburne's "Sapphics" and "Hendecasyllabics", with his later "Choriambics", show a fine natural ear for quantity, not trammelled by supposititious rules. Matthew Arnold

---

[1] Two of these being dated "Freshwater, 1861". See Clough's *Poems*, "Essays in Classical metres." Both Clough and Spedding were dear friends of Tennyson's.

[2] It should be noted that Tennyson professed to follow the structure of *Greek* alcaic verse, not the more restricted Horatian model (see *Life*, as before, p. 425).

[3] *Life*, pp. 367, 386.

made no further attempt in this line that I know of, and Browning essayed such verse only in his much later "Ixion" and possibly "Pheidippides". No subsequent work of great importance has followed these patterns, though accentual 'hexameters' and 'elegiacs' are always with us; though Mr. Watson reproduced Swinburnian cadences with fine effect in his "Hymn to the sea", and Mr. Meredith subjoined some fragments to his *A Reading of Life*.[1] Still more recent work by Mr. Robert Bridges, on the other hand, harks back to the tradition of Clough and Spedding, and shows what life may lurk in embers that had seemed altogether dead.

That tradition had been worked for most that it was worth by a writer now seemingly forgotten. Charles Bagot Cayley's "Remarks and experiments" in the Philological Society's *Transactions* for 1861-2,[2] his Preface to a translation of the *Prometheus Bound* (1867), with his later *Iliad homometrically translated* (1877), seem to me pretty well to determine the issue. It is amazing that they should not have been cited by Messrs. Stone and Bridges. Cayley's rules (given in the first two publications) differ somewhat from theirs; following Classic tradition, he shortens long vowels before a following vowel, and neglects *h* as a consonant. But in all essentials his verse is one with theirs. Accent is combatively opposed to quantity, and he is sound on the "doubled consonant" question. The experiment

[1] *Edith*, by Thos. Ashe (1873), and *Dorothy*, by Arthur J. Munby (1880), are two of the longest poems written in these metres during the last generation. For others, see my Bibliography, which is far from exhaustive, or even representative.

[2] Though this paper is for scholars only, it contains some very acute remarks on English speech and verse. In the latter he recognises "positive pauses (like the rests in a bar of music)" (p. 67), but these are only caesural or final. To say "that accent in the modern languages is the same thing as quantity in the ancient ... seems to me something like saying that noise on the pianoforte is equivalent to time on the kithara" (p. 83). His main positions are too technical to be discussed here. Another paper by him on "The pedigree of English Heroic Verse" (*Philolog. Soc. Trans.* 1867, pp. 43-54) is good but now out of date.

suggested by Spedding, and revived by Stone, was systematically tried by Cayley for nearly twenty years. There seems little likelihood of fresh fruit from a plant that has been already so assiduously cultivated.

I have declined to enumerate magazine reviews of hexameters during this decade—the veteran Whewell was still writing in its earlier years—nor need I quote the opinions of men like Dean Alford, Philip Worsley, Lord Derby, the first Lord Lytton, and others, in prefaces prefixed to their works. A tract by Lord Lindsay "On the theory of the English hexameter, and its applicability to the translation of Homer", suggested by Arnold's Lectures, is interesting on personal rather than critical grounds, since it quotes unpublished opinions of several critics; its own theory and practice are alike defective. As an "ideally good" hexameter it quotes one which I can neither understand nor scan—

Oh, by Abs! Oh, by Adnan! I am the lover of Illa!

The last Dissertation in Vol. I of Prof. Blackie's *Homer* (1866) treats the hexameter question pretty fully, and kindred papers (reprinted from these or earlier years) will be found in his *Horae Hellenicae* (1874); but this vivacious writer was sometimes run away with by theories. Calverley's paper "On metrical translation", published in 1868 and now reprinted in his *Works*, is to my mind the ablest discussion of this question from the purely Classical side, and disposed of any pretence that our accentual hexameters reproduced the structure of Greek or Latin verse. That question is but a side-issue for us, and Calverley's paper contains little that will profit the student of real English verse; but it is well to know where the arguments affecting this particular limited question can be found most convincingly stated.

I have tried to gather here all that remained to be said about this side-issue. Far be it from me to preach finality of criticism. Poets have every right to try experiments, and success is the only criterion. But this particular question does seem to me thrashed out.

Neither quantitative verse, nor accentual lines as our German school understood them, can be expected to take root in English. The first, because it transgresses our fixed speech-habit; the second, because their constitution comes short of true prosody. The latter fault can be easily remedied, as readers from the first discovered, and the lines can be treated as native English lines, their supposed structure being a myth ; the former fault is irremediable. Such is my belief, and I hope not again to return to this question, during what remains of this volume. Readers should now, at any rate, be able to distinguish between two such different things as accentual and quantitative hexameters, though eminent critics of our own day have sometimes failed to make this distinction.

A few treatises of wider outlook were published during this decade. *Lectures on the English Language*, by George P. Marsh [not in my original list], had gone through more than one edition in America before it came to us in 1862. Mostly occupied with grammar and vocabulary, it touches on verse in Chapters 23, 24, 25, dealing mainly with rhyme and alliteration. There are, however, a few remarks on structure, and some apposite quotations. Had not my attention been specially directed to this book by a correspondent, I should hardly have thought it worth mention here.[1]

In 1862 also appeared a book [again not on my first list] by Thomas Arnold, brother to Matthew, entitled *A Manual of English Literature, historical and critical. With an Appendix on English Metres.* A seventh edition of this came out so lately as 1897. The Appendix is short and slight, in the latest "revised" edition as in the

[1] From about this time onward, most grammars and literary manuals divide verse by accents alone; this may henceforth be considered orthodox prosody. It is needless to multiply examples. Fairly typical is a *Handbook of the English Tongue*, by Joseph Angus (1862), the "Prosody" Section of which (pp. 343-65) is based on Latham. Classical terms are pronounced misleading, but are still used. I shall mention only books which depart more or less from this tradition, as does the one specified in my next paragraph.

M

earliest. Guest is referred to as the sole authority, his "natural system of prosody" being adopted as regards *sections*, while yet the "classical system" is "retained provisionally". "Metre is the arrangement into verse of definite measures of sound, definitely accented" (opening words). Six kinds of feet are described, to the ordinary four being added spondee and amphibrach—which last he proposes to call *amphiambus*—but the examples given of the last are not convincing. Some remarks about hexameter verse, ancient and modern, have accrued since the first edition. As the whole Appendix occupies only some dozen pages, these references will easily be found. Nothing of consequence is to be learned from it.

Not forgetting the impetus given to metrical study at this time by Mr. Swinburne's early poems, as well as by those of some elder contemporaries, we pass on to 1869.[1] *The Rules of Rhyme*, by the younger Hood, published in this year [2nd edition, 1877], covers wider ground than its title implies, but hardly does more than illustrate traditional rules of verse by old and new examples. "Feet and caesura, metre and rhythm, rhyme and figures" are dealt with in the nine Chapters which form the first portion of the book, some lines of Pope's being quoted and commented on by way of general introduction. "Guides and handbooks" are enumerated to the extent of four [!], beginning with Bysshe. Twelve kinds of feet are specified, but it is admitted that neither these, nor the Classic rules of caesura, quite apply in English verse; in Chap. II the writer inadequately conceives the difference between Latin and English metre, and his illustrations are faulty.[2] These nine Chapters (pp. 1-63) are followed by a Rhyming Dictionary, and an Appendix (pp. 153-206) based on *The Young Poet's Guide* [this I have failed

[1] For *A Manual of English Prosody* by R. F. Brewer, published in 1869, see under 1893 (footnote).
[2] Thus "Hapless lasses" is given as an equivalent for "Miserarum est" (p. 12). My references are to the earlier edition. To the later, which seems otherwise substantially the same, was added a copy of Bysshe's "rules for making English verse".

to identify; it is apparently not by T. Hood, senior], dealing mainly with the expressional value of sounds. While this book cannot be considered trustworthy, even for beginners, it is modestly and pleasantly written, and shows acquaintance with contemporary poems—a feature not too common in books of prosody. But its view of verse is narrow and defective.

Much more ambitious and noteworthy is a book published in the same year, which I have but lately seen;— *English Versification: a complete practical guide to the whole subject*, by E. Wadham (Longmans, 1869). Here indeed is apparently a "new prosody", with nomenclature of its own; instead of iamb, trochee, anapaest, and dactyl we have *march, trip, quick*, and *revert, forward* and *backward* accent instead of rising and falling, while names like *midabout, outabout, odd-over, partlet*, occur freely—a weak accent is styled *the hover*. But when we dip below the surface this apparent novelty vanishes, and we find old ideas under new names. The writer has no conception of *time* except as *tempo* or pace (*e.g.* p. 65); 'rests' are deliberately rejected (p. 127). The melody of verse, according to him, is wholly due to vowel-sound and rhyming (p. 113); metre is a matter entirely of syllables. His "pauses" are the usual caesural divisions merely (pp. 8–9). There are no real units in our verse except lines; "division into lines appears to be the prime principle of metre" (p. 132). This too narrow view misleads his analysis throughout, often blinding him to temporal equality (*e.g.* in Shelley's "Away, away!" on p. 103), and making him believe that "the measure is broken" whenever two accented syllables come together (p. 121). Like Poe, he postulates rigid syllabic proportion, and censures any breach of it (p. 60). Yet there is much excellent stuff in this volume. The writer has thought as well as made names for himself. His first Chapter might lead us to expect success. "Rhythm, run, or singsong" is there made "the most characteristic quality of verse", it being noted that "all exaltation is rhythmic" (p. 2). The difference between Greek and English prosody is well explained (p. 4, *cf.* p. 56 and Chap. XXIII), and the tendency of English verse to accent the last syllable of a foot insisted on in opposition to the "backward run" of music (pp. 7-8, *cf.* Chap. VI). The historical origin of English verse is shortly sketched in Chapter II, and blank verse (epic and dramatic) carefully examined in Chapter III, while these and all succeeding Chapters are enriched by a profusion of apposite quotations—in some cases, if I mistake not, from the writer's own pen. Forms of versification are gone into at great length, the "hexameter" being included under "false metre and dubious" (Chap. VII). The "assertive bounce" of rhyme is a good phrase (p. 115), and though the true structure of a line like

The sun sets, the shadow flies,

is not recognised, its cadence is defended (p. 125). But, throughout my reading, I find myself continually registering dissent, which culminates on reaching the author's treatment of what he calls "cesural", "free," and "main" verse (Chaps. XIX, XX, XXII). Here the distinction between prose and verse seems to me entirely lost, through neglect of temporal equality. The "stress-rhythm" theories of a later day are most curiously anticipated and illustrated in these Chapters. Holding the opinions I do, it is impossible for me to consider the author's view of verse adequate or even sensible, and to these final Chapters I confidently appeal for proof of its insufficiency.

Equally peculiar in terminology, though of a different kind, was a tract entitled *The Laws of Verse, or Principles of Versification exemplified in metrical translations*, by J. J. Sylvester, of Cambridge, then resident in Baltimore, U.S.A., afterwards Savilian Professor of Geometry in Oxford. Prof. Sylvester's Preface and Notes to the first part of this tract (which is followed by a paper on a vastly different subject) deal, not with verse as a whole, but with one feature of it called Phonetic Syzygy, which merely means easy junction of syllables. "Rhythmic," or the technical side of poetry, it is explained in the

Preface (pp. 9–19), divides into "Metric, Chromatic, and Synectic", the first (concerned with accent, quantity, and suspensions) treating the discontinuous aspect of the Art, and the last the continuous; while this last is subdivided into Anastomosis, Syzygy, and Symptosis, the first of which deals with passing from one word to another, and the third with rhyme, assonance, *etc.* His translations (from Horace, Goethe, Schiller, and others) seek to illustrate these, especially Syzygy, and the notes explain his method. They are therefore only of comparative interest to us. As regards "Metric", he endorses Poe's view, "rendered more complete by my introduction into it of the theory of the silent syllable or rest" (p. 10)—almost as if this theory was his own discovery. In effect, his teaching goes little beyond Poe's. When he says (pp. 64–5) that "the substratum of measure is time", he refers mainly if not solely to syllabic quantity as determined by accent; and so when he says that "feet in modern metre are of equal length" (p. 66, *cf. note*). Yet I think he would have been ready to take a wider view, unless the mathematical preconceptions which he shared with Poe prevented; for he distinctly refers to musical time in some of his notes, and speaks of "acopation" and "tempo rubato" (p. 67). It is to be regretted that he did not develop his view of *metric* as well as *synectic*. The tract is dedicated to Matthew Arnold.[1]

It was during the eighth decade of last Century that a really new prosody, after some false starts, fairly began its course. The researches of Helmholtz—made accessible

---

[1] I have but just seen another *brochure* by the same author (privately printed, N.D., British Museum Catalogue says 1880), *Spring's Début: A Town Idyll, in two centuries of continuous rhyme* [*i.e.* two hundred (and odd) lines all rhyming more or less perfectly to the termination *-een*]. A Note at the end of this speaks of "two distinct schemes or strands of time and accent, in general coincident, but occasionally showing themselves independent" (p. 27). Unless *time* be here restricted to syllabic quantity, this anticipates a doctrine which I have myself tried to preach. He does, however, usually so restrict it (*cf.* p. 69, *note*, in the earlier book), and I suspect does so in this case also.

to English readers by A. J. Ellis's translation in 1875,—had laid bare the nature and working of those "tones" which create verse among other forms of vocal music; Alexander Melville Bell, by his *Visible Speech* alphabet, had for the first time given a notation capable of expressing any articulate sound. Building on such foundations, English as well as Continental scholars attacked *de novo* questions of metrical rhythm. Ellis himself, by this time President of the Philological Society, led the way; in the *Transactions* of that Society will be found papers by him, as also by Professors Skeat, Mayor, Sweet and others, still happily with us.[1] Deferring for a moment further reference to Ellis, and reserving the work of these others for examination when their separate books appear, I pause to notice briefly in chronological order one or two volumes which shared the influence of this school.

The Philology of the English Tongue, by Prof. Earle of Oxford (first edition, 1871; I quote the third, 1880), contains a Chapter on " Prosody, or the musical element in speech ". This title suggests the new outlook. Verse seeks to construct musical cadences, to emphasize the modulative element in speech—an "accordant, concentive, illustrative element", which exercises "a formative, almost a creative power " (p. 587). This it does by using *time* and *tune*, quantity and accent. Of these the latter is identified with tone, as also is emphasis, the two differing only in the objects to which they are applied; "an accented word is emphasized by the intensification of its chief accent" (pp. 595-6). Quantity is the note-mark of primitive speech (p. 589), prominent in Greek and Latin (pp. 603-4), but "a period comes... when the sonorousness of words gives place to the sentiment of modulation, whereby a musical unity is given to the sentence like the unity of thought" (p. 621). So in Anglo-Saxon verse " word-sound " was a chief feature, while its prose developed sentential rhythm; when verse adopted this,

[1] The Minutes of " Proceedings" are also often of interest, giving discussion by experts, *e.g. Transactions* for 1873-4, pp. 644-5.

the "restraint of metre" became necessary, for "metre is to rhythm what logic is to rhetoric" (p. 623). Rhythm is a national thing, metre can be transplanted; French influence "gave us a new music". Metre is "ultimately resoluble into a speciality of modulation or rhythm" (p. 624). Earle's discussion is entirely general, as is his summing up (pp. 634-40), and there is much that is highly questionable in these statements. But the point of view is widened, the *conception* of verse is broad; analysis of parts is not substituted for analysis of the whole. In this we may trace the effect of new ideas and discoveries.[1]

More of practical guidance is given by two City of London School men, Dr. Abbott and Prof. Seeley, in their *English Lessons for English People*[2] (1871). Intended primarily for boys, this book contains much that will benefit older readers, Part III being on metre. General rules applicable to English verse are formulated, but are stated much too absolutely. Thus we have the assertion that two consecutive syllables in a word cannot be metrically accented, and that when a polysyllable has two accents, these must rest on alternate syllables (*sólitáry*, not *sólitarý*, paragraph 100); while with all the emphasis of italics they state that "*three unaccented syllables cannot be found together in any English metre*, if they are all fully pronounced" (par. 107). None of these rules is invariable. To their further rule that "a pause is necessary before a trochee" they themselves quote "remarkable exceptions" (par. 138); but they admit none to the dogma "in most strict dissyllabic metre [*disyllabic* is their spelling], a trisyllabic foot at the end of the verse would injure the effect" (par. 144). Their general tendency is toward a too mechanical view of syllabic structure; their proposition that "any extra syllables may be admitted that are felt not to interfere with the regular recurrence of the accent" (par. 202) might have been

---

[1] In a good phrase he says, "The Gothic ear enjoys a precipitous consonantism" (p. 612).

[2] Misprinted "*Readers*" in my old list.

extended to other than dramatic verse. Particular scansions are often dubious; Tennyson repudiated their analysis of his line (par. 204)—

Down the long turret stair, palpitating [1].

In the main, however, sound principles are stated, and there is a refreshing absence of pedantry; 'anacrusis' is styled *the catch*. A too rigid view of syllabic structure, often leading to wrong analysis and division, is the chief fault I find in this book.[2]

Here also may be mentioned a study possessing very different characteristics. The *Fortnightly Review* for December, 1874, contained a paper by J. A. Symonds on "The blank verse of Milton", reprinted more than once, and finally in a separate volume called *Blank Verse* (my references are to the latest and best edition, 1895). This volume contains three Essays, the first a "Prefatory Note", the second historical, while the third represents the original paper. All three may be considered together, for the writer's position did not alter. It amounted, practically, to a negation of prosody. Recognising that "the notes and bars of the musical composer" give a "truer basis of measurement" than syllabic feet (p. 88), he fails to follow this out into detail, preferring to bid us trust our ears, "attend strictly to the sense and the pauses" (p. 90), and observe the "balance and proportion" of syllables, the "right proportions and masses of sound" (p. 87). Excellent advice in itself, but—as he gives it—tantamount to denying that a sonata can be resolved into its constituent notes.

[1] See the discussion referred to in recent footnote.
[2] The "Prosody" Section of Dr. Abbott's *Shakespearian Grammar* (1869; third edition, 1870, revised and much enlarged) goes on the same lines, and seems marred in places by the same fault. Monosyllables are frequently made dissyllables, even in so strong a case as—

Twelve *year* since, Miranda, twelve year since,

which should surely be accounted a nine-syllable line. As a collection of instances, and monument of careful study, this book (especially in the later edition) deserves all praise.

"Analysis by feet" is odious to Symonds; he deals with the "rhetoric of verse rather than prosody" (p. 1). His Prefatory Note shows small technical knowledge. Originally, he had laid it down that "quantity forms no part of our prosody" (p. 84); now, he admits that "both Quantity and Accent have a common element of Time" (p. 10), but thinks that "in many words quantity is hardly distinguishable from accent" (p. 7), selecting curiously as his example the Latin word *Tityre*. This attempt at technicality, made with "diffidence", carries no weight. On the other hand, the historical account of our blank verse, from Marlowe to Tennyson ("the most original and greatest living writer of blank verse," p. 67), is full of interest, and there is much excellent criticism both there and in the third Essay. The volume deserves reading as an exposition of the general effects of verse, of the mutual relations between sense and sound; but it deliberately abandons any attempt to analyse these. (For his own statement see p. 85 *seq.*) The original Essay is well summarized and criticised by Prof. Mayor in his *Chapters of English Metre* [*infra*, 1886], Chap. IV, being there ranked as a production of the "aesthetic or intuitivist" school. From that school students of practical prosody get little or no help.

Returning now to A. J. Ellis, I would first single out his paper on "The physical constituents of accent and emphasis" (Philological Society's *Transactions* for 1873-4, pp. 113-64) as representing his mature views of these. Length, pitch, and force, with other ingredients, are here (pp. 115-26) clearly defined by our foremost phonetic scholar, and he considers these three mutually independent (p. 148, *note*). "Specific varieties, due to pitch and force, are the main sources of accent; emphasis requires, in addition, the use of expressional varieties of *form* [*i.e.* quality or *timbre* of the voice], and also the adoption of differences of length" (p. 118). Specific differences of pronunciation may be either "fixed" or "free" (p. 125). English accent can be shortly defined as "fixed force with free pitch" (p. 128); in French speech, pitch, force, and length seem all "practically free", so that it has "no accent, only emphasis" (p. 138); ancient Greek speech is considered in p. 142 *seq.* Classical students will learn from these last what speech meant when (as a general rule) each syllable had its relative length and pitch determined beforehand, independent of expression, while varieties of force were left to the speaker's choice. Only thus can they fully realize the nature of ancient 'quantity', only thus measure the gulf which yawns between Greek verse and ours, even when the rhythmic as well as metric relations of the former are duly taken into account.

But it is with Ellis's view of English verse that we are directly concerned, and for this we must go to a later paper. Brief reference is indeed made to our metrical structure in the one just referred to (pp. 130–2), but it is treated more fully and systematically in pp. 435–49 of the *Transactions* for 1875–6 (*cf.* also pp. 456–69), the main substance of which is reproduced in Prof. Mayor's *Chapters on English Metre*, Chap. V. It must be owned that his treatment is heroic. In his *Elements of Phonetics* (1848) he had distinguished three degrees of both accent and quantity—the latter there termed "long, brief, and stopt"—but now he would have us distinguish no less than nine degrees of each, with correspondingly numerous gradations of "pitch, weight[1], and silence", making altogether forty-five differing possibilities to be taken into account.[2] Rather than be tortured with such minute analysis, Prof. Mayor would "rush into the arms

---

[1] This word he borrows from Steele (to whom he does justice), but employs it in a sense of his own; see my next paragraph.

[2] Prof. Mayor speaks of "forty-five varieties *of stress*", making this word cover all Ellis's five qualities. If *force* alone be dealt with, it is obvious that the possible combinations of ascending force in a dissyllabic foot would be thirty-six, with the same number of descending; while if the other four qualities may be combined with these in any order, the total of possible combinations would be counted by millions! I do not, however, imagine that Ellis conceived all five qualities to be necessarily present in every such pair of syllables.

of the intuitivists". But of course this analytic detail is not put forward as necessary to enjoyment of verse. For all practical purposes, Ellis himself says, three gradations instead of nine will serve, thus reducing the variations to a more manageable number. And, after all, the question is one of fact. Can it be denied that Ellis's complicated tabulation corresponds to possible varieties of syllabic sound? It is well that all critics, especially those who regard syllables as constituting the entirety of verse, should be made to realize how exceedingly complex the relations of those syllables can be. Something more simple and definite than these relations must inspire the quick appreciation of verse shown by children and savages. How does Ellis handle this simpler element?

In his earlier paper (*loc. cit.*) Ellis had made our verse-rhythm depend "mainly on periodical succession of clear force-accent or emphasis.... Length [of syllables] has no part in the fixed laws of English verse-rhythm, but has much influence on the oral effect." He now says that "English rhythm is primarily governed by alternations and groups of strong and weak syllables", but "materially influenced by alternations and groups of long and short, high and low, heavy and light syllables, and great and small pauses"; the tabulation of these in the case of simple alternations has just been dealt with. In a previous paragraph he had stated that "our English verse, though based on alternations of force, is materially governed by length and pause, ... and is more than all perhaps governed by *weight*". On this last element he insists much, defining it with precision in the remainder of his sentence. To me it seems that the "very complex phenomenon" so defined is really a combination, partly of metrical *ictus*, partly of elocutional expression which, as Prof. Mayor says, forms no necessary part of verse-rhythm. Adornment is insufficiently distinguished from essentials, delivery from structure. And this brings us to what I think most open to criticism in Ellis's view, *viz.* its indefinite treatment of rhythm. That he was conscious of temporal relations is clear; his recognition of "rests", his use of the word "periodicity", sufficiently prove that. But they find no prominent place in his analysis. Rhythm is to him wholly a matter of syllables, created and conditioned by their relations, whether or no they adjoin each other or are separated by intervals of silence. Apart from them it would cease to exist. This point of view is natural to the metrist, still more to the philologer whose whole life has been spent in studying syllables; but I cannot think it a true one. Analysis of individual bricks does not give us the secret of the arch which is made of these. Even if we take into account mortar as well as bricks [that is, in this case, silences as well as sounds], and reckon the strains and thrusts to which they are subjected, we are still far from having realized the meaning of an arch. To form an adequate idea of verse, we must survey it as a completed whole as well as in its component parts.

In all that affects individual syllables, however, Ellis is a master. I leave readers to study his exposition in detail; the sentences cited will be easily found in Prof. Mayor's book. In the discussion already twice referred to, Ellis gave it as his opinion that the unit of heroic measure was "indiscriminately either dissyllabic or trissyllabic" [his spelling];[1] and his views throughout are similarly liberal. Indeed, they became increasingly liberal as he went on. In an Appendix subjoined to this later paper he owns himself convinced, on further consideration, that "my rules do not form, as I thought, the sole conditions of rhythmical verse". He clung to the idea that the last foot of a line should be typical, but admits that even this rule has exceptions. In his scansion he adhered to the orthodox *foot* (which he preferred to call a *measure*), instead of reckoning altogether by accents; but he thought the Classical names both "mis-

[1] He subsequently explained, in a passage not cited by Prof. Mayor, this statement as meaning that *any one* foot could be one or other, not that all five feet could be trisyllabic at once (*Transactions*, 1875–6, p. 435). Neither critic was prepared to admit the possibility of the latter alternative.

leading" and "utterly insufficient for English purposes". He "found it of great practical advantage to be able to speak of a *strong* syllable, quite independent of the origin of its strength"; with most writers that practical advantage would be apt to accompany evasion of true analysis.

It may be said, therefore, that Ellis did invaluable work as regards details—work which should have finally exploded some antique fallacies—though he left much still to be done toward perfecting a general conception of verse. How far this latter work has since been done my succeeding pages will seek to show. Meantime, all that he wrote about verse deserves study. *Essentials of Phonetics* has been already mentioned. In his great book on *Early English Pronunciation* (1869 seq.), which threw a flood of light on much that had been dark before, occur some passages which are superseded by the later and fuller expositions we have passed under review. His *Basis of Music* (1862) is perhaps sufficiently popularized in two undated books, *Speech in Song* and *Pronunciation for Singers*, both containing much that is *ad rem* for us; his Preface to the second reviews his own work of thirty years. The article on "Speech-sounds" in the *Encyclopaedia Britannica* (1887) is by him. His tracts entitled *Hints on the quantitative pronunciation of Latin* (1874) and *The English, Dionysian, and Hellenic pronunciations of Greek* (1876) still remain unequalled to my knowledge for general handling, though some minor points may need revision. If his early devotion to mathematics left traces on both his matter and his style, they are not unwelcome in regions where clear thinking is somewhat a stranger. As a prosodian we consider him, and as such his place is a high one. He did much, and suggested more. For the most part, subsequent English prosody has progressed along lines marked out by him. Where it has been fruitful, it draws fertility from his ideas, from his way of regarding the subject; where these are neglected, it remains sterile and unprofitable.

Singularly different is the line taken in *A Treatise on*

Versification, by Gilbert Conway (1878), the single-sentence Preface to which announces its author's desire to show "what are the laws which rule, *or ought to rule*, the mechanism of English verse" [I italicise four words of dangerous import]. The 113 pages of this book are not divided into Chapters, nor furnished with index or table of contents; but they contain elaborate footnotes referring to the opinions of very many writers. Conway's own view makes our verse wholly the creation of force-accent. He goes so far as to declare that English speech is uttered in "strict monotone" (p. 5), and that no word has ever more than one accent (p. 7); also that "there can be no rhythm where there is no forcible sound" (p. 16, *note*), though most of us have seen a bar of music containing only 'rests'. Accordingly, the idea that our heroic line contains "five feet necessarily" seems to him as absurd as Steele and Chapman's ideas with regard to Latin hexameter (*ibid.*, *note*). The type and model of English verse is Italian, from which he derives rules which he thinks ought to be obeyed, and for transgressing which he is quite ready to blame our chief poets. A large part of the book (pp. 60–88) discusses hiatus and elision, the latter being distinguished from contraction. "Elision" is merely *blending* unaccented vowels by rapid articulation, as we all do constantly in speaking (p. 61, *note*); but actual contraction is claimed in the case of "hypermetrical syllables" (p. 88 *seq.*). Thus, in Say's often-quoted couplet, he allows *many a* to stand as a case of blending, but *amorous* must be written "am'rous".[1] Milton comes in here for criticism (p. 96 *seq.*), as earlier he had been accused of inconsistency.[2] "English hexameter" is briefly referred to on pp. 107–8, and onomatopoeia on pp. 109 *seq*. While the learning shown in Conway's footnotes commands respect, his main contention seems

---

[1] His rule is, "elide the elidable syllables, and cut out the mute" (p. 92, *note*). As if the mid-syllable in *amorous, delicate, beautiful, manifest, etc. etc.* were in any sense "mute"!

[2] "Consistency of practice ... it is vain to seek in the versification of Milton" (p. 67).

to me altogether faulty, and singularly at variance both with the work last reviewed and with other work almost immediately to be considered.

The year 1880 is memorable in our prosodic history. Not because Ruskin then published his *Elements of English Prosody*. This tract, indeed, is the work of a man of genius, brought for the first time in his life face to face with metrical questions, and attacking them with characteristic self-reliance. How little his attempt satisfied himself, how little also he had studied such matters as the effect of accent, his Preface tells. The acute intellect of Ruskin fastened at once on essentials. He saw that metre and music were akin; that the former, too, contains "measured rests, filling up the time required, as in bars of music" (p. 2); that "the primal essence of a poet is in his being a singer" (p. 32), actually and not metaphorically. He recognised that usually [he says "always"] it must "depend on the reader's choice to fill up the time with his voice, or to give an interval of silence" (p. 3). But when he comes to apply these excellent principles he is soon in difficulties, which his wayward genius disposes of anyhow. He starts by assuming that the most beautiful verse violates its own law, and this notion remains with him throughout. Employing somewhat peculiar terminology—*feet* he calls "metres", a *trochee* he prefers to name "choreus",[1] keeping the former term [which he writes "troche", though a *spondee* is with him always "spondeus"] for what most writers call *pyrrhic* or *dibrach*—and representing "metres" by musical symbols, as others had done before him, he reduces all quoted verse to his Procrustes-measures, letting the accent fall where it will. Readers should never accept his statements without scrutiny. They need not believe that the first example on p. 7 is rightly divided; or that "bonnie lassie" and "Aberfeldie" are reversed in accentuation (pp. 8-9); or that a word like *crustacean* could not begin a "really melodious"

[1] This term properly applies to any foot used in a chorus, and some writers make it include three-syllable feet.

heroic line (p. 10); or that there is entire difference of cadence between

> The Assyrian came down like the wolf on the fold

and

> Should the soldiers of Saul look away from the foe (p. 18);

or that the structure of Scott's "Coronach" ought to be called "a trimetre with two syllables in rest" (p. 24); or that Byron wrote "purely constructed and errorless verse" (p. 54). His whole scheme of defining the time of "metres" positively as well as relatively (p. 5) seems to me fallacious, as much so as making *deliberateness* characteristic of ancient Greece (*ibid.*). Technically, indeed, I should say that Ruskin more often goes wrong than right; what redeems his tract is its emotional receptivity. He *felt* the cadence of particular lines, felt it deeply and truly, and tried (arbitrarily and capriciously) to translate his feelings into prosodic theory. Not thus is true theory reached; yet the record of feeling has its value, coming from such a man. And, with all its faults, Ruskin's wild speculation at least aims in the right direction; students "in St. George's schools" will get from him a truer idea of what verse really is than if they had read a hundred treatises based on the old lifeless orthodoxy. But they must not think him infallible.[1]

Nor was this year rendered so memorable by the work of Edmund Gurney [omitted in my Bibliography], though his book on *The Power of Sound* (4to, Macmillan, 1880) is full of interest. Chapter VII discusses rhythm in general, making it consist in "stimulation at fixed degrees of time", its essential quality being "continuous satis-

---

[1] *Rock Honeycomb* (1877), referred to on the title-page of the *Elements*, and forming Vol. II of *Bibliotheca Pastorum*, will not reward search metrically, though it comments on "some broken pieces of Sir Philip Sidney's Psalter". The "Essays on Scott and Byron" mentioned at the end of the *Elements* appeared in the *Nineteenth Century* under the title "Fiction, fair and foul"; but only the third of these (Vol. VIII, p. 394) contains even casual reference to prosody.

faction of expectation " (pp. 127, 128). Chapter XIX is on " the sound-element in verse ". Not the mere presence of accented syllables, but their regularity of occurrence, constitutes verse; they come " in the vast majority of metres at equidistant places " (p. 425). Going on to compare music and verse, he thinks it immaterial whether we place the accented syllable first or last in a foot, and proposes an extraordinary scansion—

By the wá-|ters of Báb-|ylon we sat dówn | and wépt—

remarking that such a case of four unaccented syllables occurring together is rare (p. 427 [1]). He asserts that stress is "never reversed" in the last foot of English blank verse, an assertion which from his lips shows considerable ignorance; and makes some rather questionable statements about our " trochaic " verse (pp. 430, 431). He declines to admit "rests" as integral to structure (p. 432, *note*). On the whole, I cannot think Gurney adds much to our actual knowledge of English verse, though his remarks on Classic metre are noteworthy, and his treatise may rank high as a contribution to the study of sound in general.

What makes the year memorable from our point of view is that it saw published *The Science of English Verse* (New York, 1880 [2]), by the American poet Sidney Lanier.

---

[1] Compare, by the same author, *Tertium Quid* (2 vols. [of essays], 1887), Vol. II, p. 213. This comes in an Essay on "The appreciation of poetry", where he breaks a lance with Theodore Watts[-Dunton] over Poe's "Ulalume" (p. 201, *note*), and discusses Shelley's "Thy brother Death came and cried" (pp. 211–12), and " Fresh spring, and summer, and winter hoar" (p. 214, *note*). But the paper deals with matter more than form. Earlier in the same volume, an Essay on "Poets, critics, and class-lists" refers to "regularity of recurrence" as common to verse and music (p. 158, *cf. note*), and opines that the musical element in verse constitutes but a small part of its effect. I have enjoyed making belated acquaintance with these volumes, though by no means concurring in their conclusions as regards metre.

[2] Succeeding editions are apparently page-for-page reprints of the first. My copy, dated 1898, has nothing to show that it is not a new book, except the words "copyright, 1880." It contains an

This book seems still insufficiently known here; in its own country it has long been a textbook, and has founded a school of critics, prosody being much more earnestly studied there than with us. The distinctive note of the book is that it makes rhythm not a mere accident or ornament, but the essential basis, of verse. That idea, trite as it may seem, had not been systematically and scientifically worked out by any previous English writer known to me. Many had dallied with it, but none had followed it up to its legitimate conclusions. If I cannot, with some of his American admirers, think that Lanier has spoken the last word about English verse, I gladly join them in proclaiming the importance of his book, which to many people came as a revelation.

Lanier was at this time a teacher in the newly founded Johns Hopkins University at Baltimore, which has had a long and honourable connection with prosody. He was a practical musician, playing the flute in professional orchestras. As a poet his posthumous fame has steadily increased. In every way, therefore, he was well qualified for the task he undertook.[1] A singer who knew that he sang, he studied the mechanism of his singing, studied English verse as it was made by himself and others. He sought to analyse its musical structure, approaching it almost entirely from that side; there lay, perhaps, his

error in pagination, the first leaf of text being pp. 21, 22, while the last leaf of contents bears the same figures in Roman numerals. There is a full table of contents, but no index.

[1] Details of Lanier's life will be found in the memoirs by William Malone Baskerville (1876) and Edwin Mims (1905). A Southerner by birth, he fought in the Civil War, and suffered permanently in health from hardships and imprisonment. In youth he "could play on any instrument". See also his *Letters*, edited by his widow (1899). The lectures from which his book is formed are said to have been written in six weeks. Another set of lectures on *Shakspere and his Forerunners* (2 vols. 4to, London, 1902—the other books mentioned above are published in America) show full and careful reading. They repeat briefly his main views on prosody, but add nothing to his exposition. Personally, Lanier was much beloved. I shall refer later [*infra*, 1888] to a memorial volume written by friends and admirers.

weakness as well as his strength. It was work that greatly needed doing; let us see how he did it.

His Preface defines his aim, which is to give "an account of the true relations between music and verse", and deals shortly with a few predecessors, Steele's attempt being strangely disparaged. Then the first Chapter treats introductorily of sound, and the next eight Chapters (grouped as " Part I ") of our English verse-sounds and rhythms. " Part II," in one Chapter, describes the " tunes " of verse, and " Part III ", in five Chapters, its " tone-colors "—a phrase more familiar in music. These last Chapters—dealing with rhyme, alliteration, and syzygy—show especial marks of haste, as if time or strength failed their writer. For the same year that saw this book published saw also its author's death. He died, leaving his task unfinished, his best songs perhaps unsung. But enough is left to judge him by, in prosody as in poetry; the main lines of his theory of verse-fabric are clearly marked out.

The assertion with which Chapter I opens, *viz.* that verse impresses wholly by its sound apart from its meaning, is perhaps too absolutely made, but takes us at once into prosody's true domain. " The study of verse must begin with the study of sounds;" and they should be studied with reference to duration, intensity, pitch, and *timbre* or "tone-color" (p. 24). These are accurately distinguished and defined, the first being expressly stated to include " the correlative duration of the *silences* between sounds, which ... are quite as necessary to many forms of verse as are the sounds thereof" (pp. 32–3); and verse is affirmed to consist of " such sounds and silences as can be co-ordinated by the ear" (p. 33). Now force, or intensity, cannot be so co-ordinated with exactness (pp. 38–9), and therefore plays a subordinate though important part in verse, whose primary factors are duration, pitch, and tone-colour. Rhythm depends primarily on duration, and only secondarily on other elements (pp. 39–40); and verse-rhythm contains all the factors of musical rhythm, spoken words being sounds uttered by instruments of one particular class, to wit, our vocal organs (pp. 48-50). The characteristics which distinguish these sounds from other varieties of musical sound relate to *timbre* and *tune* (pp. 50-2). Speech, and therefore verse, has an elaborate notation of tone-colours (the alphabet), and uses every interval of tone, not only a chosen number. These characteristics distinguish verse from music; as for prose, "scientifically considered, it is a wild variety of verse" (p. 57). To observe and classify the phenomena of rhythm, tune, and tone-colour, so far as they can be indicated through the medium of spoken words, is therefore the aim of prosodic science (p. 58).

These important conclusions, developed in the three "Parts" which follow, are in substantial accord with the work of A. J. Ellis (to whom he refers in this connection, p. 27, *note*), Lanier's "color" being what Ellis calls "form". The composite structure of this last is duly noted. Parts II and III, however, dealing with the "tunes" and "colors" of verse, occupy collectively only about a fourth part of Lanier's exposition, three-fourths being devoted to Part I on rhythm. On this last our attention must be concentrated. What Lanier says about tune and tone-colour is for the most part admirable, though I must ask readers to receive with incredulity the assertion that " no rhyme but a perfect rhyme is ever worth a poet's while " (p. 299). But it is in Part I that his really constructive work is done, and done with thoroughness, though he modestly asks that it be considered as only an outline to be filled up by further research (p. 251). It is from Part I that we learn, both generally and in detail, what was Lanier's conception of English verse.

Though a musician, Lanier does not wholly adopt musical methods and rules. He does not, like musical textbooks, make time depend on accent. Only in "secondary rhythm" does accent, like other factors, play its part; " primary rhythm " consists entirely of co-ordinated durations. When a clock beating uniformly says "tick-tick" (p. 63), we instinctively make it say either "tick-*tick*" or "*tick*-tick"; but this apparent difference is imaginary, and merely shows our tendency to superimpose secondary on primary rhythm. "Accent can effect nothing, except in arranging materials already rhythmical through some temporal recurrence" (p. 65; *cf.* the syllogistic "demonstration" in the long *note* which begins on that page). English speech habitually utters syllables in definite and simple relations of equality or proportion (p. 60), and it is by this definiteness of relative duration that rhythm in prose or verse is created. These syllables therefore possess "quantity" (p. 68 *seq.*), not fixed but shifting, yet determinable by the ear, in virtue of which they can be grouped into divisions of equal or different length. Verse groups them in equal divisions or *bars*[1], each of which is "exactly equal to any other bar" (p. 82). In doing so, it employs "secondary rhythm" (pp. 69–78), and also "tertiary rhythm" or phrasing (pp. 79–87); but its essential base is equality of duration. It further groups these bars into lines, stanzas, and whole poems, so that six methods of grouping have to be considered (p. 95), *viz.* by quantity, rhythm, phrase, line [which he designates "metre", pp. 88, 91], stanza, and poem. To these the next six Chapters are devoted, what has been summarized in this paragraph occupying Chapter II, while Chapter IX [the last of "Part I"] briefly discourses of "rhythm throughout... Nature".

Chapter III continues the discussion of primary rhythm, and illustrates how English words in themselves constitute a system of rhythmical notation, their accents being arranged so as to enforce the rhythmical accent. Here he protests against the common notion that our verse is created by accent, even as expressed more guardedly by Ellis (p. 98), and insists that (in verse as in music) rhythms "exist in virtue of the simple time-relations between the units of sound" (p. 99). Then he expounds at length the temporal structure of verse-units, taking as his first example Tennyson's "Break, break, break". His exposition assumes that syllables correspond to and can be represented by musical notes, the time-values of which

[1] *Cf.*, later, p. 150, *note*.

he therefore explains, noticing particularly the " triole " or group of three sounds uttered in time of two. This occupies the rest of the Chapter (summed up on p. 117), toward the close of which (p. 114) he anticipates future discussion by asserting that English blank verse moves to triple time, and that its feet are accented on the second syllable.

These two assertions square with orthodox tradition, but the first departs from the opinion of some of our best critics, who have recognised "even measure" in our commonest type of verse, while the second departs from the almost invariable custom of musical scansionists. All Lanier's previous exposition and examples have prepared us to find the accented syllable made to begin the bar, his early illustrations of rhythm having been restricted to 'dactylic' cadences, *e.g.*—

Rhythmical | roundelays | wavering | downward.

Now, dealing with 'iambic' verse, he surprises us by writing—

To whom | should I | complain,

instead of, as might have been anticipated—

To | whom should | I com-|plain.

No reason is assigned for the new departure; we are simply told (pp. 114-15) that the facts are so. It strikingly illustrates, some will say Lanier's inability to free himself from old tradition, others will say his clear perception that English verse-units are most commonly signalized by a rise of accent. Which view is correct need not be at present debated, but readers should note and bear in mind Lanier's practice.

His identification of our commonest verse-movement with "triple time" is made with similar confidence throughout Chapters IV and V. There is little matter for surprise in this, since any one listening merely to the syllables of a line would in most cases come, as our orthodox prosody came, to this conclusion. Yet it is disappointing that Lanier, who has so clearly taught us that a line does not consist merely of its syllables, should not have at least recognised the possibility of another view. If "even measure" underlie our iambic syllables, half the difficulties of our prosody are at once resolved, and the radical difference between metres like

<blockquote>The stag at eve had drunk his fill</blockquote>

and

<blockquote>At the silence of twilight's contemplative hour</blockquote>

is satisfactorily explained. Lanier, however, did not take this view, and we must continue studying his.

Chapter IV divides secondary rhythm into "3-rhythm and 4-rhythm", 2-rhythm being identified with "pyrrhic" feet and pronounced intolerable (p. 130), while 5-rhythm and 7-rhythm are too difficult for use in verse (pp. 132-5). A clear distinction is made between rhythmical and logical accent, the latter term covering both syllable-stress and verbal emphasis (pp. 120-3); and as clearly it is explained that the actual number of sounds [*i.e.* syllables] in a bar need not correspond with its typical number of time-units (p. 136). The general drift of this short Chapter is summed up at its close (pp. 138-40), and the consideration of 3-rhythm is continued in Chapter V—much the longest in the book—which traces its prevalence from "our father Cædmon" down to Morris and Swinburne, and finds identity of movement where most people feel diversity. Criticism which asserts sameness of structure in the metres of "The Battle of Maldon" (p. 147) and the "Ormulum" (p. 159), the "Cuckoo song" (p. 161) and the "Canterbury Tales", the "Song of ever and never" (p. 171) and Hamlet's soliloquy, seems to me to miss its mark. Even were fundamental rhythm the same in all these, their differences would outweigh that sameness. The gulf that separates Langland's verse from that of Chaucer (p. 165) is not bridged by saying that both wrote in 3-rhythm, or even that one is "ancient heroic measure" and the other "modern" (p. 183). Of course Lanier knew this well, indeed he states it himself on the page last cited; but this does not suggest to him any doubt. It does not prevent his declaring (p. 184) that the overwhelming bulk of English poetry since the 14th Century is written in 3-rhythm. He goes on to deal with Shakespeare's verse by methods that would make metre of almost any words. That famous line in *Measure for Measure*—

Than the soft myrtle; but man, proud man ...

is pronounced undoubtedly correct, because "rests" occur freely in verse (pp. 189-97)—as if they were usually "rests" of this kind! What remains of this Chapter is taken up with analysis and glorification of Shakespeare's verse, in which I find little to quote except his remark that "in every line, five rhythmic accents are always present or accounted for" (p. 215), and his recognition of inverted accent (p. 217). At the end he asserts that variation from type must have been as common in Greek and Latin verse as in English, and quotes Elizabethan authorities as to the prevalence of dissyllabic feet, especially that "cunning" testimonial given by James VI (of Scotland) when he assumed that no other foot need be taken into account.

Three short Chapters conclude Part I, and need but brief mention. Chapter VI treats of 4-rhythm verse, distinguishing (p. 225) the true classic dactyl from the spurious triple-time 'dactyl' of English prosody, but strangely finding the former in "Hame came my | gudeman, and | ...." (*ibid.*), and misdividing Jean Ingelow's "It's we two, it's we two" (p. 228, *e.g.* 3rd line). He recognises the "ponderous pulse of march-time" in Classic hexameter (p. 227); our quadruple rhythm he considers to have usually a comic effect (p. 229). Judgements like this last are apt to be falsified by events, and the great development of 4-rhythm since Lanier's day (as in the hands of Mr. Rudyard Kipling) makes it open to question. Chapters VII and VIII deal very slightly with "tertiary rhythm", noting the time-beating functions of rhyme and alliteration, and desiderating omission of line-division in such "rhythmic but unmetric verse" as Shakespeare's (p. 235). Chapter IX refers (as had been done before, p. 186) to the " patting " of rhythmical periods by negroes, and notes the universality of periodic rhythm in the processes of Nature. The comparatively brief remainder of the book, as said before, is concerned with matters bearing only indirectly on rhythm.

It will be seen that it is for principles rather than conclusions that I hold Lanier's book valuable. Particular scansions often seem to me quite erroneous, as when he makes consist of trisyllabic feet the poem beginning "Agincourt, Agincourt" (p. 179); and his habit of letting accents come irregularly in successive feet[1] seems to me destructive of true analysis. And, though he fully recognised *rests*, he does not in my opinion make nearly enough use of them, actually (for example) showing "ocean" a spondee in his notation on p. 232. His musical preconceptions, I think, led him too much to make syllables embody rhythm—as in this word "ocean"; and I doubt if he sufficiently realised that suspensions of sound may occur when in no way dictated by meaning or sentential rhythm. Other and larger regions where I question his analysis have been already indicated. But criticism must yield to praise so far as fundamentals are concerned. It is Lanier's glory to have brought these finally to light. Temporal relations are shown by him essential to verse; whether or no we accept his reading of these matters comparatively little. The "new prosody" takes in his book a step which can never be retraced. I have said that to

[1] He represents the first line of *Piers Plowman* as divided thus—
In a sóm-|er séson | whan sóft was | the sónne (p. 163);
a line of Shakespeare's thus—
Would bé | as heávy | to mé | as ódi-|ous, bút (p. 215);

and so on. His *feet* are of course represented by musical notes; Classical names are not so much rejected as quietly put aside. The gain in accuracy and precision is immense, but must be considerably neutralized for musical readers by eccentric occurrence of accent.

many the book came as a revelation; its reading first showed myself how far prosodic science had advanced during the eighth decade of last Century. The name of Sidney Lanier is imperishably associated with that advance; he led its triumphant attack upon the fortresses of prejudice and superstition. If he made mistakes, they may well be forgotten in view of his great achievement. He showed, once for all, where the foundations of true prosody lie, for which reason 1880 must always be memorable in the annals of our subject.

During the final twenty years of last Century speculation about verse was constant. The elaborate metres used by our chief recent singers—by Tennyson, Browning, D. G. and Miss Rossetti, Mr. Swinburne, and others—had compelled enquiry and made tradition of little account. My notes will become briefer as we reach well known books by living writers; and I shall cease to distinguish what was or was not included in my previous Bibliography. Appendix B will show which books and papers have been added to that; here, my wish is to concentrate scrutiny on what helps insight into true principles. Sometimes I have failed to get sight of articles mentioned by correspondents, particularly those printed in the United States; more fortunate students may profit by my bare enumeration of these. Let me add that I shall always be delighted to hear of any important additions to my printed lists, but it is hopeless to attempt making these lists cover all ephemeral journalistic work or guide-books to English literature. Most of the latter only repeat old ideas about prosody, as do even the latest grammars; where there is anything novel, I shall be glad to have my attention drawn to it.

Outcast Essays and Verse Translations, by Shadworth Hodgson, appeared in 1881, and the volume has been several times reprinted. I quote the first edition, in which pp. 207-360 are occupied with a discussion of "English Verse". Distinguishing three kinds of "stress" which correspond in an ascending scale to language, metre, and poetry (pp. 215-16), the writer also (like

Ellis and Lanier) distinguishes four elements in language, *viz.* time, pitch, force, and colour (p. 223). Of these last, time is quantitative, the others qualitative (p. 224). Unlike his predecessors, however, he does not make time the basis of verse, but assigns that function to colour (p. 231). "English metres do not aim at dividing time into equal or proportionate lengths; they aim at a response of phrase to phrase, and sound to sound" (p. 236). Patmore's isochronous bars are rejected; did they exist, they and not stress would be the chief source of metre (*ibid.*). The whole conception of *feet* is therefore set aside, and replaced by counting "stresses". I cannot deem this analysis right, and think it errs through regarding "time" as synonymous with syllabic quantity. It is quite true that our verse does not depend on quantity of syllables, and I agree with most of the remarks to this effect on pp. 293–8, where it is shown that such quantity is not a factor essential to English metre, though still " a condition which must be reckoned with ". But it does not follow that our verse bears no relation to time. The writer's exclusive devotion to stress sometimes affects his scansion. I doubt his division of the " Bush aboon Traquhair" (p. 281) and " Come into the garden, Maud " (p. 283), also whether each pair of lines in Browning's "After" corresponds precisely to one line of " Saul " (p. 287), and whether Lamb's

I have had playmates, I have had companions,

repeats the structure of Latin hendecasyllabic metre (p. 336). It does not seem to me helpful to say that both

She bounds before the gale

and

This is a spray the bird clung to

are "lines of three stresses" (pp. 285, 286). I certainly challenge the statement that " stress laid on a short acute syllable makes it long, e.g. *cano*" (p. 258). Though the main prosodial teaching of the Essay must be held defective, there is much excellent criticism of verse otherwise, and of such matters as our English "impatience of form" (p. 229), and our tendency to "rush at the meaning" in speech (p. 232). Particularly good is the distinction made between *colour* and *tone* (p. 301), and the proof that mere pitch without emotional "tone" does not create emphasis (p. 302). Hexametrical and other experiments are discussed on pp. 329-42. The Essay is followed by some translations from Homer and Horace which, like most 'accentual' lines, often postulate imaginary stresses to the reader's bewilderment, *e.g.*—

A'nd as whén in heaven, around the moon in her brightness.

Perhaps the 'elegiacs' on p. 386 are the most satisfactory of these attempts.

The *Saturday Review* during February and March, 1883, contained some papers by Prof. Fleeming Jenkin of Edinburgh, reprinted in the *Memoir* of him by Robert Louis Stevenson (1887), Vol. I, pp. 149-70. Beginning as a review of Guest's book, the second edition of which had just been published, these papers go on to expound a new and original theory of English verse-structure, which is held to contain both feet and sections. The latter are word-groups, just as in prose, but shorter, five syllables being the outside limit (p. 159); feet are formed by accent and occupy "dissimilar and irregular periods" (p. 150). Thus we get "two coexisting rhythms, one due to the grouping of sections, and one to the grouping of feet"; while caesura is due to the fact that "the number of sections never coincides with that of the feet" (p. 159). These sections are not joined at random, but show continuity of beat throughout a line. "In beating time from beginning to end of each line one stroke will fall on each accented syllable," except where it falls on a pause; "but neither in verse nor prose does a beat ever fall on a weak unaccented syllable" (*ibid.*). "Time, number, and rhythm" are thus the three elements of verse (p. 161). "The beat upon the accents marks the time, the feeling of number is given by the constant number of feet and ... of sections. The group of syllables within the section, and the group which these syllables form within the line, give the primary sense of rhythm; and underlying this varying rhythm we have the secondary rhythm due to feet which by their approximately uniform arrangement assist in giving" a "sense of unity" (*ibid.*). In a normal line, he had already said, "the number of sections is constant" (*ibid.*). Applying this theory to our heroic metre, he finds that "the normal English heroic line is an iambic of five feet, broken into four sections by one major and two minor pauses" (p. 162). Representing the minor pause by one dot, the major by a colon, he thus divides a line from Pope (p. 160)—

Gó·, wóndrous creáture, : moúnt· where scíence guídes :

Here there are six beats; some lines have only three, others have seven or even eight. The proof of his theory, he thinks, is that unless lines are read by their sections they cease to impress us as being metrical; read Milton's blank verse otherwise than by its proper sections, and it becomes prose (p. 169).

It is a striking theory, and strikingly put. The crude view which finds five accented syllables in every heroic line Jenkin rejected; "those who classify by accents are fain to call many syllables accented whose sole claim to that honour is given by their length" (p. 156). He saw that two elements combine to form our verse. Had he reversed their functions, making rhythm invariable, syllabic structure changeful, I think he would have come very near the truth. Why he refused to let the rhythmical beat fall on a weak syllable I cannot understand. It surely does so in a line he quotes from Milton—

Of Oreb or of Sinai ...,

and in many other instances. His recognition of pause is sometimes too arbitrary, as when he insists on expanding into an 'Alexandrine' the line—

Crouch for employment : ʌ but pardon, gentles all—

declaring that, otherwise, "scansion seems ... impossible"

(p. 165). An enthusiastic actor, he evidently gave chief attention to verse as delivered on the stage. He rightly strove to "search for the main laws of rhythm by listening to the actual sound" of verse (p. 156); but the child crooning its sing-song must be listened to along with the "well-graced actor" if we would grasp the full meaning of these laws. Jenkin believed that "scansion was originally based upon a measurement of time" (p. 167), but not that it remains based on it to this day. That the number of beats in heroic metre may vary from three to eight is simply incredible. The test of every line in this metre is that it can be adjusted to five beats; what we cannot so adjust ceases, for us, to be heroic metre. Failure to give due importance to time leads Jenkin to identify quantity with accent, to write *famine* and so forth, to "count any syllable long which receives a secondary accent" (p. 165)—in fact, to invent imaginary criteria of "length". As against Dr. Johnson, he explicitly maintains that "the beauty of a line cannot be determined by noting how closely it approaches to the central type" (p. 162); but any line which transgresses his canon he condemns, be Pope or Milton the culprit. So that this gallant attempt to throw off traditional fetters was not wholly successful; the essayer remained a slave to accentuation, and in his devotion to it neglected the true basis of verse. To make grammatical pauses constitute rhythm is to confound elocution with structure, and this seems to me the fundamental error in these ingenious and captivating papers.

To the same year may be assigned a paper on "The physiology of versification" by Oliver Wendell Holmes, since it came out in his collection of Essays styled *Pages from an Old Volume of Life* (Boston, 1883); the real date is doubtless earlier. This short Essay of six pages treats of "the relations of verse to the respiratory organs", claiming that length of lines is determined by rate of breathing, and suggesting that accentuation may have to do with arterial pulsations. The normal proportion of respirations to pulse-beats being one to four, and twenty octosyllabic lines occupying a minute in average reading, accents and pulsations during that time will both be eighty. Personal equation plays its part; Spenser must have habitually breathed more slowly than Prior, Anacreon more quickly than Homer. Such speculation may seem fanciful, but it is precisely the application of phonetics and physiology to verse that has made prosody practical; whether Holmes's conclusions are scientifically valid I cannot pretend to determine.

The title of a small book by C[harles] Witcomb *On the Structure of English Verse* (1884) raises hopes which are hardly fulfilled. Structure is made to depend wholly on accent; accentual feet are postulated in the usual way. Good examples are given, but criticism otherwise is unnecessary. The last Section is on "imitations of Classical metres".

Not much about prosody will be found in the Philological Society's *Transactions* for 1885-7, but I would draw attention to one paper read on December 19, 1884, by Mr. James Lecky, of which only an abstract appears in the "Proceedings", pp. ii–vi. Beginning by desiring a phonetic notation for prosody, and contending that the stress-mark should be placed before rather than on a syllable, he proceeds to define rhythm and metre in unusual terms, making *metre* signify pulses of equal length, and *rhythm* denote stress-groups of proportional length (pp. iv–v). The latter is divided into *binary* and *ternary*, but "a stress-group may have a ternary effect when only containing two syllables, and a binary effect when containing three" (p. v). Five grades of stress are recognised, degrees of length and pause being also shown by symbols. *Basic* and *anacrusic* verse are illustrated by

   Hence in a | season of | calm | weather,
   Though | inland | far we | be.

"Archaistic influence" affects our verse, lyric poetry alone being now spontaneous and natural (*ibid.*); it is queried whether Classic prosody was not determined by accent, since "the grouping of syllables into metres [*cf.* above] is only possible by means of stress" (p. vi). Much is debateable in these statements, and there seems some confusion between quantity of syllables and length of groups in the opening remarks, but the condensed report may be to blame. I regret that this striking paper has not (to my knowledge) been published in any fuller form.[1]

R. L. Stevenson published in the *Contemporary Review* for April, 1885, a paper "On some technical elements of style in literature", now reprinted as the first of his *Essays in the Art of Writing* (1905), to which edition I refer. With his accustomed grace of diction, he dwells on points too often forgotten by professional prosodists. He founds, indeed, on Prof. Jenkin's theory, and pushes it beyond truth when he says that heroic lines cannot contain less than three or more than five word-groups, that five is the "forbidden number" (pp. 21–2), and that a line of heroic metre could not begin with feet like "Mother | Athens" (p. 24).[2] But his general view of verse is fresh and helpful, being shown in such sentences as the following. "Music and literature, the two temporal arts, contrive their pattern of sounds in time" (p. 9). "The rule of scansion in verse is to suggest no

---

[1] A short report of it appeared in the *Academy* for January 10, 1885 (pp. 31–2).

[2] A line of heroic metre may consist of only *one* word, as in Carey's burlesque—

Aldiborontephoscophornio,
Where left you Chrononhotonthologos?—

or of *two* words, as in Wycherley's line [this reference I owe to a newspaper quotation]—

Inhospitable hospitality.

I see no reason why it should not consist of *ten* words, each bearing an equal prose-accent. As to "Mother Athens", heroic lines beginning with similar cadences can be found, as already noted, in our best writers. "Five word-groups" are of course quite legitimate, *e.g.* Milton's—

And swims, or sinks, or wades, or creeps, or flies—

though it may be noted that Milton himself printed this line without a comma after "swims".

measure but the one in hand; in prose, to suggest no measure at all" (p. 26). "The eccentric scansion of the groups is an adornment; but as soon as the original beat has been forgotten, it ceases to be an adornment" (p. 25). "The laws of prosody... have one common purpose; to keep alive the opposition of two schemes simultaneously followed" (*ibid.*). [This last sentence recalls Prof. Sylvester's theory, *cf. ante*, 1870, footnote.] With these compare such phrases as "the double pattern of the texture and the verse" (p. 17), the illustration of a juggler keeping up several oranges at once, and the final reference to a versifier's "five preoccupations" (p. 32). I venture to think that a more adequate view of prosody than any yet met with is hinted at in these extracts. The last pages of this Essay deal with recurrent sounds in prose and verse, *e.g.* Milton's "FugitiVe and cloistered Virtue". Such matters are beyond our present purpose, but must assuredly be reckoned with in any complete analysis of verse.

The nineteenth volume of the *Encyclopaedia Britannica*, published in 1885, contained Mr. Watts-Dunton's famous article on "Poetry". Its merits have been universally recognised, but small part indeed of its space is given to metre. The question whether metrical structure can be dispensed with by poetry is examined in the first pages, without our being told what that structure is. We hear later of "caesuric effects", of "recognised and expected metrical bars" (p. 262, 2); also of "those lighter movements which we still call, for want of more convenient words, anapaestic and dactylic", the use of alliteration being commended as helpful to these latter (p. 258, 1). "Questions of versification," it is said in this connection, "touch... the very root of the subject" (*ibid.*). The "rhythmic life" as well as the "inspiration" of poetry are insisted on throughout, Dionysius and Hegel furnishing apposite texts. The common origin of verse and music, and their gradual growing apart, are handled on p. 260. It is noted that in a line of George Eliot's—

Of the unspoken; even your loved words...

"the main accent falls upon a positive hiatus" (p. 257, 2). Nothing like a reasoned analysis of verse-structure, however, is attempted in this article, nor is any theory of scansion put forward; its pages are occupied with discussion of higher subjects. The *Encyclopaedia*, it may be added, contains no article on Prosody.

A paper dated 1885 on "Quantity in English verse", by Thomas D. Goodell, appears in the *Transactions* of the American Philological Association (Vol. XVI, pp. 78–103). Prof. Goodell being an accomplished Grecian,[1] his paper naturally starts from and refers to Greek metre, but by no means in a narrow spirit. Indeed, he blames older prosodians for approaching our verse with Classical prepossessions instead of "simply listening" to its own cadences. Equally, however, he blames those who ignore all resemblance between ancient and modern metre; Greek verse had its accentual beat, ours has temporal structure. Lanier first [?] showed this, taking the true starting-point, though his method was faulty (p. 80). In English verse as in Greek, "rhythm is a definite arrangement of times," each time-group containing at least one syllable of increased "force or stress", so that our verse is really "based on word-accent" (pp. 81–2). An English versifier must so arrange words that their chief accents " shall coincide with and distinctly locate enough of the rhythmic ictuses to enable the voice unconsciously, or at least with slight effort, to locate the other rhythmic ictuses" (p. 83). Substituting "mind" for "voice", this last sentence seems to me unexceptionable. Following Lanier, he finds only $\frac{2}{4}$ and $\frac{3}{4}$ time in our verse, the latter immensely preponderating (p. 85); for notation he uses four (Greek) signs of syllable-length, with four of pause-length. This coincides with Steele, whose work seems unknown to him, for he believes himself first to suggest that the 'initial trochee' is a trisyllabic foot (p. 89). Initial

[1] I need here only mention his *Chapters on Greek Metric* (New York and London, 1901), a book full of suggestive hints about verse-rhythm generally.

feet, and anacrusis, often "insist on more than their due share of time" (pp. 90–1). I shall not debate particular scansions, but cannot think that the last line of Emerson's "Rhodora" varies in time from its predecessors. Rules of quantity are laid down on pp. 100–2, seven for triple-time verse, six for quadruple rhythm. In this latter "the rhythmizing instinct favours equality, . . . as in triple time inequality" (p. 102). Among questions omitted (see last paragraph of paper) are the relation of ictus to word-accent, that of verse to prose, and the employment of "rest or pause" within the line. These are serious omissions, but even so the paper is most instructive, whether or no one can accept all the writer's conclusions. Its terminology appeals to scholars rather than to the general public, but its clearly stated argument can be followed by even the casual reader.

Prosodic discussion was now being warmly taken up in America, from which in the same year 1885 came two first books by writers who continued its study, Prof. Gummere's *Handbook of Poetics* and Prof. Raymond's *Poetry as a Representative Art*. In the former, "Part III" is on metre, the other two Parts dealing with subject-matter and style; of the three Chapters into which Part III is divided one discusses general principles of metre, the next classifies English metres, the third deals shortly with one or two special types of versification. The first of these Chapters forms an admirable introduction to the study of our verse. Concisely and without undue dogmatism—indeed, pointing out dubieties as he goes—the writer analyses the actual structure of our metre, starting from the postulate that "measured intervals of time are the basis of all verse", and laying down that "Time is thus the chief element in Poetry, as it is in Music and Dancing" (p. 135). With excellent caution he states that "when the ear detects at regular intervals a recurrence of accented syllables, it perceives Rhythm" (p. 134), not making rhythm a creation of accent (*cf.* p. 141). Word-accent and verse-accent are distinguished (p. 139), without prejudice to the avowal "Accent is the chief factor of modern verse" (*ibid.*). Rightful deduction is perhaps exceeded when the indubitableness of Greek feet being signalized by stress is unhesitatingly assumed (p. 138); and, though pauses are well recognised (pp. 145-7), such recognition does not necessarily imply approval of the disputed line—

Than the soft myrtle; but man, proud man. . . .

When, in the next Chapter, metres are classified, the reckoning is by "stresses"; these, however, are not the actual prose-stresses of particular words, but those found in "the simple plan of the rhythm, uninfluenced by the actual words" (p. 200). From this "metrical scheme" a poet continually departs, urged both by need of variety, and by the intractability of language (p. 199); but it remains always in his mind. Two such departures are to be found in "hovering accent" and "wrenched accent" (*cf.* p. 142). The difference between iambic and trochaic metre is said to be "very slight" (p. 169). On the whole, without professing concurrence in every position taken up, I do not know where to find a safer and better textbook of prosody than this. Published by Ginn and Co. of Boston, I imagine that it can be easily procured from their London Agency.[1]

George Lansing Raymond is the author of a whole series of books on comparative aesthetics, whose dates of publication do not indicate their place in the series. The volume I have named is logically preceded by two more general books, one of which appeared only in 1900, and

[1] Interesting papers by Prof. Gummere will be found in *The American Journal of Philology* for 1886, No. 25, pp. 46-78 on "The translation of Beowulf", and *Modern Language Notes* (Baltimore) for 1887, No. 6, pp. 159-62 reviewing Prof. Mayor's book. Both refer much to verse-structure. Compare also in the latter for 1886, pp. 35-6, his "try" at defining the basis of English prosody. A later volume by the same author will be noticed in the Postscript to this Chapter. His Essay on "The Ballad and communal poetry", in the *Child Memorial Volume* (Boston, 1897), I have been unable to see, but there is a very full summary of it in "Gayley and Scott" (*infra*, 1899), pp. 266-70.

followed by four others, of which *Rhythm and Harmony in Poetry and Music* (1895) alone concerns us. His books are published in both London and New York. Covering so wide a field, they naturally paint with a broad brush; and, their author being a teacher of oratory, approach verse mainly on its elocutional side. *Poetry as a Representative Art* deals chiefly with the expressional function of verse, and dwells almost entirely upon its accentuation. Time is not wholly ignored—"a poet has only to arrange his words so that the accents will recur *at like intervals*" (p. 28; cf. 25, 45), but it is usually made merely a matter of pace, and force as well as duration is considered "essential to the effects of rhythm" (p. 35). It is fair to quote the author's own saying: "some may doubt that accent is the basis of rhythm and tune, but it is really about all that the majority of men know of either" (p. 27). Every speaker has "a rhythm and a tune of his own" (p. 20), and verse-forms are "traceable to the pause and accent of ordinary conversation" (p. 32). Differing profoundly from this view, as from the statement that accented syllables necessarily are longer than unaccented (p. 33), I find myself differing often from Prof. Raymond's analysis. He does not seem to realize the difference between ancient and modern verse (*e.g.* pp. 29–31, 46–7), or between the prosaic and the prosodial value of syllables (p. 31). Trisyllabic feet are supposed always to represent rapidity (Chap. IV), whereas triple time has its slow as well as its quick movement. The "endeavour to interpret the meanings of metres" (p. 64), dividing them by initial, medial, and terminal accents (p. 60), is surely pushed too far. (Musical scansion, it will be observed, is rejected; iambic is distinguished from trochaic metre: p. 67.) Condemnation is prompt when a poet's practice violates the critic's theory, as in the case of run-on lines (p. 40)[1]. When the writer goes on to discuss pitch and tune, figures, indirect

[1] In the first line so quoted, a misprint has survived successive editions. I have noticed some others, not surprising in a work of such proportions.

and alloyed representation, *etc.*, there is less to except against; quotations are profuse and delightful. But his view of fundamental structure does not change, nor do I find it materially altered in the later volume, though that is well brought up to date, and makes more use of *rests* (*e.g.* in a passage from "Marco Bozzaris" on pp. 41–2). It is strange that one who has studied Lanier should remain insensible to his demonstration of "time" in its true sense. The aesthetic effect of verse not seldom depends on its temporal fabric.

My record for 1886 contains only one separate book, which has been already mentioned, *Chapters on English Metre*, by Joseph B. Mayor [second edition, " revised and enlarged," 1901 ; my references are to the first edition]. Its breadth and catholicity, within self-assigned limits, deserve all praise. But the limits are strait. To Prof. Mayor, as to others whom we have reviewed, syllables constitute verse, and their accents its regulative principle. "Where the accent recurs in obedience to a definite law, there we have verse. And the kinds of verse are classified according to the intervals which separate the accents, whether an interval of one syllable or of two syllables" (p. 4). Scansion means dividing lines into syllabic feet, which he notates by three figures indicating degrees of stress, and also calls by the familiar Classic names, metaphorically used. *Time*, in his exposition, is only pace or duration ; as rhythm, it is explicitly rejected (p. 53).[1] That this view is insufficient I need hardly again argue ; its want of finality is shown in these "Chapters". Feet which Prof. Mayor thinks *iambs* other writers make *spondees* or even *trochees*; verse which most critics call iambic he pronounces anapaestic (p. 32, referring to a line in *Samson Agonistes*). He is himself occasionally in doubt whether a metre be anapaestic or iambic (pp. 109, 115, about Tennyson's "The Flower"). For, in truth, accentuation is an uncertain guide. Our word-accent, and still more our sentence-accent, are too

[1] *Cf.* (p. 55) "Nor do I recognize any given time for two syllables."

fugitive and capricious to be made the sole basis of verse. If metre depends wholly on them, it becomes a chaos, and prosody is impossible. Prof. Mayor acutely recognises syllabic diversity, but ignores the temporal uniformity which gives that its whole value. This is clearly shown in, for example, his dissection of Tennyson's "Cauteretz" (pp. 104–5), and amusingly by his confession of the difficulty he long felt in scanning Byron's poem beginning "Bright be the place of thy soul!" (p. 112). Because in this latter piece sometimes one, sometimes two, and sometimes no syllables precede the first beat, doubt was felt about the metre. When *time* is given its due place, such doubts are not felt. The lines are seen to be all in one and the same metre, whether particular places be filled by sound or by silence. Whether the poet writes "E'er burst" or "Ever burst" at the beginning of the third line is a matter purely of euphony; metrical structure remains absolutely the same. The "routine scansion" which Prof. Mayor rightly defends (p. 6) is primarily based on time.

Otherwise prosody in this volume is sane and liberal. Trisyllabic feet are admitted to every station, even the last, in heroic verse. Monosyllabic feet are recognised, though a sentence on p. 53 referring to them disappears from the second edition. Only "amphibrachs" are barred (pp. 45, 94–6),[1] being avoided by such desperate dividing as "the ra-|pid of life | " (p. 109) and "With such | *dexte-*|*rity* | to inces-|tuous sheets" (p. 179), or by supposing an "extra-metrical syllable", *e.g.* (p. 153)—

But how | of Caw-|*dor?* | The thane | of Caw-|dor lives.

Having no test of metre except feet, the writer would fain limit the number of exceptional feet in a line (p. 73), but honestly quotes lines which disprove his canon (*ibid.*, footnote); change of feet is to him change of metre.

---

[1] I suspect a misprint in one exceptional case (p. 78)—
Epic|ure|an and | *the Stoic* | severe.
Prof. Mayor's usual scansion would be "the Sto-|ic severe".

This may avail in ordinary verse, but in less usual metre soon breaks down. Thus, in the hymn "There is a happy land" (p. 127), the sixth line of each stanza is pronounced irregular. A time-scansionist sees that they are in the same metre with the lines which precede and follow. Supply obvious 'rests', and the three lines in the first stanza run thus—

> Oh ! ∧ | how they | sweetly | sing ∧ ,
> Worthy | is our | Saviour | King ∧ |
> Loud ∧ | let his | praises | ring ∧ !

There is no irregularity in these lines, any more than in Browning's couplet—

> Morning, evening, noon and night,
> "*Praise* God !" sang Theocrite.

Attention to time removes all difficulty. On the other hand, the words of "O come, all ye faithful" (p. 133) have no claim to rank as English verse. Apart from the tune, its second stanza produces no metrical effect whatever, but is simply prose.

A prominent feature of this book is its discussion of other prosodists, and admission of their replies. The short introductory Chapter is followed by criticism of Guest, Abbott, Symonds, Ellis and others; then we have Prof. Mayor's own views upon "metrical metamorphosis", naming and classification of metres (the illustrations to this Chapter are from hymns), and the blank verse of Surrey and Marlowe, Shakespeare (two Chapters), Tennyson and Browning. No pretence is made to completeness (Preface, p. vii). The book is based on lectures, some read before and criticised by the Philological Society; Ellis's remarks on Shakespeare's blank verse will be found on pp. 165–71. The second edition adds three new Chapters, on the views of Messrs. Skeat and Bridges, Shelley's metre, and the English hexameter; the last adds little to previous discussions. "Revision" is of the slightest, but a list of feet has been added. No fairer-minded or pleasanter guide than Prof. Mayor could be desired, and his book abounds in copious quotation; the student is given every opportunity of forming an opinion for himself. But the doctrine of verse set forth in its pages appears to me radically defective.[1]

Though no other separate book appears on my list for 1886, I should like to mention an article entitled "Studies of rhythm", by G. Stanley Hall and Joseph Jastrow, which appeared in *Mind* during this year (Vol. XI, pp. 55-62). This short paper is the first of a series of experimental enquiries into rhythm by American scholars, to which I shall refer again later [*cf.* Bolton, 1894, and references there], and which show how much more seriously (as already said) prosody is taken by our Transatlantic cousins than by us. At present it may suffice to say that this paper claims to find a good deal of subjective "illusion" in what we have been wont to regard as objective rhythmical facts.[2]

Under date 1887 I formerly placed references to various books by Prof. Saintsbury. Others would now have to be added, with particular mention of his "Introduction" to a new *Rhymers' Lexicon* (1905). But all are superseded by his elaborate *History of Prosody* (Vol. I, 1906), noticed in the Postscript to this Chapter. The earlier passages merely hinted at a view of "equivalence" to be some day developed and expounded. They cannot, therefore, have influenced contemporary theorizing, except by showing that a critic and scholar of high rank was dissatisfied with current methods and results; so we need not at present stay to examine them.

The first appearance of *Milton's Prosody*, by Mr. Robert Bridges, was as an appendix to the Clarendon Press edition of Milton (1887). Through successive editions as a separate issue, it retains marks of its birth, and of subsequent additions, even the latest (1901),—which I

---

[1] Prof. Mayor's *Handbook of Modern English Metre* (1903) will be mentioned in the Postscript to this Chapter.

[2] A paper in the same volume (pp. 393-404), "On the time-sense," by Lewis T. Stevens, contains nothing that bears directly on verse-rhythm.

shall quote,—speaking of "to fill up the spare pages of this sheet" (p. 82). Originally a "tabulation of Milton's practice", it has grown by multiplied Appendices, each separate and independent, into a discussion of verse-structure generally. The original tabulation was a masterly piece of work. If "laws" are sometimes made too absolute, the guiding principles of Milton's practice are analysed with loving care, and amply illustrated.[1] But it is with the Appendices that we are mainly concerned, particularly with those on "metrical equivalence" and "rules of the common lighter stress-rhythms". In these, as elsewhere, Mr. Bridges champions a view in which time is ignored. It is, I think, only twice referred to, and that hypothetically (*cf.* pp. 33, 103); and it certainly plays no part in his theoretical exposition, which makes verse depend either on feet or "stresses". The fact that stresses do not occur when expected only moves him to condemn the practice of our best poets (p. 73 *seq.*, *cf.* p. 96, *etc.*), and to proclaim the desirability of a reformed verse, in which stresses are to be constant. How such verse is to differ from prose I do not find stated; it can differ only by virtue of temporal relation between the stresses, and then comes the question whether the stresses are really indispensable. Besides, who is to guarantee perception of the stresses? All previous attempts in this direction have failed, because the stresses were not self-evidencing. Even the choruses in *Samson Agonistes*, to my mind, do not make their structure clear. Divorced from time, stress in English has never proved a sufficient basis of metre; lines do not "read themselves". And, divorced from time, no mere succession of prose accents will create an impression of verse. Ingenious as the rules given in "Appendix J" are, and sound as is the incidental criticism of other systems, these rules by themselves only explain how to make verse smooth; they do not touch its guiding principle.

[1] Two points of detail are "corrected" by Mr. Bridges in the *Athenaeum* of January 30, 1894 [*cf.* Postscript to this Chapter].

The high place held by Mr. Bridges both as critic and poet makes his teaching carry weight. Yet experience seems to me against him. As with his later quantitative essays (before referred to), so here, the experiment has been well tried already. Leigh Hunt worked on similar lines in dramatic verse. Frere, in his renderings of Aristophanes, wrote blank verse of similar looseness. Nay, did not the successors of Shakespeare, Ford and Massinger and Webster, trust too much to stresses in their verse, and did not Milton restore temporal structure? Are we to run the same cycle? Not Mr. Bridges himself, but some of his followers, write verse which is indistinguishable from prose; some of them deny that the two differ. Even in the master's beautiful poem "London Snow" I for one miss temporal fabric. Critics are slow to appreciate new departures; my judgement may be biassed. But poets, also, sometimes depart in wrong directions. I cannot believe that, even in the hands of a singer like Mr. Bridges, verse which lacks the foundation common to all verse can be more than tuneful prose.

Apart from theory, *Milton's Prosody* is a book to spend hours over. Consummate metrical skill is in evidence throughout; criticism often seems divination. Students should remember that with Mr. Bridges "elision" does not mean cutting out but some form of slurring; it is used as "a term of no definite meaning" (p. 52). "Stress" is also a general term (p. 78). They must be prepared to learn that Milton "came to scan his verses one way, and read them another" (p. 18); also that in *Paradise Lost* he attempted "to keep blank verse decasyllabic by means of fictions" (p. 19). With the fuller statements given in this book they may like to compare its author's Note at the end of his *Feast of Bacchus* and of *Nero, Second Part*, and to study the "six-stress" lines of the former along with the "five-stress" lines of the latter. Among the *Shorter Poems* some are of great interest metrically, and have much influenced younger writers. The verse as well as the prose of Mr. Bridges must be taken into account in dealing with English prosody, and critical differences need not blind any one to the great merits of both.

The *Andover Review* (Boston, U. S. A.) for March, 1887, contained a paper on "The laws of English tone-color", by Albert H. Tolman. Prof. Tolman has, I believe, written much on prosody in the *Atlantic Monthly* and elsewhere, but this is the only magazine article of his I have seen. Into short compass it packs much illustration of the phenomena in question, observation of which he seems to consider modern, and due to German guidance. The scientific explanation of such facts we owe to Germany, but the facts themselves—alliteration, "vowel-echoing," *etc.*—were noted by Eighteenth Century metrists. Rhythm is not a subject of study in this paper.

Next year, however, in a memorial volume already referred to, *The 46th Birthday of Sidney Lanier* (Baltimore, 1888), this writer ably criticises Lanier's conception of verse. A pupil of Lanier's, he duly honours his master's work, pointing out that he "sought to explain English verse as a present fact" (p. 39), and declaring that "so long as man's heart-beats are separated by equal intervals, he will never distribute accents without reference to time" (p. 40). But he also points out that Lanier, essentially a lyrist, laid too much stress on the singing elements of verse. "He treats the rhythmical accent of verse almost as if it were a thing independent of everyday accent." "In rendering music, we add accent to musical sounds; in reading poetry, we find it in spoken sounds." "In free blank-verse . . . not so much of the expression is committed to the rhythm; the words have a substantive, an independent meaning, which the separate tones of a piece of music do not have" (p. 41). Hence come "frequent omissions of the rhythmical accent even in bars that are filled with sound", and "a bewildering variety of equivalent forms of the bar"; but "the fundamental rhythm . . . is clearly heard through all interruptions". Such original and telling criticism makes one wish to know more of Prof. Tolman's work. On the fundamental fact of 'isochrony' he is evidently sound.

In 1888 appeared a remarkable book entitled *Accent and Rhythm explained by the Law of Monopressures* (Blackwood, Edinburgh; published anonymously, but understood to be by a Scottish clergyman; "Part I" only). The teaching of this book has been adopted by Prof. Skeat, first in the "Introduction" to Vol. VI of his *Chaucer*, then in a paper on "The scansion of English poetry", read before the Philological Society in January, 1898. As prosody owes in other ways much to our veteran philologist, and his work should precede that of younger men, I take the above together, there being no substantial difference in their views. Both writers reduce the "monopressures" or accentual units of our speech to four types and no more, exemplified in the first book by the words *mind, remind, minded, reminding*, which may be represented by the simple signs I, ⌐, L, ⌐ (Prof. Skeat prefers figures *one* to *four*[1]). They claim that all verse is resolvable into these forms, which give a true scansion as opposed to the conventional false one. A familiar line would then be thus divided [it will suffice to link the words]—

The-curfew tolls the-knell-of parting day,

sense and "monopressure" coinciding. Two objections to this analysis surely present themselves. Does not a word like *unity* present a different type? Is the pressure on its final syllable more obvious than that on the final syllable of a word like *abundant* or *remorseful*?[2] May not a word of even four syllables contain but one "monopressure"? Apart from this, does resolution into these groups throw light on verse-structure? They are not

---

[1] He also uses *T*, *A*, *C*, and *E*, being initial letters of the illustrative words *tone, ascent, cadence, extension*, while a Roman *t* denotes secondary stress.

[2] The anonymous author's way of dealing with such words will be found on p. 46 of his book. I am not sure whether Prof. Skeat endorses it.

distinctively units of verse. They are merely the raw material which verse and prose alike use. *How* the maker of verse constructs from these a fabric essentially different from that of prose speech is the very question which prosody asks, and it is not answered by saying that prose and verse use the same raw material. I cannot, therefore, see that this method is helpful, though phonetic details are ably handled in the anonymous author's book, and though Prof. Skeat's later paper deservedly ridicules our ordinary scansion. If their view be pushed so far as to deny the possibility of three consecutive unaccented syllables, our recent verse is conclusive against it. Whenever a fourth syllable is squeezed into triple-time measure, three out of the four syllables must be without metrical accent; and such instances are far from uncommon.

In 1888 was also published Prof. Sweet's *History of English Sounds*, rewritten and greatly altered from its first form of 1874. In this new edition paragraphs are numbered throughout, at an average rate of nearly four to a page, making reference easy; and there is a fuller table of contents. Noticeable among additions are the recurring paragraphs on "metre and stress". While Prof. Sweet does not, like his elder colleague just dealt with, advance any complete theory of verse-structure, he gives in these paragraphs hints from which a true phonetic basis of verse might, I think, be well constructed. Take such sentences as the following. " Quantity and stress are as essential elements of metre as time and barring are of music." ... " In practice it is impossible fully to harmonize the natural quantity and stress of a language with the artificial quantity and stress of metre ; one or other must go to the wall." ... " The stress-groups of ordinary speech amount to nothing more than prose ; " to make them into feet, we " lengthen or shorten syllables without scruple " (356). Yet " unconscious respect for natural quantities influences our best poets " (357). " Syllables that are quite stressless in ordinary speech can in verse take the full stress that is required by the metre" [this is said of "Middle English four-stress metre"] (609). Compare the references to Chaucer and the *Ormulum* (614 *seq.*), to "Modern English" (755-64), and to "Living English" (935-44). Prof. Sweet recognises three degrees of both quantity and force (16, 19), and seems to identify accent entirely with the latter. He enters into niceties about long and short consonants as well as vowels which have perhaps little value for us, metre depending on broad and simple principles. No detail, indeed, is too small to be noticed by metrists, and even these probably should not escape attention. It is, however, to the general view of metre typified in the above extracts that I would particularly direct remark, and that seems to me as sound as the rest of the book is above any criticism of mine.

Amusing is the contrast between these books and one on *The Poetry of the Future*, by James Wood Davidson (New York, 1888). Its writer wishes to abolish "the trammels of metre and stanza" (p. 109), and with these are to depart also rhyme, alliteration, refrain, and most other embellishments of verse (pp. 96-7). We have really, he thinks, only "four feet, each accented on the last syllable" (p. 40); for it is a "universal law" that "the pause produced by the stress of accent marks and makes the end of the foot" (pp. 58-9). Trochaic and dactylic metre he scans as commencing with a monosyllabic foot, and recognises only two possible forms of rhythm. Whatever clashes with this he condemns, and would fain amend, even in Milton's verse. "Had the poet not been in too great a hurry," he could have written the line as Mr. Davidson thinks better (p. 87); when he does not, in another case, we are told—"It is unrhythmical. It is prose" (p. 158). Such criticism needs no comment; yet much in this book shows acute observation. But to its author verse is merely a "succession of syllables" (p. 29), and "accent is the foundation-idea of the whole system of English prosody" (p. 176). He has, in fact, still to learn what really constitutes the "metre" which he seeks to abolish.

For the next year or two my notes are confined to American writers. A *Theory of the Origin and Development of the Heroic Hexameter*, by Fitzgerald Tisdall (New York, 1889), I have not seen; nor yet a book on *The Versification of Pope in its relation to the Seventeenth Century*, by William Edward Mead (Leipzig, 1889). *Modern Language Notes* (Baltimore) for 1890 contained a paper on "Certain considerations touching the structure of English Verse", by William Hand Browne, a teacher in Johns Hopkins University (Vol. IV, pp. 97–101, double columns numbered 193–202; I use the latter for reference). Vigorous and confident, this paper lays down rules of much precision. Though Lanier is praised at the outset as the first person who studied English verse as it is, not what other people said about it, his method is not followed in detail. *Feet* are said not to exist in our verse; the amphibrach in particular is pronounced wholly impossible (col. 193). English verse is "decorated prose", decoration involving symmetry and proportion (194). Its decorative patterns are framed by contrast of strong with weak syllables, in the proportions of one to one, one to two, or one to three, the last being a recent invention (195–6). Variations are got by dropping either one or two accents, reversing either one or two, or by combinations of these (197). "Any variation is allowable that does not obscure or equivocate the genus" (198), as Milton does with his "bottomless pit". [The present love of multiplying trisyllabic feet in heroic verse would receive short shrift from Prof. Browne.] 'Time' has not yet been mentioned, but comes in when twenty lines from "To be or not to be" are examined. *To die* " is the exact analogue of the short appoggiatura in music, the time of which is taken [subtracted] from the following note" (*ibid.*). In *natural shocks*, " three syllables are uttered in the time of two; ... this is the triplet, the exact analogue of the triplet of music" (199). Pause may replace a whole foot (*ibid.*, *cf.* 201). So he comes to deal with *caesurae* (199–201), making an incidental remark on French caesura which is no longer correct; and here at length he finds his unit of structure. The "stave" formed by caesura is "the unit of verse-formation" (201). This conclusion recalls that of Fleeming Jenkin [*ante*, 1883]. I cannot agree with it, or with division by syllables instead of beats; nor do I think rhythm adequately treated. But the paper throughout is full of point and suggestiveness.

Briefer mention may serve for some other writings. A paper in the same volume of *Modern Language Notes* on "The inventor of the English hexameter", by F[elix] E. Schelling,[1] contains nothing *ad rem* for us; nor is there much to our purpose in a paper on "Beginnings of the Classical Heroic Couplet in England", by Henry Wood, printed in the *American Journal of Philology* for 1890 (Vol. XI), though it discusses Waller's reputed improvement of that metre, and his debt to French poets. *English Versification for the use of Students*, by Rev. James C. Parsons (Boston, New York, and Chicago, "copyright 1891"; second edition, 1894), needs mention only as an unpretentious summary of accustomed rules. *A Primer of English Verse, chiefly in its aesthetic and organic character*, by Hiram Corson, LL.D. (Boston, 1892), adopts Latham's notation by $a\,x$ and $x\,a$, and deals mainly with assonances and other "colors" of verse, not without interesting criticism of these. And Edmund Clarence Stedman's book on *The Nature and Elements of Poetry* (Boston and New York, also London, 1892; a reprint, with additions, of lectures which had appeared in the *Century* magazine during that year) deals with higher matters than the technique of verse. In the second Lecture, indeed, it is pointed out that rhythm means vibration, and vibrations both cause and express emotion, wherefore in passionate utterance speech grows rhythmic (pp. 51–2). But the lecturer soon after declines to "enter the workshop of the poet", though, speaking to a Baltimore audience, he praises the teacher who there demonstrated laws of rhythm (pp. 61–2). For the most

[1] Other papers by this writer (not seen by me) are mentioned in Appendix B.

part, however, like Mr. Watts-Dunton—whose article he calls "the best modern essay upon the subject" (p. 25)—he deals with the matter and not the form of poetry.

A book called *Orthometry*, by R. F. Brewer [1] (London, 1893), is a substantial compilation on old lines, adding little or nothing novel. Regularity of accentuation is pronounced the differentia of verse (p. 1), but quantity is recognised (p. 22), and a pause is allowed "rarely" to take the place of a syllable (p. 143). Trisyllabic feet in which vowels come together are said to be made dissyllables by a "nice ear" (p. 121); whence the following line is practically taken to consist of nine syllables thus divided (p. 145)—

I | whōse văst | pĭtў ăl-|mŏst mākes | mĕ dĭe.

The book contains a rhyming dictionary, and—what deserves special mention here—the fullest bibliography yet published in any English treatise on metre (pp. 280–96). Some entries in it need explanation. "Okell" is probably a misprint for Odell. "Haslewood" must be the editor of Puttenham's and other *Ancient Critical Essays*, who did not himself write on metre. "Trussler" and "Longmuir" merely edited rhyming dictionaries. If "Bain" means Prof. Bain of Aberdeen, I know nothing of consequence on metre by him; in one book he has a chapter on "The definition of poetry", but declines to go into questions about metre. Why should "Canon Daniel's Grammar" [1881] be mentioned more than a score of others which have the usual Section on Prosody? Any attempt at a list of prosodists, however, is welcome in the almost total dearth of such; this list is later and fuller than that of Crowe [*ante*, 1827], and there is hardly another between.

It would be hopeless to keep count of articles and reviews in the daily or weekly press, but I may mention

---

[1] This is a reissue, greatly enlarged, of *A Manual of English Prosody*, by Robert Frederick Brewer, B.A. (12mo, Longmans, 1869), in which its view of verse was already defined.

that during some ten years from 1893 onward the *Literary World* (London), then a weekly journal, contained a succession of papers dealing with the rhythmical structure of verse, explaining double and treble beats and freedom of "syllabism" within these beats, and laying much stress on "relative accentuation" as a key to syllabic cadence. References to these will be found in that Journal's issues for June 5 and 26, 1903. Their writer seems to have been unaware that any prosodist except Ruskin had anticipated any part of his view—which shows that a survey like the present one may have its uses. A book or pamphlet based on these papers would be a desirable addition to prosodic literature, for there is fresh work in them, though I cannot accept all their conclusions in matters of detail. The writer, however, would do well to acquaint himself with what has been accomplished by predecessors along the same lines.

A singularly interesting paper on "Rhythm", by Thaddeus L. Bolton, appeared in *The American Journal of Psychology* for January, 1894 (pp. 145–238).[1] Some thirty pages at first sketch the physiological basis and historical development of rhythm. Statements not in themselves novel combine here to fresh result. With Lanier's view of primary and secondary rhythm (p. 157) is linked a Guestian theory of syllabic groups (p. 158), while feet are also recognised, and assumed to be separated by pauses (p. 173). It is stated that "the two-rhythm was apparently the prevailing rhythm in the history of our language" (p. 160); but by 'two-rhythm' is apparently meant, here, merely a grouping into couples. "Poetry has never lost the time-element entirely" (p. 169); "the simplest unit of English poetry is the time between two accents, . . . and this must be constant" (p. 172). The emotional effect of rhythmic utterance, its origin in and production of a "trance" condition, are ably explained (pp. 163, 165, 171). The

[1] *Cf.* also pp. 310 and 488 for some additional memoranda.

attempts by Lanier, Corson, and Poe to "construct philosophies of English verse" are shortly noticed (pp. 174-6), disagreement being intimated with Corson's view that "feeling unifies, intellect analyses". The bulk of this paper, however, is taken up neither with theory nor criticism, but with a record of experiments; and this gives it great value. Observation was applied to determine "what the mind did with a series of simple auditory impressions in which there was absolutely no change of intensity, pitch, quality, or time-interval", and then how it treated "regular variations with respect to the intensity or time-interval of the sounds in this series" (p. 178).[1] The results are exceedingly interesting. Absolutely uniform sounds were mentally arranged in groups. The net result of a long series of experiments with varied intensity (pp. 186-228) was to show that increased force suggested a fictitious idea of prolongation; while conversely, as appears from the shorter record of experiments with varied time-interval (pp. 228-34), prolongation suggested fictitious increase of force. An accented sound tended to come first in a group, a longer sound last; "if the recurrent difference is one of duration, the longest impression comes last" (p. 232). Curiously enough, "a change from a 3-group to a 4-group gave rise to a feeling of slower pace" (p. 236); while a succession of changes from 2-groups to 3-groups, or *vice versa*, produced "a very disagreeable feeling" (p. 237). These facts have obvious bearings on metre. The writer holds they prove that "the most common foot in modern poetry is accented on the last syllable" (p. 234). Might it not be safer to say that when we attend mainly to stresses we incline to make these begin feet, but to terminate them when we attend mainly to time; that both methods are legitimate, but the latter preferable (unless otherwise shown invalid) because in our verse temporal relations are more impor-

[1] Details cannot be given here. The sounds were *clicks*, produced by a machine, and as far as possible the auditors were kept in ignorance as to what results were observed or expected.

tant than stress-values, though both are essential? Some further applications of the "general principle" to verse are suggested on pp. 237–8, tending perhaps to inculcate a too rigid theory of verse-structure, rather akin to Poe's. But the whole discussion is fruitful in a great many ways, and the paper must be considered a 'document' by all interested in verse-rhythm.[1]

The *Contemporary Review* for November, 1894, contained an article by William Larminie on "The development of English metres" (Vol. 66, pp. 717–36). This seems written with two purposes—to inculcate regard for quantity, and to advocate a form of *vers libre*. The first part, with its "fourfold" division of quantity (p. 720), pushes criticism too far. It is quite true that Browning was apt to let stress override quantity (*ibid.*, *cf*. p. 736, *note*); but when it comes to rewriting cadences of Poe, Swinburne, and Tennyson (pp. 722–5), one should remember that smoothness is not the sole virtue for a poet. Quantity is perhaps made too much a fetish; but recognition of it is so rare in our prosodies that one welcomes even an exaggerated respect for it. Why should Mangan's lines be praised above others, when they contain quantities like those marked in the following?—

> Shall I hear the thrŭsh sing from his lair . . .
> No more sĕe the bĕe bearing honey.

As for the proposal to substitute Biblical or Ossianic prose for verse, on the ground that "the burden of technique . . . has become too heavy to be borne" (p. 727), poets must be left to consider it. Certainly, if it is adopted, alliteration and assonance will have to play a larger part even than they now do in our verse. National partiality, one suspects (as *in re* Mangan), has something to do with the praise of assonance (pp. 731–5) and the question (p. 736) "Can the august poetry of

---

[1] Those so interested should refer to Hall and Jastrow [*ante*, 1886], to Hurst and McKay [1899], and to a group of writers named together in the Postscript to this Chapter.

England condescend to take a hint from the Cinderella of the West?" It should not be above doing so, and it would have to learn no unfamiliar lesson; meantime, need we despair of old forms? Some of Mr. Larminie's statements seem rather questionable, *e.g.* " Italian has no quantity, but it has stress ; French has neither" (p. 726). Nor will all agree with him about "the unnecessary burden of rhyme" (*ibid.*). But as a whole the paper is fresh and interesting, provoking thought even when it does not convince.

In *English Poetry from Blake to Browning*, by William Macneile Dixon, Trin. Coll. Dublin (1894), the first Chapter discourses on " Poetry and its relation to life", making rhythm the essential quality of verse, and stating—almost in the very words of Mr. Stedman [*ante*, 1892]—that "rhythm represents emotion, and it gives rise to emotion" (p. 9). I do not, however, find any attempt made to determine the precise nature of this rhythm.

A paper in *Mind* for 1895 (New Series, Vol. IV, pp. 28–35) on " The difference of time and rhythm in music", by Dr. R[ichard] Wallaschek, might seem beyond our province, but will be found to contain apposite matter. It insists that our sense of 'time' is wholly subjective, speaks of "the merely mental character of time-division in music", even says that "in spite of an accentuation which is likely to suggest triple time, the observer may still follow duple time in his thought" (p. 29). There is, according to this writer, only one musical time, *viz.* "evenness" ($\frac{5}{8}$ and $\frac{7}{8}$ time being designedly irregular: p. 30). "There is no 'time' in the heart-beats themselves," though from Aristotle onward men have said that there is (p. 32); birds' songs have *tempo* but not *Takt*, the latter denoting our perception of the motion (p. 34). It will be seen how this affects the question of relation between spoken words and rhythmical periods[1].

[1] Readers who wish to pursue this subject farther are referred by Dr. Wallaschek to his book on *Primitive Music* (Longmans, 1893), which contains "an inquiry into the origin and development of

In 1895 was published the first volume of Dr. Courthope's great *History of English Poetry*. Chroniclers of our literary annals seem rarely to find time for prosodic study; as with Warton's and other histories, scant room is given to metre. The denial of any link of connection between Anglo-Saxon verse and Chaucer (p. 4) will stagger many. The latter half of Chap. II (pp. 70-8) sketches the change from quantitative to accentual verse, and suggests that our heroic metre derives from iambic trimeter as modified by French poets. Vol. II (1897) mentions briefly Surrey's reforms in verse (p. 92), and in Chap. X deals cursorily with the Elizabethan quantitative attempt, Fraunce being singled out for praise. It is not, I think, till Vol. III (published in 1903), in the first half of Chap. XIV, treating of Milton's verse, that questions of scansion are referred to; and then—besides a reference to Mr. Bridges—we merely have a contrast drawn between the views of Guest and Prof. Mayor, preference being given to the latter. It seems clear that, with so many large matters to consider, the historian has not found time to study the philosophy of verse, or to read our principal prosodists.[1]

During 1896 I find for mention only an anonymous tract of twenty-four pages, reprinted from the *Manchester Quarterly Review*, and understood to be by Mr. H. D. Bateson.[2] It consists of two parts, the first an "Introduction to the study of English rhythms", the second a discussion of the metre of *Christabel*. Both are very slight, and raise more questions than they

the music, songs, instruments, dances, and pantomimes of savage tribes... with musical examples".

[1] *Life in Poetry: Law in Taste* (Macmillan, 1901), by the same author, refers in the second Lecture of Part II to "Poetical expression", discussing the necessity of metrical form. An earlier volume, *The Liberal Movement of English Literature* (1885), hardly touches prosody.

[2] This has since been separately published (1904), without alteration except by a preface prefixed and a short list of prosodians added.

solve; the general tendency is to rely on accent, coupled with caesural pause (pp. 7-8). "Isochronous divisions of accents" are said to be "familiar to the English ear" (p. 12). A distinction between common and triple rhythm is suggested (p. 2), and elasticity of structure highly praised, while yet the writer tries to state "limits within which the variation of the metre is confined" (p. 21).

The closing years of the Century saw pamphlets, magazine articles, and newspaper correspondence about metre in considerable profusion, among them some efforts of my own. As a whole, these served chiefly to show how uncertain were most people's ideas about English prosody. Not staying to enumerate these, I pass to more outstanding contributions. It will be borne in mind that, also, some first or second editions of books already mentioned came out during these years. Prosody was to a certain extent 'in the air' at this time, and in the air it rather tended to remain, seldom touching solid earth. Yet, as will be seen, some publications had importance.

New Essays towards a Critical Method, by John Mackinnon Robertson (London and New York, 1897), contains an Appendix on "accent, quantity, and feet" which shows thought and wide reading. It evidently began as a defence and eulogium of Poe's "Rationale", and too much adopts his view. For want of any clear distinction between stress and quantity, the first three Sections—dealing with Classic verse, the Foster-Gally controversy, and accent generally—leave us pretty much where they found us. And when the writer passes to modern verse, he seems at first to adopt Poe's fatal premiss " there is no time-unit " (p. 361), and legitimately to conclude that "prosodical method . . . is essentially incapable of reduction to scientific bases" (p. 355). But footnotes added later show that reading Lanier's book has modified this view. He indeed defends Poe against Lanier, and successfully criticises the latter on particular points (pp. 355, 364, *notes* beginning on); but the conception of rhythm as a series of sounds and silences, which he mistakenly believes Lanier the first to state clearly (p. 362, *note*), has evidently impressed him. I feel sure that a critic so able as Mr. Robertson will come increasingly to lay weight on this side of the balance. Unless we realize that verse is a stringing of words to time, and that this may be accomplished by divers methods, varying with varying speech-habits, prosody cannot be sound. Mr. Robertson had originally gone far in this direction; he was aware of the "fluctuant relativity" of metre (p. 361), he knew that "time-space between syllables" was a factor of verse (p. 362); it needs but to give this due importance. There is much that is interesting in his fourth Section, dealing with our own verse, and still more in the fifth and last, which discusses French verse with ripe knowledge, disposing of some ancient crudities. I cannot, however, believe that Racine's line—

> Je ne le croirai point ? Vain espoir qui me flatte !

"comes pretty near *Arma virumque cano* in total rhythm" (p. 374, *note*). Neither French nor Latin metre falls within the purview of my present work, but a remark like this seems to manifest settled confusion between two different things; which confusion mars the effect of much that is otherwise admirable. One may hope in future editions to find it replaced by that clearer view to which the author's judgement already inclines.

A small book of much learning is that on *The Foreign Sources of English Versification, with special reference to the so-called iambic lines of eight or ten syllables*, by Charlton M[inor] Lewis (Halle, 1898). Building on German authorities, the author in five of his six Chapters traces the progress of metre from primitive forms, through Classical verse, to our own day. Only in the sixth and last does he reach English verse; indeed, only in the last Section of it (p. 99 *seq.*) does he discuss its structure, treating of "the syllabic principle in modern English verse". It might suffice to quote his pronouncement: "Our verse is of a very complex constitution, and any description based upon feet or accents alone, or on both together, is not adequate to cover all the phenomena" (p. 103). With this I heartily agree, but wonder if our meaning is the same. For, speaking (p. 102) of a line in Shelley's *Cenci*—

The house-dog moans, and the beams crack; no more—

he says that the first words would be pronounced in precisely the same way if they occurred in a line of 4-foot *Christabel* metre, *e.g.*—

The house-dog moans, and the beams are cracked.

Here I must differ. The essential difference between the two metres lies in this, that the words are adjusted to a slightly different rhythm in each case; and it is precisely this process of *adjustment* which has to be reckoned with in addition to prose feet and accents. This may seem a small matter, but it is one of vital importance; for it is this element, apt to be ignored by the scholar in his study, which constitutes the life of our verse.[1] Coming to details, it is hardly correct to say that no 9-syllable heroic line has been written since Elizabethan days; Keats has a famous one (with redundant final syllable), and one or two others exist. I doubt if Milton wrote "Belus or Serāpis"; in any case, better instances of 'treble initial inversion' can be found than either that or " How the lit lake shines, a ..." (pp. 99–100). Shelley, for instance, has the line—

Harmonizing silence without a sound;

and Mr. Watts-Dunton has—

Water, water! Blessed be God, he says.

When points like these, however, are the only ones to mention, criticism might almost as well be silent; and

---

[1] I am glad to notice that both as regards this point, and as regards that next mentioned above, the author has modified his statement in *The Principles of English Verse* (1906), for which book see Appendix B under that date.

this last Chapter seems on the whole as judicious as its predecessors are erudite and informing.

Laborious study is also shown in a treatise on *Word-stress in English*, dealing with "the accentuation of words in Middle-English as compared with the stress in Old and Modern English", by George J. Tamson (Halle, 1898). Following German models, Dr. Tamson collates examples from our verse with admirable industry, but leaves general conclusions to be drawn by others.

In 1898 was also published a pamphlet *On the Use of Classical Metres in English*, by William Johnson Stone. I shall not be suspected of favouring its attempt to revive quantitative metre when I say that no more remarkable Essay had appeared for years. The whole notion that Latin laws of quantity can be transplanted into English seems to me absurd. The young writer's historical knowledge was incomplete; some of his chief predecessors were unknown to him. His view of accent was crude, and soon underwent modification, as appears in the second edition,[1] printed (posthumously) along with the 1901 edition of *Milton's Prosody* [*ante*, 1887]. What made the Essay remarkable was its clear grasp of 'quantity'. At a time when few English writers recognised its existence, most prosodians subordinating it to or mixing it up with stress, Stone fastened intuitively on it as a fact. To this day critics stumble over his complete recognition of it; they will not believe that he meant his verses to be read "with the natural accent unimpaired". I regret that these verses do not appear in the revised edition. No doubt they had faults, but the paper seems incomplete without them. Reviewers were terribly puzzled by them; even the best came to grief in scansion. Not one, that I saw, noticed the few occasional slips, of which one occurs in the line—

As the arrow-scattering goddess Artemis hunts on a hill-side.

To me, this shows the unreality of the whole attempt,

[1] Where the title becomes "Classical Metres in English Verse".

but another explanation is obviously possible. Stone's rules I shall not discuss, but they showed true phonetic feeling; the "doubled consonant fallacy", in particular, surely received its quietus from him. It is this sense of phonetic quantity, quite apart from the use he made of it, that I find altogether admirable. "Will Stone" was a born prosodist, and his death at twenty-six was a loss to science as well as to his friends. His paper is sparklingly written, and entertains where it does not convince. In correspondence—I did not know him personally—he was fair and open-minded, ready to receive as well as give. The alterations introduced into his revised text show widening reach and deepening insight. Fundamental disagreement with his methods and aims should not blind any one to the ability with which they are planned and carried out.[1]

A view of verse as unique as Stone's, though in a different way, came from a teacher of long and high repute, Prof. James Wilson Bright of Baltimore. Readers in this country first noticed a condensed review in the *Athenaeum* (July 8, 1899) of a paper submitted by him to our Philological Society. This paper has apparently not been published, but its conclusions were doubtless those stated in the same writer's articles on "Proper names in Old English verse" (*Publications of the Modern Language Association of America* for 1899, Vol. XIV, No. 2, pp. 347–68), and "Concerning grammatical ictus in English verse" (see *An English Miscellany presented to Dr. Furnivall in honour of his 75th birthday*, Clarendon Press, 1901, pp. 23–33). Utilising ideas furnished by Sievers and other grammarians of the German neo-philological school, Prof. Bright denies that 'inverted accents' are either real inversions or parts of a trisyllabic foot, claiming that in such cases the usual force-accent is supplemented by a pitch-accent on the apparently unstressed syllable. He also rejects trisyllabic feet in strict heroic verse except after a pause,

[1] Appendix A [1899] notes some quantitative lines by Mr. Stone's father, which I missed on their publication.

reducing them to dissyllables by synaeresis, syncope, *etc.*; this is not mentioned in these articles, but in works by his pupils [see next paragraph]. " Unbroken continuity " of practice is said to exist " from Swinburne back to the *Beowulf*" (first paper, p. 357); by studying it we shall find " the true basis for the scansion of English verse " (second paper, p. 25). Such a thesis, maintained by so learned a critic, must indeed give us pause; we seem back in the Eighteenth Century. I do not know what " essential laws of rhythm " (p. 362) require absolute uniformity of syllabic recurrence. As to "pitch-accent ", Prof. Bright would probably not make too absolute the distinction between that and " force-accent ", but would be content to say that pitch predominates in one case, force in the other. Even so, how shall his proposition be established ? Familiar instances like *rose-gardén* and *well-watér* prove nothing ; they admit of other explanations. Is it credible that in every case such as Milton's

And tow'rd the gate *rolling* her bestial train

we have a specialized pronunciation—that metrical stress somehow falls on the second syllable of *rolling*? Besides, Prof. Bright surely gives away this part of his case when he admits that 'inversion' may occur in one foot, the first (p. 362). If in one foot, why not in others ? Why, particularly, not in the second foot, when it is obvious that Milton's 'double trochees' imitated Italian models ? What grounds are there for making 'inversion' possible only after a pause? The grammatical facts put forward by Prof. Bright are, I think, of great value in helping us to understand the phenomenon of 'hovering accent', but do not justify the conclusions drawn from them. After reading carefully the Professor's two papers and some by his pupils I remain unable to see that his view of syllabic structure has been proved or even made probable.

Some pamphlets by pupils of Prof. Bright are mentioned in Appendix B. One of them, by a writer no longer living (George Dobbin Brown), tries to prove dissyllabic

Milton's pronunciation of *Aegean* in the well-known phrase—
  Of Lemnos, th' Aegean isle.

The fact that Milton himself spelt the word with a diphthong in the second as well as the first syllable seems fatal to this hypothesis. A vast amount of research is evidenced in these pamphlets, but their central position is always assumed, never established by argument.

In a class of its own stands a paper by Prof. W. P. Ker on "Analogies between English and Spanish verse (Arte Mayor)," dated December, 1898, but printed in the Philological Society's *Transactions* for 1899-1901, Part I, pp. 113-28. Favourers of 'amphibrachic' verse will like to know that Prof. Ker gives the structure of the lines he is considering, double feet being separated by caesura, thus [I correct an obvious misprint]—

$$\cup \perp \cup \cup \perp \cup \mid \cup \perp \cup \cup \perp \cup \text{ (p. 114).}$$

Much useful information about the origin of pure triple-time English verse is given in this paper, with appropriate quotations. A significant sentence may be noted. "The triple time of common dance tunes, with periods of eight bars, was found congenial to verse, and was allowed to shape the prosody of verse" (p. 124).

Experimental research into rhythmical facts found expression in an article on "Time-relations of poetical metres", by A. S. Hurst and John McKay, which appeared in *University of Toronto Studies* for 1889 [*cf.* Appendix B]. Observations conducted by tapping in connection with inaudible scansion (to avoid vocal distracting elements) produced some curious results. Dactyl and trochee were found of shorter duration than anapaest and iamb (p. 66); the rhythms of dactylic and anapaestic metre revealed themselves as different (pp. 70-1). In amphibrachic metre, there was "a tendency ... to speak the accented syllables a little shorter than the others" (p. 65). The writers' general conclusion is that accent is not the sole regulator of our metre (p. 68). As their methods and results have not escaped challenge, further consideration ot them may be reserved for the Postscript to this Chapter, but their paper well repays perusal.[1]

A book of prodigious importance for students was and is Professors Gayley and Scott's *Introduction to the Methods and Materials of Literary Criticism* (Boston, U.S.A., 1899). Into small compass is packed an amazing mass of information, critical and bibliographical, on verse as well as on wider matters of literary interest. While Chapter VII, on "The principles of versification", naturally contains most that is relevant for us, other Chapters should not be neglected, and will not be by any one who even glances at them. This is a book which the student should "sell his bed" to buy; it is simply invaluable to every literary worker.[2] Messrs. Gayley and Scott, who have here laid us under so deep a debt, are also known by independent publications. Among other things may be mentioned Prof. Gayley's *Classic Myths in English Literature* (Boston, 1893), which contains some 'hexameter' translations by the author; and his *Representative English Comedies* (Macmillan, 1903), in which there is an appendix on Greene's prosody. For two striking papers by Prof. Scott, see the Postscript to this Chapter.

One or two minor publications, later than the foregoing, remain for mention. *A Note on the Scansion of the Pentameter and its Use in English Poetry* (1900), by F. K. Harford, is sufficiently characterized in my Bibliography, but should be read by any one to whom its contention is novel. The second of two papers in the *Cambridge Review* (March 1, 1900) "On English Hexameter Verse", by Edward Carpenter, has some thoughtful remarks on the possibilities of this metre, with specimen lines.

---

[1] Two papers by Dr. Scripture, occupying Vol. VII (1899) of *Studies from the Yale Psychological Laboratory* (of which he is director), deal only with elocutional matters. Important work by him, however, will be mentioned in the Postscript to this Chapter. For further details see Appendix B.

[2] In a work of such magnitude, a few mis-references are inevitable. I have noted one or two only, but would suggest that any found should be reported to the authors, as a small acknowledgement of great obligation.

Among Essays not treating directly of structure is one in *Longman's Magazine* for December, 1900, on "Rhyme", by Frank Ritchie, which pleasantly puts together a good deal of information. This might fitly close the Century, so far as date is concerned, but a work of larger scope has still to be noticed.

My last entry for 1900 is one which doubtfully comes within a survey limited to native writers discussing their own prosody; but since Messrs. van Dam and Stoffel's *William Shakespeare: Prosody and Text* is written in English and published in England it can hardly be omitted, and with it may be named a later work by the same authors, *Chapters on English Printing, Prosody, and Pronunciation (1550-1700)*, published at Heidelberg (1902). In these books a gage of defiance is thrown down before our chief critics, the former one asserting that "no editor has up to now thought it worth his while to make a full and close study of Elizabethan prosody" (p. 428); while the latter wages unflinching war against any "extra syllable" in heroic verse as quoted by scansionists hitherto, without actually denying the possibility of such a syllable (p. 112). It is a pretty quarrel, which we can leave to those concerned; Prof. Churton Collins, as will be noted in the following Postscript, has not been slow to reply. Us it does not directly concern, since we deal with modern English; trisyllabic feet are undoubtedly used by modern poets, whatever Chaucer or Shakespeare did. The "burden of proof", however (p. 113), it seems to me, rests with those who assert a difference between Elizabethan and Victorian verse in this respect. And personally I should query this initial statement in the former book: "The rhythmical arrangement of syllables is the sole essential principle that determines the outward character of poetry as compared with prose" (p. 3). Unless "arrangement" here covers much more than the syllables themselves, this statement is seriously defective; its prosody is unreal, a concoction of the laboratory. The authors' main thesis is defended with determination, and cannot be lightly set aside. Taken along with Prof. Bright's view, it shows how little certitude, how little finality, has been reached by prosodic study. Here is a cardinal point on which contradictory opinions still prevail. At the end of the Nineteenth Century, people are still asking whether a bar of verse may—or, at least, for several Centuries did—contain now two and now three syllables. We may think that the question answers itself; but such is not the belief of all experts. The very foundations of English prosody are still in doubt. Its "essential principle" cannot be said to have been placed beyond question.

[For some notice of later publications see following pages. I cannot better utilise this blank space than by quoting a few sentences from the first volume of Prof. Saintsbury's *History of English Prosody* (*infra*, 1906), relevant to my last paragraph. Speaking of 'decasyllabic verse', he says (p. 174): "It is only by means of this mixture of trisyllabic feet that the extraordinary variety and charm of English poetry ... can be attained; and it has been almost invariably by those who used them most that the attainment has been most successful and complete." "The Bysshes, and even the Johnsons, cannot prevent persons with an ear from reading the apostrophe *with* the syllable it has vainly tried to expel, and giving value to the i and y syllables to which they impotently refuse value." Elsewhere (p. 205) he praises "the blessed trisyllabic swing and swell", and reminds us (p. 307) that "In English, by the grace of God and the Muses, the poetry makes the rules, not the rules the poetry." These excellent sayings I unreservedly endorse.]

POSTSCRIPT

WITH the Century I purposed to stop. But the considerable number of important publications which have come out since suggests carrying the record down to date, at whatever disadvantages of limited information. Some of these have been already mentioned, but others await remark. A briefly summarizing conclusion also seems desirable.

Prof. Gummere must lead the way. *The Beginnings of Poetry* (Macmillan, 1901) is a weighty work, gathering together the results of long research into "the rise of poetry as a social institution" (Preface). Its first two Chapters discuss various theories about the origin of verse, from the "sexual cry" to the tribal dance; the second Chapter, particularly, traces with infinite learning all accounts and explanations of primitive metre, the "latest word of science" being sought in Meumann (p. 81). The writer's own view is fully given. Verse is "rhythmic speech, with mainly emotional origin".... " By *rhythmic* must be understood a regular recurrence which clearly sets off such speech from the speech of prose" (p. 30). "All writers on poetry take rhythm for granted until some one asks why it is necessary;" then, after discussion, "a respectable minority (but still a minority)" holds it non-essential (p. 31). Prof. Gummere is not one of that minority. As a contribution to the philosophy of verse this book ranks high; but it is a book for scholars rather than the general public. The ordinary student will be content to let specialists discuss the matters of which it treats, and will still use the author's *Handbook* [*ante*, 1885] for immediate necessities. And our survey, confined to practical issues, must dismiss this work with short notice but sincere praise. It were easy to quote pages of interesting matter, but they would not advance our search. The book is beyond all else a storehouse of information and thought on its particular subject.

In 1901 was also published *The Musical Basis of Verse*, by J. P. Dabney. As the title indicates, this deals wholly with the rhythmical aspect of verse-structure, looks to Lanier as sole precursor, and credits him with being first to use time-scansion (Preface, p. viii). It does not, however, follow him slavishly, but rejects his view of 3-beat rhythm, and his accentuation of feet on other than the first syllable (*ibid.*). Musical methods are adopted wholesale, accent always beginning the "bar", and metre on its technical side being made matter of *vibration* (p. 17); differences are recognized between music and verse (pp. 24, 26-7), but they are differences only of degree. In the main, I need hardly say, this commends itself as a right view, if less altogether novel than the writer supposes; but it is urged with too unquestioning faith. Nothing which seems to conflict with it can be good. Measuring from accent to accent, and drawing no distinction between rhythm-accent and word-accent,[1] the author postulates uniform structure, and condemns all departure from this. "It is bad writing to put upon the accented beat of the measure any weak monosyllable" (p. 32); yet our best poets do it. "Wrenched accent" is "inadmissible" (*ibid., note*); they think otherwise. "If we adopt direct attack [*i.e.* verse without 'anacrusis'], direct attack must be uniformly preserved" (p. 48); Milton's *L'Allegro* and *Il Penseroso* contradict this. Historical knowledge is not this author's strong point, nor has he studied comparative metre. He is not even aware that ancient hexameter moved to common time, but identifies it with our triple-time metre (pp. 63, 181, *etc.*). J. A. Symonds and Prof. Mahaffy are his authorities for ancient times, Mr. Gosse and others for modern. But within its own limits the book is excellent. Insistence on *movement* as a line's chief feature shows true insight. The distinction between 2-beat and 3-beat rhythm

---

[1] This distinction he positively rejects (p. 58), declaring that "syncopation in verse is not conceivable" (p. 31, *note*).

[4-beat being apparently not recognised] (p. 30) is practical, and avoids the frequent fallacy by which a trisyllabic foot is supposed to imply triple time. Indeed, some scansions will surprise in an opposite direction, as when Coleridge's—

'Tis the middle of night by the castle clock,

is pronounced to be in 2-beat rhythm (p. 42), and also Shakespeare's—

Come away, come away, Death (p. 45);

while the assertion (p. 50) that Pippa's song—

Overhead the tree-tops meet,

is "really in 3-beat rhythm" seems hazardous. Differences over such matters, however, must be expected; principle is the great thing, and that is embodied in the words, "The 2-beat and the 3-beat rhythm are as antipodal and as distinct from each other as oil and water" (p. 53). I see little use in crowding pages with rows of crotchets and quavers; the question arises— Do these represent syllables, or only beats? My belief is that they represent the latter, and that identification with syllables is misleading. Still, musical notation teaches the rudiments of rhythm, and so far this book is helpful. Its second and third Chapters are the most distinctive; their weak side appears in such statements as that Scott took his four-foot verse from Wordsworth (p. 70) and that Byron was "a master of technique" (p. 85), their strength in descriptions like that of the "bounding swiftness" of most 3-beat rhythm (p. 76). The Chapters which follow are interesting in themselves, but add little to previous knowledge. Unequal as the book is, and even dangerous sometimes as a guide, it is refreshing through its whole-hearted devotion to rhythm. *Pause* is of course recognised as integral, but is used with comparative rareness. There is much very apposite quotation from contemporary or recent writers.

The *Modern Language Quarterly* (London) for December, 1901, and April, 1902, contained two papers by R. B. McKerrow on "The Use of so-called Classical Metres in Elizabethan Verse." Mr. McKerrow, to whom I am indebted for several pieces of information (*cf.* Appendix A), is a distinguished student of the period referred to, and these papers give an independent scholarly account of that curious eddy in the river of our poetry. I do not always agree with their phonetic judgements, and think injustice is done to Stone in this connection; but these are points not worth dwelling on here. I trust these papers will be published separately some day, or rather will form the basis of a more detailed and exhaustive account of the Elizabethan quantitative experiment. Such an account is still a desideratum.

Experimental scrutiny of our verse-measures produced some striking results during 1901 and 1902. To the former year belong papers by Messrs. Wallin, Triplett and Sanford, and Squire, particulars of which will be found in Appendix B; to the latter belongs *Elements of Experimental Phonetics*, by Edward Wheeler Scripture (New York and London, 1902). This latter work sums up results obtained by investigators, including the above-named, to whom its author was guide and friend. Dogmatic theorists about rhythm—particularly those who approach it from the musical side—would do well to study these results. They will find that things which they have been accustomed to regard as objective facts are relegated to the domain of subjective impressions. Dr. Scripture distinguishes between physical and mental constituents of accent, and between auditory and motor factors of the same, the most characteristic property of auditory accent being "impressiveness" (p. 506). This bears out the view of accent suggested provisionally in the first pages of our study. He does not find it sufficient to identify accent with force. Where Bolton heard only greater intensity in the 'tick-*tick*' of a clock, he claims to find pitch and quality slightly altered too; we seem to hear it say 'tick-*tock*' (p. 522). And he recognises but three "necessary properties" of a tone—

pitch, duration, and intensity; quality, *timbre*, or tone-colour is one of the extra properties which "may be added" (p. 89). It is very interesting to find the latest belief of science coming back to agreement with earlier ones; this tripartite division is as old as the Latin grammarians, perhaps as Aristotle. Dr. Scripture's large book is full of suggestive ideas; space allows me to cite only these few. His governing notion is division into "centroids", that is, groups not unlike the "monopressures" of an earlier critic [*ante*, 1888], but considered as resulting from other elements in addition to *force*. This conception naturally reappears in the work of his pupils or co-workers, and will be much canvassed. I doubt myself if it is a complete representation of the facts. But the observations and conclusions of this writer are of the highest importance.

The researches on which his book is based were conducted mainly by *tapping*. There is an evident danger in this method, that the act of tapping may influence mental or audible recitation, creating fictitious regularity. Of this the observers were aware; one couple remark, with much acuteness if some *naïveté*, that their method would be "fatal to poetry". Of course no great verse is a matter merely of temporal rhythm; other elements differentiate "Propria quae maribus" from a line of the *Aeneid*. Nursery rhymes, with their bold rhythmical effects, are well suited to this method, and this pair of writers apply it mainly to them, recording their "auditory forms". Mr. Wallin got some amusing results from setting people to read a crabbed passage from Browning which was new to them; the difference was very marked when they read it as prose and after discovery that it was verse. Mr. Squire's is the longest and most philosophical of the three papers. He experimented first with German then with American children, and found that the former showed more tendency to "qualitative accent" and greater intervals of pitch. Little is said in any of the papers about the relation of verse to musical time.[1] Messrs. Triplett and Sanford scan by stresses; to them, "peas [*sic*] porridge hot" is identical with "the short meter stanza of the hymnbook" (p. 365). They find, however, that "there is a rough equality in the figures for the intervals, except where they are lengthened by pauses", or made irregular to bring out the meaning (pp. 375-6, *cf.* 379). Mr. Wallin holds that prose is measured as well as verse, and that "centroid intervals" are not uniform (p. 113 *seq.*); yet "no recurrence of centroids can be rhythmized unless the length and regularity of the intervals fulfil the requirements of the rhythmical time-sense", which "may differ slightly for different individuals" (p. 128). To Mr. Squire, on the other hand, "temporalness, in its connotation of regular succession, is the basal principle of rhythm," and "temporal changes can alone (intensity and pitch remaining constant) produce a pleasing rhythm"[2] (p. 541). All the writers agree that there is much self-deception; Mr. Squire thinks that "the objectively long may appear shorter and unaccented" (*ibid.*), and noted that "some individuals were inclined to hear the high as the more intense, others the low" (p. 549). In opposition to Messrs. Hurst and McKay [*ante*, 1899], Messrs. Triplett and Sanford found iambs quicker than trochees (p. 380), and Mr. Squire found it impossible to get his children to group by amphibrachs at all. The differences of opinion among these papers enhance one's feeling of their good faith and vivid reality; they read like what they are, transcripts from life. I regret that we have as yet nothing of a similar character to show in this country.

Bold departure from tradition characterizes *An Introduction to the scientific study of English Poetry*, by Mark H. Liddell (New York, 1902), in which it is

---

[1] They agree in making the 2-group naturally precede the 3-group; Mr. Squire alone identifies these with Lanier's 3-rhythm and 4-rhythm respectively. He speculates on the probable origin and development of these groups (pp. 535, 540).

[2] So can also "intensive co-ordination" by itself (*ibid.*).

maintained that "accent is not the determining element of English verse-forms" (p. 22). "Thought-groups," not temporal periods, are made the units of verse in our language, and "rhythm-waves" are considered without reference to their duration. I do not think the writer was cognisant of the researches last mentioned; he makes no reference to them, and seems to work on lines of his own. Realizing the essential difference between Greek verse and ours (Book I, Chap. V, and *passim*), Prof. Liddell pushes this to a denial of quantitative relations in our metre. In simpler words, he ignores the fact that our syllables, too, are set to time after a fashion of their own. Through ignoring this, his able analysis fails to carry conviction as a complete account of the matter. The first half of his volume (Book I) deals with general questions, the second half (Book II) with English verse-structure more particularly. In the second Chapter of the former he makes his leading assumption (see especially p. 45 *seq.*), and I think the example on p. 47 may test its truth. He finds only "rhythmic prose" in the following [I alter one phrase to avoid bisecting a word]—

> Duncan is in his grave. After the fitful
> Fever of life he sleeps in peace. For fate
> Has done its very worst—nor steel, nor poison,
> Malice domestic, foreign levy, nothing
> Can touch him further.

I submit that this would pass anywhere for verse; not good verse, but still verse; and that this is so, not because we count the syllables, or because the printer has arranged them in lines, but because we relate them to equal time-periods. Shakespeare's music, his "rhythm-phrases", and the rest, are superadded to this; they beautify the verse, make all the difference between doggrel and poetry, but they do not create the structure. That depends on our perception of *time*. Without that, even the best words are prose; with it, even the weakest may be verse. Shakespeare himself cannot evade this law; it is because he uses it so subtilely, so masterfully, that his verse is so wondrous. Here, if any where, is the "one factor" so often "overlooked in studies of Verse Form" (p. 85).

There is much that is valuable in this book, with much that invites criticism. Its introductory Chapter seems rather captious. Who, nowadays, makes poetry "supernatural", or upholds Lindley Murray's scansion? In Chapter II, 'inversion' is supposed to occur only "after a pause", "where the thought took a new turn" (p. 48); is this true of Shakespeare's—

    And yet dark night *strangles* the travelling lamp,

or of Shelley's line—

    And wild *roses*, and ivy serpentine,

or of many similar instances? The analysis of speech-significance in this and succeeding Chapters may seem protracted, but is necessary for the writer's purpose, to demonstrate his "five rising waves of attention-stress" (p. 59)—a conception which, taken by itself, is surely no whit less mechanical than counting feet or syllables or accents. In the one place where, speaking of English verse, allusion is made to the element of time (pp. 171–3), this is identified with capacity for being set to music; but the two things are quite different. On the other hand, the analysis of stress in Chapter XI is perspicacious, especially the distinction between a force and its result (p. 208) and the proof that accent can shorten sound (pp. 212–14). But what gives chief value to the book is its dissection of speech into "thought-moments", "emotional pulses," "waves of attention energy," illustrated by painstaking analysis. I do not, indeed, accept the identification of these with "rhythm-waves" (p. 217), or believe that in itself a "grouping of thought-moments would be a rhythmic Verse Form" (p. 87). Still, we have here a fact of speech, for which room must be found in our theory. Comparing this book with that on "The Musical Basis of Verse" recently mentioned, we see how complicated is the problem. Mr. Dabney and Prof. Liddell represent opposite wings of the prosodic army; the main line of advance, I think, is between their extremes, each of which has truth, but not the whole truth.

The Relation of the Rhythm of Poetry to that of the Spoken Language, by C. W. E. Miller (Baltimore, 1902), I have been unable to see. It will be noticed that in American literature 'poetry' is, more frequently than with us, used for 'verse', and 'verse' for 'line'; both usages are hostile to clearness. Turning home, what have we to show in these years? New editions of chief books [*cf.* Mayor and Bridges] provoked much newspaper reviewing; but little solid teaching resulted. Two papers mentioned in my Bibliography for 1901 are wrongly ascribed to "Peter" instead of Thomas Bayne; they hardly call for note. In an edition of *Milton's Lycidas*, by H. B. Cotterill (1902), Appendix I "On Rhythm in English Verse" gives a bright but sketchy view of verse regarded musically, and speaks of "counter movements of stress and length, like the cross-play of wavelets on an ocean roll" (p. 105). The "Ptolemaic" theories of Mr. Bridges are rejected, triple time is assumed for our 'iambic' measure, and anapaestic retardation is invoked to explain every case of 'pyrrhic *plus* spondee'. Mrs. Woods, on the other hand, in her Preface to *The Princess of Hanover* (1902) adopts Mr. Bridges' view of verse, and adds little of her own. Defending "nine-syllabled lines", she does not tell us why these are not found in *Paradise Lost*; defending Cockney rhymes, does not advert to Tennyson's repudiation of these. Rightly ridiculing "rhymes to the eye", she with equal justice vindicates imperfect rhymes from wholesale condemnation, but might have added that many of them are conventional survivals of what once were perfect rhymes. It will be noted that this Preface is the first piece of work by a woman-writer chronicled in this volume. Great advantage may be expected from women turning their attention to prosody; they bring fresh minds, not dulled by traditional fallacies. They have already begun to discuss Latin metre; surely English is worth their examination. Since Mrs. Browning can hardly be said to have entered the field, we may hail in Mrs. Woods our first woman-prosodist, and trust that her example will be largely followed.

Imaginations in the Dust, by L. H. Victory (1903), contained an "Essay on Elementary Metres", based mainly on Ruskin, but short and practical. My own *Study of Metre*, in the same year, attempted to popularize more 'actual' views of verse-form. Prof. Mayor followed up his larger book with a *Handbook of Modern English Metre* (Cambridge, 1903), intended for educational use, which covers wider ground than his *Chapters*, going on to consider the aesthetic effect of particular metres and of individual words. Rhythm is still wholly a matter of syllables, scansions seem sometimes most questionable [*e.g.* the lines said to be "in the same metre" on p. 91], and there are one or two slips, such as thinking that Wordsworth never closed a sonnet with rhyming couplet (p. 147). The examples are good and up to date, but the method of analysis far from adequate. *English Verse*, by R. M. Alden (New York, 1903), I regret not to have seen, but hope to see soon.[1] "Some remarks on the study of English verse," by Henry van Dyke, in the *Atlantic Monthly* for October of that year, begin by asserting that "the science of English verse is still in its formative stage", and rightly urge that it must be based on the practice of poets, yet do not get beyond counting by syllables and their stresses, these last being "structural factors". But four papers by Ernest Newman, in the *Weekly Critical Review* (Paris) for the four weeks of September, 1903, discuss "The rationale of English verse-rhythm" in a manner far removed from ordinary journalism, and constitute a real study of the subject. Mr. Newman is evidently a musician, and pushes the musical view as far as it will go. In the last analysis, he is "left with the trochaic line alone as the skeleton upon which English verse is hung"; in other words, nearly all our lines are in $\frac{3}{8}$ rhythm, and what seems departure from it is usually but variation of it. This

---

[1] *Cf. infra*, p. 268. The correct date is 1904.

rhythm may be determined either by accent or quantity, or by "the two in coincidence"; and all bars are equal to one another. I do not think this view gives the whole truth, or that it could withstand such experimental investigation as we have lately considered; but it puts one side of the truth forcibly. The other side relates to that quantity, that syllabic residuum, which Mr. Newman would fain subordinate entirely to rhythm; and to the possibility of maintaining a double time in our consciousness. The essayist's style is clear, his comments on other prosodists pertinent and pointed; Lanier receives due credit. These papers should certainly be extricated from their obscure place of lodgement, and re-issued after consideration of the other works mentioned in this Postscript.

In 1903 Mr. Bridges published his first quantitative poem *Now in wintry delights* [Daniel press, Oxford; for others see Appendix A], which I name only to mention the beautiful sample of phonetic script which it contains. In January, 1894, he contributed to the *Athenaeum* newspaper three articles headed "Miltonic elision", maintaining that in real trisyllabic feet "the extra (elided) syllable is always to be slightly pronounced" (p. 114, first column); his cogent and well illustrated argument in support of this should surely be conclusive. Prof. Churton Collins, in his *Studies in Shakespeare* (1904) condemns Messrs. van Dam and Stoffel's "amazing theories about Shakespeare's metrical system, and their still more amazing re-arrangements of his verse as prose" (p. 331), but himself opens the door to chaos by denying that laws of rhythm can be definitely formulated (p. 327). I do not understand what is conveyed by such scansions [or rather *pictures*] as

If ăftĕr ĕvĕrў̆ tĕmpēst cōme sŭch cālms;

and cannot admit that in

From Dis's waggon; daffodils . . .

"the ear tells us that rhythmically there is no deficiency" (pp. 329, 330). On such principles anything may be verse; meantime, the uncertainty of Shakespeare's text makes all such discussion rather nugatory.

A book entitled *How to write Verse*, by George J. H. Northcroft (1904), does me the honour to borrow my account of the basis of English metre, especially in its fifth Chapter, without further acknowledgement than a complimentary reference at the end of that Chapter. It covers the whole field of verse-making, and forms a useful introduction to that art. *Forms of English Verse*, by Charles F. Johnson, N.D. [1904], gives a good summary of metrical types for young readers. *Feet* are discussed on pp. 12-14, "equal time-beats" being held fundamental; "scanning is simply pronouncing the accents at isochronous intervals." In his short Preface the author remarks that "an ingenious physicist may at any time prove that the acoustic basis of verse is something different from what it has been supposed to be", but that will not affect our enjoyment of metre. A booklet *On Anglo-Saxon Versification from the standpoint of Modern-English Versification*, by Edwin B. Setzler (Baltimore, 1904), hardly comes within our scope, as it deals wholly with Old English verse, of whose syllabic structure it makes a careful study. The author is not a disciple of Prof. J. W. Bright [*ante*, 1899].

Late in 1904 was published a substantial pamphlet on *The Basis of English Rhythm*, by Mr. William Thomson, of Glasgow. I have discussed it elsewhere.[1] In private letters Mr. Thomson, besides pointing out some inaccuracies in my statement (see below), has assured me that I totally misunderstand the drift and purpose of his Essay.

---

[1] *Metrical Rhythm* (pamphlet, 1905). Some slips require correction. On p. 8, line 20, "seven quavers" should be *six*. On p. 16 I assumed that Milton's word "melancholy" was scanned like one of Mr. Gilbert's four-syllable feet; but they are four syllables in time of four, it is four in time of three—this distinction I should not have overlooked. On p. 23 Mr. Thomson says I overstate agreement between us as to temporal equality, since he admits duple feet in triple rhythm, and *vice versa*. I regret to find that agreement on this fundamental point is less complete than I had supposed.

I shall therefore not characterize it here farther than by saying that it uses musical notation more skilfully than I have seen done elsewhere or had conceived possible, but that in my judgement its scansions give the prosaic rather than the prosodial value of syllables and their accents. "Triple Time" is made to preponderate overwhelmingly in both our prose and our verse. The Essay is certainly one to be reckoned with by all critics of metre.

In June, 1904, and again in December, 1905, Prof. F. N. Scott of Michigan University [*cf. ante*, 1899] contributed two remarkable papers to *Modern Language Notes* (Baltimore). The earlier is on "The most fundamental differentia between poetry [not merely verse] and prose", which he traces to a radical difference of impulse, that which produces prose being the desire of communication, that which produces poetry the desire to express feeling, separately or in communion with others. The later paper, on "The scansion of prose rhythm", claims to find crescendoes and diminuendoes in prose speech which obey fixed laws, and which collectively he designates the "motative arc" (*nutation* and *motation* are his names for the rhythms of verse and prose respectively). He makes prose rhythm depend mainly on pitch, verse rhythm on "stress" [force]; but surely goes too far when he says (p. 717) that "stress or energy" is "the principal element" of our metre. The "simple experiment" by which he seeks to demonstrate this introduces time as well as stress under the name "pauses", and this other "element" is essential to its success. Both papers, however, deserve attentive reading.

The limits of my survey have not allowed me to mention any work by foreign writers, even the monumental *Englische Metrik* of Prof. Schipper, still our most exhaustive treatise on the subject, or the brilliant critiques of some younger French writers such as M. Paul Verrier. But they do not forbid my including a *brochure* by a compatriot, though written in French and (privately) printed abroad. This *Étude comparée de la versification française et de la versification anglaise*, par Thos. B. Rudmose-Brown (Grenoble, 1905), was reviewed in the *Athenaeum* of September 16, 1905, and contains a careful study of some writers previously unknown to me, particularly Fredrik Wulff. I hope its young writer will soon develop his theories of *le syllabisme* and *le non-syllabisme* with fuller detail and in English dress.

In 1906 Mr. John Davidson appended to his *Holiday and Other Poems* a Note "On poetry", in which he declares rhyme a "decadent" thing, though capable of being used for "crescive" work, and praises the "nude" beauty of blank verse—as if *Paradise Lost* were less richly clad than the *Essay on Man*! A paper in *Macmillan's Magazine* for June on "Rhythm and rhyme", by George Bourne, vindicates the place of temporal beat in verse, without touching disputed questions. But the metrical event of the year is the commencement of Prof. Saintsbury's great *History of English Prosody*. This long projected and long expected work seems planned as a history rather of our verse itself than of what critics have said about it; the first volume (alone published as I write) carries the tale from the "Origins" down to Spenser. Such a record, dealing with the form and not the contents of our poetry, is very badly wanted to-day; in English, we have had nothing of the kind since Guest, and he is altogether 'impossible'. It would not be easy to find any one so well qualified as Prof. Saintsbury for the task to which he has now set his hand. Yet I think most readers of this first volume will share my surprise at the resolute way in which its author declines to discuss the phenomena which he chronicles. All the questions which have interested us during this survey, and which we have seen battled over during two Centuries of enquiry, he puts aside as "previous questions". A true Englishman, he confines himself to fact, and eschews philosophy (*cf.* p. 7, *note*; the Introductory Chapter generally; and *passim*). Whether this attitude can be maintained through succeeding volumes remains to be seen. When he comes to consider prosodical criticism, to traverse the ground we have traversed, it will surely be necessary for him to express opinions of some sort, to say on what foundation he conceives his doctrine of "equivalence" to rest. Succeeding volumes will show; none awaits them with keener interest than myself. I gladly close my survey with this first volume of a work which—as I ventured to anticipate—bids fair to take the place too long occupied by '*Guest*', and become our textbook for the history of English verse.[1]

What, then, is the upshot of the whole matter? This, for certain; that we have as yet no established system of prosody. Much analytic enquiry has yielded no synthesis authoritative and generally accepted. It is a strange fact, so late in the history of our literature; Greek metrists would have viewed it with surprise. That the synthesis will come is surely past question. When it does come, I suspect it will be found less and not more complex than its many predecessors. It will not come on lines of Greek prosody. Our syllables do not directly express time, are not regarded by us as primarily measures of time; any attempt to prove that they do so in our ordinary verse must fail, and any attempt to make them do so in verse of novel pattern seems to me ill-judged. Yet—keeping to our ordinary native fashion of verse—syllables must be somehow marshalled and arranged, if they are to produce patterns differing from those of prose speech. They must be brought into relation with some overruling law, through whose dominance they become materials of prosodic structure.

That this law is a temporal one I cannot doubt. Verse without time-measure is about as conceivable as weaving without thread. All talk of stresses and thought-groups and emotional climax and centroid recurrence is so far beside the mark; it omits the most necessary factor. Verse depends first and always on time-rhythm; it "contrives its pattern of sounds in time". Different

[1] For a paper on the technique of English verse, by C. F. Keary, and for *The Principles of English Verse*, by Charlton M. Lewis [*cf. ante*, 1898], see last entries in Appendix B.

ages, different speech-habits, modify its manner of doing this; but it must always do it somehow. Failure to apprehend this truth has made lifeless much of our metrical criticism. Verse considered apart from time is a dead thing, a corpse for the dissecting theatre of grammarians; the life is fled, how then can their analysis find it? The same mistake was made by Greek and Latin prosodists of the later Empire; they dealt with part of the question as if it were the whole.

Whether we have yet rightly apprehended the relation of our verse to time is another matter. We may have formed too narrow conceptions of rhythm. Hitherto we have borrowed these mainly from music; do all its methods necessarily hold good in dealing with speech? That there is close kinship between verse and music is evident, and as yet we have no language save that of music in which to express temporal occurrences. But this language does not always seem appropriate. In any case, English syllables do not by themselves create or constitute rhythmical periods. They are, at most, set or adjusted to such periods, often with perceptible coercion. This enforced adjustment, in my belief, gives our verse its charm and character. Theories which consider only one or other side of this double structure cannot be adequate. The correlation, the interaction of both elements is the very thing we have to analyse. Most prosodic investigation takes too limited a view of the problem; some of it has got so out of contact with truth that it sees no difference between verse and prose.

The reality of this double structure seems easily demonstrable. Does not some of even our most brilliant verse suffer from the perpetual hammer-beat of syllabic accent, leaving the ear no liberty, but monotonously enforcing rhythm? Such verse is felt to have the hardness as well as the clearness of resonant metal. On the other hand, in the work of our most accomplished singers—even in such exquisite work as that of Miss Rossetti—is there not sometimes a tendency to let syllabic and temporal beats wander too far apart, so that occasionally the ear is puzzled to bring them together? In all verse, are we not conscious of slight divergence between the uniform temporal beat and the varying syllabic accent? To say that these habitually coincide is surely doing despite to our judgement.

There is, therefore, still room for much independent enquiry. We have first to determine, theoretically and experimentally, what is the real basis of our verse. Laboratory work can be of use here, if free from preconceptions, and if its methods do not create phenomena instead of recording them. The basis once made clear, endless labour can be expended on contributory factors. All details of syllabic structure, vowel and consonant character, stress-value, 'tone-colour,' expressional significance, and the rest, will find place in a complete theory. Much has been already done in this regard, and much remains to do. But these things can be rightly seen only in perspective of the whole. Our first need is to view verse intelligently as a composite total—now at length, looking back on the experience of Centuries, to discover what English verse really is. That the discovery has still to be made, may well seem surprising; but the fundamental disagreements revealed throughout our survey show plainly that such is the fact.

We may reasonably look with expectation to what the next few years will bring. If the whole truth has not yet been reached, it is now recognised as attainable; our best prosodic analysis is saner, wider, more catholicly minded than ever before. Study of temporal sequence, in particular, has made a beginning. It is in that direction that advance may be most confidently expected, as it is in that direction that advance is most desirable. Many experts, fortunately, are aware of this, and are seeking to extend our knowledge on this side. From their efforts much gain should result. To them more especially, but also to all who are interested in prosody, I trust this book may be of some use, and I proffer cordial salutation.

APPENDIX A

BEING

ADDENDA TO AND *CORRIGENDA* IN MY PREVIOUS LIST OF ENGLISH QUANTITATIVE VERSE

14th Century? Macaronic verse might be supposed to yield 'hexameters' earlier than any I have cited. Thus, in Wright and Halliwell's *Reliquiae Antiquae* (1841), Vol. I, p. 90, we find condemnation of those who *mumble, skip*, or "*leap over*" part of the Office:—

Momylers, forscyppers, ovrelepers, non bene psallunt.

In the same book, p. 291, this line has grown into two, all English but for *quoque* and *sic et* instead of *and*. Finally, in Wright's edition of *Latin Poems attributed to Walter Mapes* (1841), p. 148, *note*, comes this wholly English line on the same theme:—

Momler, forscypper, stumler, scaterer, overhipper.

It is English, but is it quantitative? I think Latin and English were both read by accent, and hence the false quantities in both. Other instances can doubtless be found; probably the same rule will always apply. The wonder is that such lines are not more numerous. Usually, when Latin and English lines alternate, the latter follow native measures; compare, for example, the piece at second reference above. When, however, such lines do occur, I think they should be regarded as accentual, not quantitative.

[For a reference which suggested this note I have to thank Mr. Eric R. D. Maclagan.]

The same argument applies to a supposed couplet by Chaucer (see Skeat's edition, Vol. II, p. 419, and *cf.* Introduction to that volume, p. xxiii, *note*; also Saintsbury, *Hist. of Pros.*, Vol. I, pp. 8, 10). If the words which conclude the first "Metre" of *Boethius* are meant to form an 'elegiac' couplet, as Prof. Saintsbury seems to hold, accent and not quantity is their basis.

J. Payne Collier (*Bibl. and Crit. Account*, Vol. I, p. xli) opined that the words with which Chaucer "commences his prose version of Boethius" were intended to form two hexameter lines, "as correct as many of those" in Stanihurst. Few will agree with him.

No truly quantitative verse, apparently, was produced in England before the 16th Century, and Bishop Watson's lines quoted by Ascham may be considered our earliest extant specimen of such.

16th Cent. I omitted to mention a line in which, according to Fuller, Queen Elizabeth addressed some grammar-school boys (see Walpole's *Royal and Noble Authors*, Vol. I, p. 31):—

Pērsĭŭs, ā crāb-stāffe; bāwdў Mārtĭāl; Ōvĭd, ā fīne wāg.[1]

Her Majesty had been Ascham's pupil, and this is clearly meant to be quantitative. But if one of these boys had confused two Latin quantities as she confused *body* and *bawdy*, would he have 'scaped a whipping? She doubtless pronounced *Ovid* with a long *O*.

1576. Mr. R. B. McKerrow has directed attention (in *Modern Language Quarterly* for December, 1902; I regret having missed this before) to a book previously unseen by me. This is *Houres of Recreation . . . done first out of Italian into Englishe by James Sandford Gent.*, the second edition. At the end of this volume come "Certayne Poemes Dedicated to the Queenes moste excellente Maiestie", which are on unpaged leaves, and did not appear in the first edition (1573).[2] One of these is in 'elegiac' couplets, repeated in five different languages—Greek, Latin, Italian, French, and English. The last is specially interesting, because it antedates all our published quantitative lines except Ascham's, and is the first recorded attempt at writing 'pentameters' in English. I quote it entire, preserving the spelling, but adding symbols of quantity as seem necessitated by the metre.

Ēnglānd wĭth thĭs vērse dŏth drēsse yŏu vĭrgĭn ăn āltăr,
　Whŏm nŏt wātĕr, ŏr āyre, Ĭrŏn ŏr āge căn ănŏy,
Āge vŏlătĭve ēates nŏt sŭch vērse ăs dĭd tŏ thĕ Grēekes būĭld
　Lāstĭng prāise, nŏr thăt Rōme ĕvĕr ēngrāvĕd ēarst.
Thēn rĕtĭrĭng Ĭ my stēppes, āftĕr thēĭr glŏrў wĭl ēnsŭe,
　Mūrdrĭng ŏblĭvĭŏn, yŏur wĭll Ĭ glŏrўe tŏ lĭve,
Ānd wĭth thĭs mĕsūred vērse yŏur hŏlўe nāme shăll ăbrŏde sprĕade,
　Sĭth yŏur hŏllў făvŏur hēlpĕth ăn hŏllў fūrў.

---

[1] As before, I add symbols in all cases of quantitative verse, to show quickly which syllables are accounted 'long' and which 'short'. Footdivision my readers can supply for themselves. The last syllable of each line is marked *long* or *short* according to the general scheme of the metre, irrespective of actual [supposed] quantity.

[2] This had a different title: *The Garden of Pleasure . . . etc.*

It will be seen that quantity ("measured verse") is attempted, with little success, though *volatīve* and *engrăved* may represent contemporary vocalisation. *Retīring*, in the fifth line, evidently copies the French *retirant*. The sixth line is unintelligible as it stands; "your glory will I make to live" is what it ought to say. Was Sandford a pupil of Ascham, or did he follow Continental exemplars? It looks as if the latter influenced him most. How little it profits to reproduce Elizabethan spelling is shown by *holy* being spelt first "holye" and then "holly", without metrical reason so far as concerns the first syllable at least. *Ing* is clearly reckoned 'long'. The lines are certainly curious, in themselves, on account of their date, and for their polyglot character.

1580. By an extraordinary pen-slip, I stated (*English Metrists*, 1903, p. 13) that Gabriel Harvey was "some twenty-five years junior to Sidney". He was several years senior. Sidney was born in 1554, Harvey is usually stated to have been born in 1545, but some authorities say 1550. I cannot imagine what caused this blunder. It is the only serious one I have detected in those hastily printed pages; notice of any other will oblige.

Gabriel's younger brother John is mentioned by him in the third of *Three proper . . . letters* [see Bibliography] as having written some quantitative lines, he himself correcting them. They will be found in Haslewood, *Anc. Crit. Essays*, Vol. II, pp. 270-3. Gabriel's 'quantities' are only too faithfully followed, *e.g. If sŏ bĕ, blĕssed, majĕsty*. I quote one couplet, as usual encomiastic of Queen Elizabeth:—

Nŏt thĕ līke Vīrgĭn ăgāine, ĭn Āsĭa ŏr Āfrĭc ŏr Ēurōpe,
Fŏr Rŏyāll Vērtūes, fŏr Māĭēstĭe, Bŏuntĭe, Bĕhāvĭōur.

Observe *like, in, Asi-* [*a* elided], *or* [as if *Oorope*]. It is interesting to see *behaviour* made a trisyllable. Being mere exercises, I omitted these from my former list.

Can any Elizabethan scholar tell me what proof there is that Gabriel Harvey was a member of the "Areopagus"? He is commonly assumed to have been, perhaps because he was "Leicester's man", and so presumably acquainted with Sidney; but I have found no definite authority for his inclusion.[1]

1588. HAKE (JOHN). There are said to be some 'hexameters' in *A Touch-stone of Wittes*, by this writer; but I believe

[1] I see that Mr. Spingarn [*cf.* Appendix B, 1899], like myself, places Harvey outside the Areopagus.

no copy of the book is to be found. Warton (*Hist. of Poetry*, Hazlitt's edition, Vol. III, pp. 203–4) speaks as if he had seen it; his editor had "never met with it" (*ibid., note*). Schipper (*Engl. Metr.*, Vol. II, p. 11) and Gayley and Scott (*Lit. Crit.*, p. 498) briefly describe the book, I know not on what information. Warton says it is chiefly compiled, "with some slender additions," from Webbe's *Discourse*; the others make it derive from Fraunce.

1588–9. Mr. M⁽ᶜ⁾Kerrow (*loc. cit.*) points out that 'hexameters' were used in the "Martin Mar-prelate" controversy. In the original *Epistle* (1588; Arber's reprint, pp. 18, 19), two alternative lines are suggested for an epitaph on Dean Bridges, viz.:—

> Hēre līes Jōhn Brīdgĕs, ă wōrthĭe Prĕsbȳtĕr hĕ wăs;

and

> Hēre līes Jōhn Brīdgĕs lāte Bĭshŏp, frĭĕnd tŏ thĕ Pāpă.

At the end of *Mar-Martine* (1589; anonymous tract, ascribed to Lyly, *cf.* Bond's *Lyly*, Vol. III, pp. 423–6), come six lines of reply, as follow:—

> Hēre hāngs knāve Mārtĭne, ă trāitrŏus Lĭbĕlĕr hĕ wăs
> Ĕnĕmĭe prĕtĕndĕd bŭt ĭn hārt ă frĭĕnd tŏ thĕ Pāpă.
> Nŏw māde mĕat tŏ thĕ bĭrdes thăt ăbŏot hĭs cărkăs ăre hāglĭng.
> Lĕarne bў hĭs ĕxāmplĕ yĕe rŏute ŏf Frŭrĭtăn āssĕs,
> Nŏt tŏ rĕsĭst thĕ dŏĭngs ŏf ŏur mŏst grăcĭŏus Hĕstĕr,
> Mārtĭn ĭs hāngd fŏr thĕ Māstĕr ŏf ăll Hȳpŏcrĭtĭcăl hānglĭes.

The savage vigour of these lines makes one think Nash may have had a hand in them; he pretends to approve the spelling "pruritan" in *The Return of Pasquil* (1589). Grim comment is supplied by the fact that one author of the *Epistle* was actually hanged. In the British Museum copy of *Mar-Martine* [apparently unique], the last of the above lines is so much cut away as to be barely legible; Mr. Bond thinks "one or more" other lines may have followed.

It may here be noted that Mr. Bond (Vol. III, pp. 448–9) gives as Lyly's some 'hexameters' which really belong to Sidney; *cf. Athenaeum*, April 4, 1903, p. 435.

1592. NASH (THOS.). In old list, *dele* first three words in "The Apologie of Pierce Penniless".

New edition of *The Works of Thomas Nashe* [sic], ed. R. B. M⁽ᶜ⁾Kerrow, 3 vols. (A. H. Bullen), 1904.

1595. SABIE (FRANCIS). [*Cf. Engl. Metr.*, 1903, pp. 23–4.] See *Dict. Nat. Biogr.*, but what it tells does not amount to much.

1599. Anonymous [*cf.* old list]. *The First Book of the Preservation* was reprinted by Payne Collier in his *Illustrations of Old English Literature*, Vol. II (3 vols. 4to, 1866, privately printed).

For a modern reprint of several works mentioned above, see Appendix B, 1904, Smith (G. Gregory).

[The foregoing includes what few additions can be made to my former list of Elizabethan quantitative writings. It is much to be wished that students of the period would note any samples of pseudo-Classical verse they come across; some may be still uncatalogued. The next two Centuries have yielded no fresh *trouvaille* of this kind, and succeeding entries refer mainly to specimens which I have not before had occasion to characterize.]

1750? I did not mention Cowper's solitary piece of 'sapphics', placed among his posthumously published "Early Poems", therefore probably written about this date; I cannot believe it was meant to be quantitative. If it was, it contains such dactyls as *dĕlāy ŏf execution, Jūdās mŏre ăbhorred, pēnce sŏld hĭs*. But if Cowper read his lines—as most people do read English quasi-sapphic measure—by accent, giving four beats to the long lines and two to the short, these difficulties vanish. The first stanza would then divide thus:—

> Hatred and | vengeance, | my eternal | portion,
> Scarce can en- | dure de- | lay of exe- | cution,
> Wait with im- | patient | readiness to | seize my
> Soul in a | moment.

So read, they differ from those of Dr. Watts, with which otherwise they might well be paralleled for loose quantity as for terrible subject; Watts's lines are as faulty by accent as by quantity, Cowper's have a real and natural swing. If I am right, therefore, they should not be considered quantitative lines.

1802. The metrical pieces in Odell's *Essay* [*cf.* text, 1806], pp. 178–86, written at or before this date, deserve notice. Such a 'sapphic' line as—

> Gŏds ăbŏve mĭght ēnvў thĕ fŏnd ădōrĕr

would easily pass for quantitative. But Odell, who seems to have thought out his structure for himself, disregards positional length, and makes "emphasis" instead of duration of syllable his basis. *Hollow* is to him a trochee, and *essences* a dactyl. His lines are therefore really constituted by accent, but on a basis of strict feet; the above line, for example, cannot be read like one of Cowper's. If verse of this type is to be written at all in English, Odell's is probably the best way to do it, avoiding at once the futility of supposed quantitative and the roughness of purely accentual metre. It is pretty much the way in which, to compare great things with small, Mr. Swinburne's "Sapphics" are written. Odell's first stanza runs thus:—

> Gods above might envy the fond adorer,
> Him who near thee sits, in a silent rapture,
> Thus to hear thee tenderly speak, and see thee
>   Tenderly smiling.

It will be seen how near this comes to orthodox quantity; the structural difference between "tenderly smiling" and "painfully silent" is as nought to an English ear. Other specimens follow, the longest being a translation from the *Iliad*, of which these are the first two lines:—

> Sing, O Muse, the destructive wrath of Pelead Achilles,
> Source of abundant toil and grief to the host of Achaeans.

1805 and 1842. DEAN WILLIAM HERBERT, who as a young man 'cut up' Mitford in the *Edinburgh Review* [*cf.* text and old list, 1805], wrote quantitative verses more [*ex hyp.*] correct than any predecessor. These, like his *Review* article, can be seen in his *Works* (1842), Vol. II. The 'sapphic' stanza of which I quoted one line in my text reads thus (p. 70 in that volume):—

> Ŏ līquĭd strēamlĕts tŏ thē māin rĕtūrnĭng;
> Mūrmŭrĭng wātĕrs, thăt ădōwn thē mōuntāin
> Rūsh ŭnŏbstrūctēd; nĕvĕr īn thē ōcĕan
>   Hōpe tŏ bē trānqŭil.

Rūsh is a false quantity, due doubtless to spelling; *liquid, bē tran-,* perhaps *rēturning,* seem questionable. But these are exceptional. Compare a set of 'alcaics' (p. 214), of whose eight stanzas I give the last:—

> Ŏ hĕar ălōft, thōu Quēen ŏ' thē bĕautĭfŭl!
> Sĕrēne thē sŏft āirs trĕmblĕ ăt hĕr cōmĭng;
>   Dĕlīghtfŭl ēnchāntmĕnt ăwākĕns
>   Āll thĕ bŏsŏm's trĕmŭlŏus dĕvōtĭon.

Here *ăt her* follows Latin precedent; I notice nothing else to query. In another 'alcaic' stanza (p. 155), *of his* can be similarly explained; *gentle movement*, first written, is altered in *Errata* to *gentle action*. Both Herbert's verses, and the pages in which they occur, should be read; notice especially, on p. 71, the stanza contrasted with that first quoted above. His arguments do not convince me, either about Greek verse or about English; the former are now out of date. But they are always interesting.

1838. GUEST (Skeat's ed., p. 550 *seq.*) seems to think that all "the experiments which have been made during the last three centuries" had an accentual basis; in them, "instead of the accent representing the sharp tone, or the ictus, it has been considered as a substitute for the long quantity" (p. 551). Their rhythm was loose, and they "followed the triple rather than the common measure," besides neglecting pauses (*ibid.*). "German hexameters" share this condemnation (p. 552). He thinks that by dividing centrally, and avoiding false accentuation, a satisfactory metre might be evolved; and offers some lines of his own as a "test" (p. 553). Though these are not quantitative, I give three as a sample; the *colon* indicates his "middle pause".

Sing the wrath, O Goddess: Achilles' wrath the Pelides!
Deadly it was, and whelm'd: with many a woe the Achaians,
Many a soul it sent: of hero brave into Hades.

No doubt, lines of this length tend to break into halves, but I do not think this tendency should be exalted into a canon. Otherwise the lines read fairly well; accentuation is clear, and there are no harsh masses of consonants. "The Pelides" comes in oddly; the first syllable of "Pelides" had obviously no 'long' sound to Guest. Such experiments, at their best, do but little toward naturalizing an unfamiliar metre. That, as a rule, can be done only by poets.

1844. SHADWELL (LANCELOT) [*cf.* old list, and text]. This writer's 'hexameters' should also be distinguished from the ruck of accentual verse, since they at least profess to follow quantity. The *Note*, or rather "Advertisement", after Book II, indeed, declares that his is "the first specimen of real Hexameter verse that has appeared in the English language"; also that "in this translation the rules of ancient art are strictly followed out, and never departed from". It is difficult to know what this means, since the pledge given of further explanation was not redeemed. Ordinary rules of [supposed] quantity are not followed; the writer's position seems much like that of Odell or Guest. I quote the first four lines of Book II:—

<blockquote>
Soundly the rest of the gods, and the horseplume-helmeted heroes,
Slept thro' the livelong night ; but, sleep staid not to Kronion :
Waking and thoughtful, he dwelt on his scheme, that the sons of Achaia
Thickly should die at the ships, and Achilleus' name be exalted.
</blockquote>

1846. OXENFORD (JOHN). In *Classical Museum*, Vol. III, pp. 279–83, short paper on "The practice of writing English in Classic metres".

Not mentioned elsewhere. This writer, like others of his time, abandons quantity as a basis, but tries to secure quantitative effect by great precision of "*ictus*". He gives one specimen, in 'sapphics', apologising for his unaccented syllables, but relying on the others. I give a sample stanza:—

<blockquote>
Wealthy Priam leaving his Troy—in safety
Led by thee—avoided the proud Atrides [;]
Pass'd Thessalian watchers, and pass'd encampments
Hostile to Ilium.
</blockquote>

1853. CLOUGH (A. H.) [*cf.* old list, 1848, and present text, 1860 *seq.*]. The "Letters of Parepidemus" appeared first in *Putnam's Monthly Magazine of American Literature, Science, and Art* [which later became "Putnam's Magazine," *tout court*], Vol. II (1853), pp. 72–4 and 138–40. The Second Letter touches on 'quantity.' Clough was still only feeling his way, and the sample lines there given are more accentual than quantitative. *Odoriferous* is still a spondee *plus* dactyl, and he has such contradictory scansions as *fŏllŏwed the yĕllŏw Menelaus*. By the early Sixties he had come nearer the position of Spedding [*cf.* below], but he never mastered the latter's rules. The "Essays in Classical Metres", printed among his poems, show this. True, he now writes *ŏdŏrĭfĕrous* and *sŏpŏrĭfĕrous*, *ĕchoes*, *shĕpherd*, *căvern*, *ăttentive*. But he also writes *sŭnny*, *swĕlling*, *fŭrrow*, *cŭrrent*, *hŏllow*, *radiănt*, *tŏ*, *ŏn that*, *manў streamlets*, *watĕr overflowing*. It can be said only that he "essayed" to write quantitative verse, not that he succeeded in doing so.

1861. SPEDDING (JAMES) [*cf.* old list, and text as above]. The only lines, to my knowledge, in which Spedding exemplified his theory, are those in the *Fraser* article. He first gives as correct quantitative metre this line:—

<blockquote>
Swēetlў cŏmēth slŭmbēr, clōsĭng th' ō'erwēarĭĕd ēyelid;
</blockquote>

then says there would be two "shocking false quantities" if it ran—

> Sweetly falleth slumber, closing the wearièd eyelid.

Later, he puts forth his *chef-d'œuvre*, eight lines, which are quoted by W. J. Stone. In them Stone had detected "two false quantities" when he first wrote; in his revised edition the phrase is "two or three". I recognise two in *procēssion* and *divīsion*, a third in *is* followed by a vowel; other syllables are dubious but legitimate. The elision in *quantity obeyeth* is of course monstrous. Spedding's practice certainly ill sets off his theory; three blunders in eight lines is bad. It shows how little reality such 'quantities' had to him.

1871. ELLIS (R.) [*cf.* old list]. In his interesting Preface (see especially p. xiv *seq.*) Prof. Ellis explains his rules, which are quite different from those advocated by later writers, or by Spedding and Cayley, of whose contemporary work he seems unaware. Entirely rejecting 'combative accent', he tries (following Tennyson) to unite accent and quantity, allows a heavily accented syllable to count as 'long', ignores initial *y* as well as *h*, but otherwise observes rules of 'position'. Thus, "*heavy level ever cometh any*" are usually trochees, sometimes pyrrhics; "*dolorous stratagem echoeth family,*" usually dactyls, are sometimes tribrachs. As a "pure iambic line" he selects—

> Thĕ pūny pīnnăce yōndĕr yōu, mȳ frĭĕnds, dĭscĕrn;

in which phonetic quantity is at least three times set aside. His rules therefore, as he sees himself (p. xvi), are almost wholly negative; they merely prevent clumsy crowds of consonants, a result which might surely have been reached by simpler methods. Brilliantly wrought as the translations are, they strike me as being neither Classic verse nor English; the "Attis", in particular, I find metrically unreadable. But both translations and preface repay study.

1886. TENNYSON (SECOND LORD). *Jack and the Bean-stalk. English Hexameters. By Hallam Tennyson. Illustrated by Randolph Caldecott.* 4to, Macmillan (London and New York).

This *jeu d'esprit*, not elsewhere mentioned by me, interests as reflecting the view of quantity held by its author's father. Aspirated *h* is ignored, and phonetic sound not always regarded, so that we find *widŏw, lŏoking, prŏtect, where an' O where, cursing him hied to hĕr bed, ăn humble obeisance, etc.* Spelling, indeed, seems more studied than sound. Accent is not allowed to replace quantity, so far as I have noticed, and is sometimes contrasted with it, as in *ĕlĕphănt*. *Ng* is sometimes reckoned one sound, sometimes two.

This entry reminds me that I have nowhere referred to some burlesque quantitative scraps by the late Laureate, quoted in his son's *Memoir* (one-volume edition, pp. 425-6; *cf. note* [a] there). They show that he was inclined to regard such metres as being usually "only fit for comic subjects". It will be remembered how Stone was "nearly reduced to tears" by a line ending in *grŭel!*

1898. Another book not elsewhere mentioned by me is *Versions from Hafiz* (small 4to, Grant Richards), by Walter Leaf, in which an accomplished scholar tries to represent Persian metre by quantitative English, symbols being placed by him over syllables for our guidance. Strict rules of quantity, here again, are not followed, unstressed syllables being regarded as "common", while accent is allowed to create length[1]; yet the general effect is quantitative, and unusual feet (*bacchius, epitritus, etc.*) are used. A favourable example is (Ode V)—

Āflāme wĭth blŏom ĭs thĕ rĕd rōse,

which reads itself. So, without marks, would (Ode VI)—

Wild of mien, chanting a love-song, cup in hand, locks disarrayed;

but we are asked to believe that this should be read—

Wīld ŏf mīen, chănt-|ĭng ā lōve-sŏng, | cŭp ĭn hānd, lŏcks | dĭsărrāyed ⏑ |.

So we are asked not to read as "bad anapaests" this line (Ode XIV)—

Āgāin sĕe | mĕ vānqŭished | ănd lāid lŏw | ŏf wīnē ⏑ | ;

but how can we fail to parallel it with

Behind shut the postern, the lights sank to rest?

Or how can we fail to read as an 'octosyllabic couplet' this other line (Ode IV)—

Ăn ĭf yŏn Tŭrk | ŏf Shīrāz lānd | thĭs hĕart wŏuld tāke | tŏ hŏld ĭn fēe | !

No, if quantity is to be a basis, it must be independent of accent; combined with accent, it inevitably takes second place in English.

---

[1] "Both quantity and accent are in many cases what the English reader makes them" (p. 14). One would like to have heard Stone's criticism of this view; his pamphlet came out in this same year.

These clever exercises only prove this anew, though they avoid the still more fatal fallacy of supposing a purely quantitative basis of English metre practicable or tolerable.

1899. W. J. Stone's trumpet-blast in favour of quantitative verse provoked illustration as well as comment. In the *Academy* for April 1, 1899, pp. 388–9, appeared some 'elegiacs' by his father, Mr. E. D. Stone, beginning [the symbols are mine]—

> Hō! jŏllў ōld pārsŏns, whŏ smōked lōng pīpes ŏf ăn ēvenĭng,
>   Smōked lōng chŭrchwārdĕns, sīpped ăt ă bĕadў rŭmmĕr.

These lines should of course be read by "Will Stone's" rules, but there are a few divergencies, *e.g. stupĭdly, birētted, ŏf horseflesh, is one, dĕckers; rustĭcal antĭphones*, as the second half of a 'pentameter', is perhaps one of the "two or three false quantities" to which the writer pleads guilty. As a whole, they well illustrate the rules, and my readers can judge for themselves the merit of such lines as—

> Rēd-tīled, smārtlў bănnēred, māde tŏ ă tĭdў păttĕrn,

or

> Wŏndĕrs mĕn rĕckŏn īt sēemlў tŏ wĕar pĕttĭcōats.

I cannot believe such verse capable of any but the comic effect happily created by it here.

In *Literature* for May 13, 1899, is a letter, signed A. E. Crawley, containing "Sappho's Litany" in stanzas appropriate to the title. I quote the first and last of the seven.

> Thrŏn'd ŭpŏn līght, Thŏu vĕrў Gŏd, Lŏve ōur Quĕen,
> Dāughtĕr ŏf Gŏd, mўstĕrў-wŏrkĕr, hĕar mĕ!
> Spāre frŏm āll lŏve's wēarĭnĕss ānd bĭttĕrnĕss
>   Mў spĭrĭt, Ŏ Quĕen!
>   *   *   *   *
> Cŏme tŏ mĕ nŏw! ănd dĕlĭvĕr frŏm āll mў
> Hārd sŏrrōws; ănd ŏf thĕ lŏngĭng wĭthĭn mĕ
> Fūlfĭl āll; ănd bĕ ĕvĕr, Ĭ bĕsĕech Thĕe,
>   Mў sŭccŏur ănd shĭeld.

Except for the ignoring of *h* in *workĕr, hear*, these lines seem perfectly to carry out Stone's rules. They are followed by this rendering of an epigram ascribed to Plato :—

> Dāy Stăr ŏf thĕ lĭvĭng wăst thŏu ŏnce shĭnĭng ămŏng mĕn,
> Nŏw thŏu'rt Ĕv'nĭng Stăr ŏf thĕ dĕad ĭn Părădĭse.

Technically faultless, this couplet leaves me impenitently convinced of the unsuitability of such structure for serious English verse.

1903. Quantitative poems by Mr. Bridges were published this year, as per my previous list. In the *Academy* of July 18 (and next year, amended, in a pamphlet of *Scattered Verses*) appeared some satirizing quantitative lines by myself, mentioned here for completeness' sake.

1905. *Demeter; a mask*, by Mr. Bridges (Clar. Press, Oxford; paper covers), contains some further quantitative experiments. The chorus which begins Act I is in 'choriambic' metre—

> Gāy ānd lŏvelў̆ ĭs ĕarth, mān's dĕcŏrāte dwĕlling,

varied by a shorter line ending each stanza, *e.g.*—

> A dĕlight dĕar tŏ ĭmmōrtāls.[1]

On p. 31 the first line spoken by Hermes professes to be in 'sapphic' metre (*cf. note*, p. 59), and four 'hexameter' lines, "hidden in the blank verse," begin with the word *daughter*. On p. 36 are two 'alcaic' stanzas, and on p. 37 an Ode in Horatian 'iambics'—which, curiously, Mr. Bridges found, "as I anticipated, the most difficult classical metre to represent in English" (p. 66). The latter begins:—

> O thăt thĕ ĕarth, ŏr ŏnlў̆ thĭs fāir ĭsle wĕr' ōurs
> Ămĭd thĕ ōcĕan's blŭe bĭllōws.

[*Wer'* is doubtless so written to show that it is a short syllable, rhyming with *her* and not with *care*; *cf.* first sentence on p. 63.]

If any one can reconcile the English ear to quantitative verse, Mr. Bridges should do it. His lines are poetry as well as verse. His phonetic feeling is all but unimpeachable. Before questioning any of his quantities, one would need to know not only his rules but his personal pronunciation; whether he sounds the vowel in *raptūrous* differently to that in *raptūre*, that in *wĕ* differently to that in *wĕedy*. To me the whole thing is a fallacy. But his technical remarks on pp. 62–6 should be read by those interested. I give myself the pleasure of quoting the two 'alcaic' stanzas mentioned above.

---

[1] One would naturally, from a quantitative standpoint, read this ᴗᴗ−|−|ᴗᴗ−−, but the author's note (p. 66) directs us to read it ᴗᴗ−|−ᴗᴗ−|⏑. His second example runs—

> Thĕ ĕchōes mădlў̆ rĕjōicĭng.

I know how these lines would scan in ordinary English verse; a pause would separate the third and fourth syllables. Their supposed quantitative structure is another story.

Lŏ whĕre thĕ vīrgĭn vēilĕd¹ ĭn āirў bĕams
Āll-hōlў Mōrn, ĭn splĕndŏr ăwākĕnĭng,
Hĕav'n's gāte hăth ŭnbārrĕd, thĕ gōldĕn
Aĕrīāl lăttĭcēs sĕt ōpĕn.
[For the pronunciation of *aerial*, see p. 66.]
Wĭth mūsĭc ēndĕth nĭght's prĭsŏnĭng tĕrrŏr,
Wĭth flōw'rў ĭncĕnse : Hāste tŏ sălūte thĕ sŭn,
Thăt fŏr thĕ dāy's chāse, līke ă hŭntsmăn,
Wĭth flāshĭng ārms cŏmĕth ō'er thĕ mōuntăĭn.

⁎ I shall be glad to receive references to any quantitative English lines not mentioned in this or my previous list. It will be understood that accentual lines are excluded. Their name is legion; enumeration of them would be neither possible nor profitable. A complete record of quantitative verse, on the other hand, is both possible and desirable. Few writers have essayed it ; their work deserves note. However little we may sympathize with their efforts, we need not grudge these commemoration. They form a separate chapter in the history of our verse, and it should be written in full.

APPENDIX B

BEING

ADDENDA TO AND *CORRIGENDA* IN MY PREVIOUS LIST OF WORKS DEALING WITH ENGLISH VERSE-STRUCTURE, BY NATIVE WRITERS.

[Books and papers criticizing the *contents* of verse are excluded. So, for the most part, are school-books, ordinary grammars and manuals of English literature, newspaper and even magazine articles, unless these contain something distinctive. Even so, my list errs on the side of inclusion, that extreme seeming preferable to the other. Notice of any *important* omission from this taken in connection with my previous list will be deemed a favour.

Books may be presumed *octavo*, and published in London, unless otherwise stated. Toward the end I have appended

---

[1] The *diaeresis* over a single vowel is to me offensive. What is there to 'divide' ? Why not *veilèd*, like *unbarrèd*? And why not *aërial*, where it is right?

publishers' names when known, to facilitate reference; with earlier volumes this seemed needless.

Wherever no remark accompanies an entry, the book or paper is described in my text, at or about the date of publication; the Index will give the exact page, if there is any difficulty in finding it.]

1610. BOLTON (EDMUND) [*cf.* old list]. *Hypercritica* is reprinted in Haslewood, *Anc. Crit. Essays*, Vol. II.

1619. DRAYTON (MICHAEL) [*cf. ditto*]. The *Epistle of Poets and Poetry* (in verse), which I had of course read before, contains nothing about prosody, though it deals with other "brave translunary things". It calls Gascoigne and Thomas Churchyard [author of *A Praise of Poetrie* (1595), not mentioned elsewhere by me, because containing nothing *ad rem*] "great meterers".

1640. BEN JONSON's *Grammar* [*cf. ditto*] seems to have formed part of a projected second volume of his *Works*; another item was his *Timber: or Discoveries*.... See "Temple Classics" edition of the latter (1902), Note at end. Though this latter treatise refers frequently to verse, it says nothing about metre.

1667 and 1679. Two books by Samuel Woodford, D.D.— viz. *A Paraphrase upon the Psalms of David* (1667) and *A Paraphrase on the Canticles* (1679)—have prefaces referring slightly to structure. Trisyllabic feet are defended in the latter, and a passage from Milton given in prose form. The date alone makes these worth naming.

1692. Dryden's Prefaces were generally referred to in my old list; that to his *Aeneid* is mentioned early in my present text. In the Preface to his *Juvenal* (1692) he discourses at length about versification rather than structure, and laments the absence of a proper "Prosodia". In a much earlier one to *The Rival Ladies* (1664) he defends rhymed couplets against blank verse, praises Waller's "sweetness", and credits him with introducing the "distich". In that to *Albion and Albanius* he contrasts our speech with French and Italian, speaks of "the effeminacy of our pronunciation", and hopes one day to "treat more largely" of sound. His Preface to *Fables, Ancient and Modern* (1700) gives some interesting details about himself and his projects. Other references can doubtless be found. The *Art of Poetry* and *Essay on Satire*, both in verse, have nothing to the purpose.

Most of the above can be read in *Essays of John Dryden*, edited by W. P. Ker (2 vols., Clar. Press, 1900)—an admirable collection for wider uses than ours.

1709. COWARD (WILLIAM). *Licentia Poetica Discuss'd; or, the true test of Poetry, . . .* [with] *Critical Observations on the Principal Antient and Modern Poets, viz. Homer, Horace, Virgil, Milton, Waller, Cowley, Dryden, &c. as frequently liable to just Censure. A Poem.* By W. Coward, Coll. Med. Lond. M.D.
Not mentioned elsewhere. A Preface of some twenty-eight pages (unnumbered). The Poem in two Books, many *notes*. Comments amusingly on the liberties taken with syllables by poets.

1710 and 1751. For Dyche and Dilworth, see text; dates erroneous in old list.

1739. *Letters concerning Poetical Translations . . . etc.*, anonymous [by William Benson; for full title see text]. The Letters are dated September—December, 1736. How, then, can there have been a prior edition in 1713 [or even in 1731]?

1747 and 1755. In old list, alter date of publication of Johnson's *Dictionary* from the first to the second of these dates. Its two volumes came out together.

1762. Add Sheridan's two *Dissertations* [see text] to other works mentioned in old list [1775], and alter date of his *Dictionary* (2 vols.) from 1789 to 1780. The *Lectures on Elocution* are in 4to.

1765. RICE (JOHN). *An Introduction . . .*, full title in text.

1773. *A New Dictionary of the English Language, by William Kenrick, LL.D.; to which is prefixed a Rhetorical Grammar* (4to). Introduction, pp. i–viii; Rhet. Gram., pp. 1–57; remainder unpaged.

1775. COCKIN (WILLIAM). *The Art of delivering Written Language*; full title in text. Dedicated "To David Garrick, Esq."

1783. Blair's *Rhetoric*, in old list. For Lecture "37" read 38.

1785. *Critical Essays on some of the Poems of several English Poets.* By John Scott, Esq.

1791. WALKER (JOHN), in old list. For *Principles of Elocution* read *Elements* of *Ditto* (2 vols., 1781); and add his *Rhetorical Grammar* (1785). The *Key to Proper Names* was published in 1798. Other books as mentioned in text.

1799. ROBERTSON (REV. JOSEPH). *An Essay on the Nature of the English Verse, with directions for reading poetry. By the Author of the Essay on Punctuation.* Preface signed "J. R., Mortimer St., August 28, 1799".

1817. *The Round Table*, by William Hazlitt [and Leigh Hunt], 2 vols., Edinburgh; paper No. XI is on "The versification of Milton", but contains nothing for our purpose. Not mentioned in text.

1819. CAMPBELL (THOMAS). *Specimens of the British Poets* (7 vols.). Second edition in one vol., ed. Peter Cunningham, 1841. Campbell's "Essay on English Poetry", from the *Specimens*, with his "notices" of poets, in one vol. 16mo, 1848.

1819. Article in *North American Review* for September, by William Cullen Bryant, "On trisyllabic feet in iambic measure." Reprinted, with additions, in Vol. V of Bryant's *Works* (6 vols., New York, 1884). This contains three "Literary Essays", the above being the third; the other two, though concerned with poetry, do not touch our subject. Vol. V is "Prose Works, Vol. I".

1820. *Blackwood's Magazine* for September (Vol. VII, No. 42), article on "Sweetness of versification", signed "J. D." Very slight. *Repetition* is much dwelt on. "The recurrence... of accents in certain places ... constitutes rhythm" (p. 642). I have no clue to authorship.

1821. *Edinburgh Review*, in old list. For "p. 143" read pp. 422–36.

1821. REV. JAMES CHAPMAN [*cf.* old list, 1818]. *The original Rhythmical Grammar of the English Language: or, the art of reading and speaking, on the principles of the music of speech* (Edinburgh).

1822. SYLVESTER DOUGLAS, BARON GLENBERVIE, translation of *Ricciardetto, Canto I*. This had been privately printed the year before. Either edition contains a long Note on versification (pp. 158–85).

1827. RUSH (JAMES). In old list [1833] for "teacher" read "physician". First edition dated 1827.

1828. *Blackwood's Magazine* for November (Vol. XXIV, No. 145), "Noctes Ambrosianae, No. 39"; discusses briefly the difference between verse and prose (pp. 642–52).

1830. BARBER (JONATHAN). *A Grammar of Elocution; containing the principles of the arts of reading and speaking ...* By Jonathan Barber, Member of the Royal College of Surgeons, London. New-Haven [Connect.], 12mo.

Not mentioned elsewhere. Follows Rush [*cf. supra*] entirely. In Section on "Measure of speech" (pp. 125–43) uses Steele's symbols, and reproduces much of his teaching.

1836? *A Grammar of English Grammars,* . . . By Goold Brown (New York). This has gone through many editions, with much enlargement. The 10th appeared in 1875. Its "Introduction" is dated "New York, 1836", which I assume to be the date of the first edition.

1841. HORNE (RICHARD HENGIST). *The Poems of Geoffrey Chaucer, modernized.* Introduction discusses trisyllabic feet [*cf.* criticism in Poe's *Rationale*]. Specimen pieces turned into modern English by himself, Wordsworth, Leigh Hunt, "Elizabeth B. Barrett," etc.

1843. O'BRIEN (WILLIAM). In old list, for "isochronous bars" read "equal intervals", and substitute *p. 19* for *p. 39.* "Isochronous metres or bars" are mentioned on p. 31 in connection with Greek verse.

1846? POE (E. A.), in old list. For 1846 read 1848.

1847. In Philological Society's *Transactions,* Vol. III, p. 95, article by Prof. Malden, "On Greek and English versification."

1847. *English Prosody,* by Asa Humphrey. Referred to by Goold Brown. I have not seen it.

1848. *A System of English Versification;* with rules and examples. By Erastus Everett, A. M. (New York), 12mo.

1848. *The American Review* for May, pp. 484–92, article on "The art of measuring verse", signed "J. D. W."

1857. PATMORE (COVENTRY) [*cf.* old list]. His Essay is omitted from last edition of *Poems* (Geo. Bell & Son, 1906), but will be found in a new edition of his whole *Works.*

1862. MARSH (GEO. P.). *Lectures on the English Language* (Murray), ed. W. Smith, LL.D., and headed "The Student's Manual of the English Language". The *Lectures* had previously appeared in America. A subsequent English edition, in 1868, is called the fifth edition.

1862. ANGUS (JOSEPH). *Handbook of the English Tongue,* 12mo (Rel. Tract Soc., N. D.). Not the same as *The Handbook of English Literature,* by the same author (*ibid.*).

1862. ARNOLD (THOS.) [junior]. *A Manual of English Literature, historical and critical. With an appendix on English metres. Cf.* "7th edition, revised" (1897; Longmans).

1867. In Philological Society's *Transactions,* pp. 43–54, article on "The pedigree of English Heroic Verse, by C. B. Cayley, Esq., B.A." [*cf.* old list, 1861].

1869. F. W. NEWMAN [*cf.* old list, 1861]. *Miscellanies.*

Now forms first volume of his collected *Miscellanies* (Trübner, 3 vols., 1869–89). See "Lecture II" on "Forms of poetry".

1869. BREWER (R. F.). *A Manual of English Prosody* (Longmans, 12mo). This is an earlier form of the same writer's book on *Orthometry* [old list, 1893].

1869. HOOD (THOS.), in old list. *Dele* reference to "the elder Hood". Authorship of *Young Poet's Guide* unknown to me.

1869. WADHAM (E.). *English Versification; a complete practical guide to the whole subject* (Longmans).

1869. ABBOTT (E. A.). *Shakespearian Grammar*, 3rd edition, "revised and enlarged" (1870; Macmillan). Also, in old list, under Abbott and Seeley (1871), read "English Lessons for English *People*".

1878. CONWAY (GILBERT). *A Treatise on Versification* (Longmans).

1880. SYLVESTER (J. J.) [*cf.* old list, 1870]. *Spring's Début...*, full title given in text. Privately printed, N. D.

1880. GURNEY (EDMUND). *The Power of Sound* (Smith, Elder & Co., 4to). By the same author, *Tertium Quid* (Kegan Paul & Co., 2 vols.), 1887; papers on verse in Vol. II.

1881. BAYNE (PETER). *Two great Englishwomen, Mrs. Browning and Charlotte Bronte: with an Essay on Poetry illustrated from Wordsworth, Burns, and Byron* (James Clarke & Co.).

Not mentioned elsewhere. The Essay touches slightly on questions of metrical form, making *lyric* the oldest type of verse (pp. xxxiii–iv).

1883. HOLMES (OLIVER WENDELL). *Pages from an Old Volume of Life* (Boston). A collection of essays, written 1857–81. Essay IX is on "The physiology of versification".

1885. STEVENSON (R. L.). Article "On some technical elements of style in literature", *Contemporary Review* for April; reprinted in his *Essays in the Art of Writing* (Chatto & Windus, 1905).

1885. GOODELL (THOMAS D.). Article on "Quantity in English verse", American Philological Association's *Transactions* for 1885–7 (Vol. XVI), pp. 78–103.

1886. GUMMERE (F. B.). To the two books named in old list [1885] add the following:—In *American Journal of Philology*, Vol. VII (1886), No. 25, pp. 46–78, article on "The translation of Beowulf, and the relations of Ancient and Modern English verse". In *Modern Language Notes* (Baltimore), Vol. I (1886), pp. 35–6 and 83–4, replies to a critic. In the same, Vol. II

(1887), No. 6, pp. 159–62, a review of Prof. Mayor. In *Child Memorial Volume* (Boston, 1897), essay on "The Ballad and communal poetry" [not seen].

1886. RAYMOND (GEO. LANSING) [*cf.* old list, 1895]. *Poetry as a Representative Art* (Putnam's Sons, New York and London). Fifth edition, 1903, in which are given titles of other books not germane to our subject, but forming part of the author's "system of comparative aesthetics".

1886. HALL and JASTROW. In *Mind*, Vol. XI (1886), pp. 55–62, article entitled "Studies of rhythm", by Prof. G. Stanley Hall and Joseph Jastrow, dated from Johns Hopkins University, Baltimore.

1887. TOLMAN (ALBERT H.). In *Andover Review*, Vol. VII, pp. 326–37, article on "The laws of tone-color in the English Language". See also next entry.

1888. *The 46th Birthday of Sidney Lanier* (Johns Hopkins Univ. publication agency, Baltimore), a memorial volume, contains a paper on "Lanier's Science of English Verse" by Prof. Tolman.

1888. DAVIDSON (JAMES WOOD), *The Poetry of the Future* (J. B. Alden, 16mo, New York).

1889. MEAD (WILLIAM E.). *The Versification of Pope in its relation to the Seventeenth Century* (Leipzig). [Not seen.]

1890. BROWNE (WILLIAM HAND). In *Modern Language Notes* (Baltimore), Vol. IV, pp. 97–101, article entitled "Certain considerations touching the structure of English verse".

1891. SCHELLING (F. E.) [*cf. ante*, p. 209]. *Poetic and Verse Criticism of the reign of Elizabeth* (Philadelphia; University of Pennsylvania Press). [Not seen.]

Also, in *Publications of the Modern Language Association of America* (Vol. XIII, No. 2), "Ben Jonson and the Classical School." [Not seen.]

1890. WOOD (HENRY). In *American Journal of Philology*, Vol. XI, pp. 55–79, article on the "Beginnings of the Classical Heroic Couplet in England".

1890. PALMER (GEO. HERBERT). In *Atlantic Monthly* for July—December (Vol. 66), pp. 526–34, paper on "Hexameters and Rhythmic Prose".

Not mentioned elsewhere. 'Hexameters' please because "less rigidly metrical" than other lines, but as "the prevalent movement of English verse is iambic", a sort of "iambic recitative" might be better, though it is difficult to make accents sufficiently obvious without rhythm (pp. 526–8). A sample version of *Odyssey*, Book XXIII, occupies remainder of paper.

1892. CORSON (HIRAM), LL.D. *A Primer of English Verse, chiefly in its aesthetic and organic character* (Ginn & Co., Boston).

1892. STEDMAN (EDMUND CLARENCE). *The Nature and Elements of Poetry* (Houghton & Co., Boston and New York; Cassell & Co., London). A "revised and extended" form of lectures delivered in Johns Hopkins University, and printed in the *Century Magazine* for 1892 (Vols. 43 and 44).

1893–4. BOLTON (T. L.). The paper on "Rhythm" mentioned in my old list was published in January, 1894 [not 1893]. My reference should read: *The American Journal of Psychology*, Vol. VI, No. 2, pp. 145–238.

1894. HALLARD (J. H.). In old list, read "Second edition (Rivington), 1901".

1894. LARMINIE (WILLIAM). In *Contemporary Review* for November (Vol. 66, pp. 717–36), article on "The development of English metres".

1894. DIXON (WILLIAM MACNEILE). *English Poetry from Blake to Browning* (Methuen & Co.).

1895. WALLASCHEK (R.). In *Mind* (New series, Vol. IV), pp. 28–35, article on "The difference of time and rhythm in music".

1895. COURTHOPE (W. J). *A History of English Poetry*, Vol. I. Vol. II appeared in 1897, Vols. III and IV in 1903, Vol. V in 1905. (Macmillan.)

1896. BATESON (H. D.), in old list. This tract now published separately (Manchester, 1904), with new Preface, and short list of writers on prosody.

1897. ROBERTSON (JOHN M.) *New Essays towards a Critical Method*. Appendix on "accent, quantity, and feet" (John Lane, London and New York).

1898. LEWIS (CHARLTON M.). *The Foreign Sources of English Versification, with especial reference to the so-called iambic lines of eight or ten syllables* (Halle, paper covers). [*Cf. infra*, 1906.]

1898. TAMSON (George J.). *Word-stress in English. A short treatise on the accentuation of words in Middle-English as compared with the stress in Old and Modern English* (Halle, paper covers).

1898. KER (W. P.). In Philological Society's *Transactions* for 1899–1901, Part I, pp. 113–28, paper read December 2, 1898, on "Analogies between English and Spanish verse (Arte Mayor)".

1899. BRIGHT (J. W.) [*cf.* old list, 1899]. In *Publications of the Modern Language Association of America* (Baltimore), Vol. XIV, No. 3, pp. 347–68, article on "Proper Names in Old English verse".

[*Cf. infra*, 1901, Furnivall presentation volume.]

1899. SPINGARN (JOEL ELIAS). *A History of Literary Criticism in the Renaissance, with special reference to the influence of Italy in the formation and development of modern classicism* (New York and London; Macmillan).

Mentioned in App. A. Part III deals with English authors, see especially pp. 298–304 on "Classic Metres".

1899. HURST (A. S.) and McKAY (JOHN). In *University of Toronto Studies, psychological series, edited by Prof. Kirschmann*, No. 3, pp. 57–75, article entitled "Experiments on time relations of poetical metres".

1900. RITCHIE (FRANK). In *Longman's Magazine* for December, pp. 114–24, article on "Rhyme".

1900. VAN DAM and STOFFEL. *William Shakespeare. Prosody and text. An Essay in Criticism. Being an introduction to a better editing and a more adequate appreciation of the works of the Elizabethan poets.* By B. A. P. van Dam, with the assistance of C. Stoffel (Williams & Norgate, N. D.).

Cf., by same authors, *Chapters on English Printing, Prosody, and Pronunciation (1550–1700)*. By Bastian A. P. van Dam and Cornelis Stoffel (Heidelberg, paper covers, 1902, in series of *Anglitische Forschungen*).

1901. BAYNE (THOS.). In old list, substitute this name for "Bayne (Peter)." The entry next following in that list may probably be credited to him also.

1901. *An English Miscellany presented to Dr. Furnivall in honour of his 75th birthday* (Clar. Press). Contains a paper "Concerning grammatical ictus in English verse", by Prof. James W. Bright [*cf. ante*, 1899]. Also contains [not mentioned in my text] "A note upon Waller's distich", by H. C. Beeching (pp. 4–9). Canon Beeching queries some popular ideas, and asserts that Marlowe always placed a strong syllable immediately before or after a weak one metrically accented, *e.g.*—

> Who builds a palace and *rams* up the gate.
> To whom you offer, and *whose* nun you are.
> Her mind *pure* and her tongue . . .

1901. BROWN (GEORGE DOBBIN). *Syllabification and Accent* *in the Paradise Lost* (John Murphy Co., Baltimore). Mentioned in text immediately after Prof. Bright, of whom he was a follower.

1901. HUGUENIN (JULIAN). *Secondary Stress in Anglo-Saxon. Determined by metrical criteria* (John Murphy Co., Baltimore). Not mentioned in text. Author was also a pupil of Prof. Bright.

[Both G. D. Brown and Huguenin are now dead.]

1901. WALLIN (J. E. WALLACE). In *Studies from the Yale Psychological Laboratory*, Vol. VII, pp. 1–142 [the entire volume], "Researches on the rhythm of speech."

1901. TRIPLETT (NORMAN) and SANFORD (EDMUND C.). In *The American Journal of Psychology*, Vol. XII, No. 3, pp. 361–87, "Studies of rhythm and meter."

1901. SQUIRE (C. R.). In the same, No. 4, pp. 492–589, "A genetic study of rhythm."

1902. SAINTSBURY (GEORGE) [*cf.* old list, 1887]. In Vol. II of *History of Criticism*, published this year, Book IV, Chap. III, is on "Elizabethan Criticism", and deals shortly with the quantitative attempt (p. 160 *seq.*); verse-structure is not otherwise much mentioned. Vol. III of this work came out in 1904, while in 1903 had appeared *Loci Critici: passages illustrative of critical theory and practice from Aristotle downwards* (Ginn & Co., Boston and London). These deal only incidentally with prosody, which however forms the subject of the "Introduction" contributed to *The Rhymers' Lexicon* (Routledge, N. D. [1905]), and will be treated with final fullness in a work whose beginning is chronicled under date 1906.

1902. LANIER (SIDNEY) [*cf.* old list, 1880]. *Shakspere and his Forerunners* (2 vols. 4to, Doubleday, Page, & Co.).

1902. SCRIPTURE (EDWARD WHEELER). *Elements of Experimental Phonetics* (New York, Charles Scribner's Sons; and London, Edward Arnold). Large book. Dr. Scripture has superintended the Yale Psychological Laboratory for several years, and papers of his have appeared in its *Studies*, *e.g.* Vol. VII (1899) is occupied by two articles by him, but they do not specially touch on verse.

1902. MILLER (C. W. E.). *The Relation of the Rhythm of Poetry to that of the Spoken Language* (Baltimore). [Not seen.]

1902. COTTERILL (H. B.). *Milton's Lycidas* (Blackie & Son). Appendix I (pp. 97–105) is "On rhythm in English verse".

1902. TODHUNTER (JOHN). In *Fortnightly Review* for February, pp. 346–60, article entitled "Blank verse on the stage". Not mentioned in text. Mainly about elocution.

1903. MAYOR (JOSEPH B.) [*cf.* old list, 1886]. *A Handbook of Modern English Metre* (Cambridge Univ. Press).

1903. OMOND (T. S.). *A Study of Metre* (Grant Richards, now Moring). *English Metrists* [Part I] (Pelton, Tunbridge Wells).

1903. NEWMAN (ERNEST). In *The Weekly Critical Review* (Paris) for September 3, 10, 17, and 24, a series of articles on " The rationale of English verse-rhythm ".

1903. GAYLEY (CHARLES MILLS) [*cf.* old list, 1893 and 1899]. *Representative English Comedies* (Macmillan). Appendix (pp. 503-11) on Greene's versification.

1903. VAN DYKE (HENRY). In *Atlantic Monthly* for October, pp. 469-75, " Some remarks on the study of English verse."

1904. BRIDGES (ROBERT) [*cf.* old list, 1889]. In *Athenaeum* for January 16, 23, 30, three papers on "Miltonic elision". [*Cf.* also Appendix A, 1905.]

1904. COLLINS (JOHN CHURTON). *Studies in Shakespeare* (Arch. Constable & Co.).

1904. SMITH (G. GREGORY). *Elizabethan Critical Essays, edited with an Introduction by* (2 vols., Clar. Press). Referred to in App. A. This contains reprints of many treatises mentioned in my old list, *e.g.* those of Gascoigne, Webbe, Puttenham, James VI, Campion, Daniel, *etc.*, besides several others; it may be said to replace "Haslewood". For some remarks on prosody, see Introduction, pp. xlvi–liv.

1904. NORTHCROFT (GEO. J. H.). *How to write Verse: being studies in the principles and practice of the art of English verse-structure* (Smith's Publishing Co.).

1904. ALDEN (RAYMOND MACDONALD). *English Verse* (New York). [Seen too late for notice here; *cf. infra*, p. 268.]

1904. JOHNSON (CHARLES F.). *Forms of English Poetry* (American Publishing Co.; and Sidney Appleton, London), N. D.

1904. SCOTT (F. N.) [*cf.* old list, 1899]. In *Publications of the Modern Language Association of America* for June (Vol. XIX, which is also XII of "new series", No. 2, pp. 250–69), paper on " The most fundamental differentia of poetry and prose". [*Cf.* also 1905.]

1904. SETZLER (EDWIN B.). *On Anglo-Saxon Versification, from the standpoint of Modern-English Versification* (stiff paper boards, Furst & Co., Baltimore).

1904. MILLER (RAYMOND DURBIN). *Secondary Accent in Modern English Verse (Chaucer to Dryden)*; J. H. Furst & Co., Baltimore.

Not specified in text. This, like the pamphlets of Brown and Huguenin [*ante*, 1901], is written by a pupil of Prof. Bright, and adopts his view without question. All three were written as dissertations preliminary to the degree of Ph.D. in Johns Hopkins University, and show careful study of our literature.

1904. THOMSON (WILLIAM). *The Basis of English Rhythm* (paper covers, Holmes, Dunlop St., Glasgow).

1905. RUDMOSE-BROWN (THOMAS B.). *Étude comparée de la versification française et de la versification anglaise: l'alexandrin et le blank verse* (privately printed, Grenoble; paper covers).

1905. SCOTT (F. N.) [*cf.* 1904]. In *Publications . . . etc.*, as before, Vol. XX ("new series," XIII), No. 4, pp. 707–28, paper on "The scansion of prose rhythm".

1906. SAINTSBURY (GEO.) [*cf.* 1902]. *A History of English Prosody from the Twelfth Century to the present day*, Vol. I (Macmillan).

1906. DAVIDSON (JOHN). *Holiday and Other Poems* (E. Grant Richards). See Note at end, "On poetry."

1906. BOURNE (GEORGE). In *Macmillan's Magazine* for June, pp. 541–9, article on "Rhythm and rhyme".

1906. KEARY (C. F.). In *Fortnightly Review* for November, pp. 811–26, "Some thoughts on the technique of poetry."

Seen too late for notice in text. A suggestive but too dogmatic paper, opinions stated as facts. The unit of verse is taken to be a phrase or line, rather than a 'foot'; our heroic line is made a sort of dimeter, characterized by two main accents. What distinguishes a prose clause so characterized from a line of verse?

1906. LEWIS (CHARLTON M.) [*cf. ante*, 1898]. *The Principles of English Verse* (New York, Henry Holt & Co.; London, Geo. Bell & Co.).

Seen too late for notice in text. A small but able book, for "general readers" as well as scholars (*Preface*). Six chapters. Rhythm is "a recurrence of similar phenomena at regular intervals of time"; "regularity of time-intervals is a *sine qua non* of rhythm" (p. 2; *cf.* p. 16 on the "ideal rhythmical scheme"). "Time," however, is still identified with *tempo* (*e.g.* p. 15), and in the first Chapter the rhythms of prose and verse are accounted equally regular, neither perfectly so (p. 14 sums up this view).

Much is said about "conflict" (first mentioned on p. 16), held to be between thought and expression. Metrical beat is assumed to create "stress" of some sort (p. 25); the effect of a weak stress is "as if a runner should put one foot in a hole and so fail to touch ground. We can perhaps imagine him going on without breaking step" [I cannot! He would certainly fall] (p. 21). "Inversions" in 'heroic' lines cause irregularity "in the metre, not in the rhythm" (p. 27), and in these the poet "does not change the total number of syllables" (p. 30). [The term 'heroic' is restricted to couplets, the other being styled "blank verse", and both "pentameter".] Yet the objection to nine-syllable lines is "purely a matter of convention" (p. 31). "Hovering accent" is discussed on pp. 35-8; Classic names of feet are admitted (pp. 39-44), with cheerful defiance of "system" (p. 44). This ends Chap. II. The remainder of the book is mainly practical, and should be useful. "Trochaic rhythm" is asserted to be less natural and agreeable than iambic (p. 104); the "rhythmical scheme" [identified with "average tempo"] of triple-time verse is pronounced to be slower than that of "iambics", though the syllables of the former are more rapidly uttered than those of the latter (p. 111). [The former's "gallop" (p. 109; *cf.* 117), therefore, must be slower than an "iambic" march!] There is some candid criticism of Browning and Swinburne in Chap. V, where also the "little book" of R. Bridges is pronounced "utterly wrong in some of its fundamental principles" (p. 121). Like Gurney, the writer finds but four stresses in the line—

By the wáters of Bábylon we sat dówn and wépt (p. 119),

which, in my judgement, reduces it to prose. The last Chapter contains a wholesome protest against doctrinaire views about tone-colour. This book should foster an intelligent and sympathetic attitude toward metrical questions.

NOTE

At the last moment, after unexpected delays, I have been able to see a book mentioned on p. 235—*English Verse: specimens illustrating its principles and history. Chosen and edited by Raymond Macdonald Alden, Ph.D.* (New York, Henry Holt & Co.: 1904 [not 1903 as in text])—and take this opportunity of saying that it well deserves perusal. The bulk of the book contains excellently chosen examples, illustrating (in Part I) the nature and (in Part II) the historical development of our verse; while Part IV gives some extracts from writers on metre. But specially noteworthy is Part III, on "The time-element in English verse". Here is briefly indicated a view of metre quite unusually complete and comprehensive, as two sentences will show. "The sounds of verse have constantly to effect a compromise between the typical rhythm to which they are set and the irregular stress- and time-variations of human speech" (p. 394). "The fundamental principle of verse is that it sets up a new order of progress which constantly conflicts with, yet without destroying, the order of progress of common prose speech" (p. 408). In view of such sayings, the division of our verse merely by "stresses", due doubtless to German teaching, seems strangely inadequate (*cf.* the introductory pages of Part I). Like many American prosodists, Dr. Alden seems more familiar with German writers on our verse than with either English critics or the latest work of English poets. He will find (perhaps has already found) in recent high-class verse longer single lines than his "eight-stress iambic", and quantitative attempts continuing those he records. But these are details. Not having seen this book mentioned by writer or reviewer here, I desire to draw attention to it as useful for teachers and interesting by reason of its references to time-structure; and regret that a bookseller's blunder prevented my receiving it in time for proper notice.

INDEX

[Where references are numerous, the more important are italicized. Bracketed figures denote a reference where the thing or person is not actually named.]

Abbott (E. A.) 167–8, 200, 260.
Addison (Joseph) 8, 18, 33.
Akenside (Mark) 108.
alcaics (Classic) 158 *note*.
alcaics (modern so-called) 158, 248–9, 254–5.
Alden (R. M.) 235, 264, *268*.
Alford (Henry) 160.
anacrusis 74, (96), 102, 107, (118), (125), (135 *note*), (144), 155, 168, 191, 227.
Angus (Joseph) 161 *note*, 259.
Anonymous 42, 64, 123–4, 205, 247.
"Anti-Jacobin, The" 6, 7, 81, 118.
appoggiatura [various spellings] 64, 100, 130 and *note*, 136, 208.
Arnold (Matthew) 157, 158, 160, 161, 165.
Arnold (Thomas, junior) 161–2, 259.
Ascham (Roger) 244, 245.
Ashe (Thomas) 159 *note*.

Bain (Alex.) 210.
Barber (Jonathan) 258.
Barham (T. F.) 149.
Barrett (E. B.) [*cf.* Browning, Mrs.] 136, 259.
Bateson (H. D.) 215, 262.
Bathurst (Charles) 147.
Bayne (Peter) 234, 260.
Bayne (Thomas) 234, 263.
Beattie (James) 67–8, 78, 98, 103.
Beeching (H. C.) 147 *note*, 263.

Bell (A. M.) 166.
Benson (William) 8, 257.
Bentley (Richard) 8, 13, 67, 83, 85.
"Beowulf, The" 196 *note*, 221.
Blackie (J. S.) 124, 160.
"Blackwood's Magazine" 108 *note*, 120, 258.
Blair (Hugh) 70–1, 72, 98, 257.
Blake (William) 86, 214, 262.
Blundell (James) 124–5.
Bolton (Edmund) 256.
Bolton (T. L.) 201, 211–13, 262.
Bourne (George) 239, 266.
Brewer (R. F.) 162 *note*, 210, 260.
Bridges (Robert) 147, 159, 200, *201–4*, 215, 234, 236, *254–5*, 265, 267.
Bright (J. W.) *220–1*, 225, 237, 263, 264, 266.
Brightland (John) 6.
Bronte (Charlotte) 260.
Brown (G. D.) 221–2, 263–4, 266.
Brown (Goold) 121, 122–3, 259.
Brown (John) 32, 71.
Browne (W. H.) 208–9, 261.
Browning (Mrs.) [*cf.* Barrett, E. B.] 136 *note*, 234, 260.
Browning (Robert) 159, 186, 187, 200, 213, 214, (228), 230, (252), 262, 267.
Bryant (W. C.) 108, 258.
Buckingham (Duke of) 8.
Burney (Charles) 69–70, 75.
Burns (Robert) 86, 128, 129, 260.

Byron (Lord) 87, 104, 111, 139, 142, 176, 199, 228, 260.
Bysshe (Edward) 6, 7, 10, 17, 46, 162, 225.

Cædmon 183.
caesura 15, 28, 45, 58, 75, 100, 101, 104, 109, 116, 119, *(126-7)*, 130 *note*, 133, (138), 141, 142, 152, 159 *note*, 162, 163, 188, 193, 208-9, 216.
Calverley (C. S.) 160.
Campbell (George) 69 *note*.
Campbell (Thomas) 108, 258.
Campion (Thomas) 265.
Canning (George) 118.
Carey (Henry) 192 *note*.
Carey (John) 98 *note*, 103-4, 107.
Carpenter (Edward) 223.
Cayley (C. B.) 159-60, 251, 259.
Chapman (James) 62, 91, *105-7*, 174, 258.
Chaucer (Geoffrey) 13, 20, 35, 55, *183*, 207, 215, 224, *243*, 266.
choriambics (modern so-called) 154, 158, 254.
Churchyard (Thomas) 256.
Classic metre, passim: *cf. espec.* 2-6, 36, 75, 93-4, 128-9, 152, 170; also *alcaics, choriambics, hexameters, sapphics*.
Clough (A. H.) 134-5, 149 *note*, 158, 159, *250*.
Cochrane (J. I.) 157.
Cockin (William) 65, 257.
Coleridge (S. T.) 58, 62, 81, *86-91*, 97, 99, *104-5*, 124, 126, 136, 142, 143, (215), (218), 228.
Collier (J. P.) 243, 247.
Collins (J. C.) 224, 236, 265.
Collins (William) 17, 74, 86.
Conway (Gilbert) 174, 260.
Corson (Hiram) 209, 212, 262.
Cotterill (H. B.) 234, 264.
Courthope (W. J.) 215, 262.
Coward (William) 257.
Cowley (Abraham) 108, 257.

Cowper (William) 17, 86, 116, 154 *note*, 247, 248.
Crawley (A. E.) 253.
Crowe (William) 118-19, 210.

Dabney (J. P.) 227-8, 233.
Dallas (E. S.) 146, 149 *note*.
Daniel (Evan) 210.
Daniel (Samuel) 265.
Dart (J. H.) 157.
Davidson (J. W.) 207, 261.
Davidson (John) 239, 266.
Denham (John) 19, 102, 108.
Derby (Lord) 160.
Dilworth (Thomas) 6-7, 257.
Dixon (W. M.) 214, 262.
Douglas (Sylvester) 113, 258.
Drayton (Michael) 256.
Dryden (John) 6, 8, 19, 33, 84 *note*, 108, 129, *256*, 257, 266.
Dunton. *See* Watts-Dunton.
Dyche (Thomas) 6-7, 257.
Dyer (John) 74, 108.

Earle (John) 166-7.
"Eclectic Review" 123-4.
"Edinburgh Review" 91-4, 111-12, 258.
Edwards (Richard) 102.
"Eliot, George" 193.
Elizabeth (Queen) 244, 245.
Ellis (A. J.) 63, 121, 137, 166, *169-73*, 180, 181, 187, 200.
Ellis (Robinson) 158, 251.
Emerson (R. W.) 195.
Evans (R. W.) 145.
Everett (Erastus) 137, 138, 259.

Fogg (P. W.) 81-2.
Ford (John) 203.
Foster (John) 20-5, 38, 43, 44, 50, 52, 57, 71, 78, 124, 216.
Fraunce (Abraham) 215.
French verse 4, 39, 51, 94, 142, 208, 209, 215, *217*, 239, 244, 266.
Frere (J. H.) 118, 203.

Gally (Henry) 20-1, 23, 25, 216.

Gardiner (William) 120-1.
Gascoigne (George) 16, 256, 265.
Gayley (C. M.) 196 *note*, 223, 246, 265.
German verse 81, 94, 97, 113, 131-2, 134, 158.
Gilbert (W. S.) 237 *note*.
Gildon (Charles) 2, 7-8, 57.
Glenbervie (Lord). *See* Douglas (Sylvester).
Glover (Richard) 10, 19, 104.
Goldsmith (Oliver) 32, 34, 74.
Goodell (T. D.) 194-5, 260.
Gosse (Edmund) 227.
Gray (Thomas) 17, 19-20, 74, 86.
Greene (Robert) 223, 265.
Gregory (George) 98-9.
Guest (Edwin) 62, 64, 93 *note*, *125-32*, 146 *note*, 154, 155, 162, 188, 200, 211, 215, 239, 240, *249*, 250.
Gummere (F. B.) 195-6, 226-7, 260.
Gurney (Edmund) 176-7, 260, 267.

Hake (John) 245-6.
Hall (G. S.) 201, 213 *note*, 261.
Hallam (Henry) 123.
Hallard (J. H.) 262.
Harford (F. K.) 223.
Harris (James) 9, 12, 33.
Harvey (Gabriel) 245.
Harvey (John) 245.
Hawkins (John), 34.
Hawtrey (E. C.) 134.
Hazlitt (William) 258.
Helmholtz (Hermann) 165.
Herbert (William) 92-4, 248-9.
Herries (John) 35-6, 37, 97.
Herschell (William) 134.
hexameters (Classic) 15, 23, 26, 27, 31, 36, 45, 61, 68, 75, *109*, 117, 118, 162, 174, *184*, (208 ?), 227, 230.
hexameters (modern so-called) (36), (41), (45), (68), 81, 84, 87, 94, (97), 98, 105, *108-13*, 118, 124, *125*, 131 and *note*, 132, *134-6*, 142, 145, (149), *157-61*, 162, 164, 174, 188, 200, 209, *219-20*, 223, (229), (236), *243-55*, 261.
Hodgson (Shadworth) 186-8.
Holder (William) 119 *note*.
Holmes (O. W.) 190-1, 260.
Hood (Thomas, senior) 163, 260.
Hood (Thomas, junior) 162-3, 260.
Horne (R. H.) 136, 142, 259.
Horsley (Samuel) 83.
Huguenin (Julian) 264, 266.
Humphrey (Asa) 137, 259.
Hunt (Leigh) 25 *note*, *136*, 142, 203, 258, 259.
Hurst (A. S.) 213 *note*, 222, 231, 263.

Ingelow (Jean) 184.

James VI (King) 184, 265.
Jastrow (Joseph) 201, 213 *note*, 261.
"J. D." (108 *note*), 258.
Jenkin (Fleeming) 188-90, 192, 209.
Johnson (C. F.) 237, 265.
Johnson (Samuel) *17-19*, 23, 26, 33, 46, 47, 53, 55, 65, 67, 74, 75, 77, 79, 97, 112, 130, 190, 225 *note*, 257.
Jonson (Ben) 6, 8, 72, 256, 261.

Kames (Lord) *25-9*, 30, 33, 52, 53, 57, 78, 85.
Keary (C. F.) 240 *note*, 266.
Keats (John) 218.
Keightley (Thomas) 147 *note*.
Kenrick (William) 41, 48 *note*, 257.
Ker (W. P.) 222, 256, 262.
Kingsley (Charles) 135, 149.
Kipling (Rudyard) 184.
Knight (R. P.) 94-5.
Knox (Vicesimus) 70.

Lamb (Charles) 187.
Landor (W. S.) 86.
Langland (William) (127), 183, (185 note).
Lanier (Sidney) 6, 63, 118, *177-86*, 187, 194, 204, 208, (209), 211, 212, 216-17, 227, 231 note, 236, 261, 264.
Larminie (William) 213-14, 262.
Latham (R. G.) 132-4, 161 note, 209.
Leaf (Walter) 252.
Lecky (James) 191-2.
Lewis (C. M.) 217-18, 240 note, 262, 266-7.
Liddell (M. H.) 231-3.
Lindsay (Lord) 160.
"Literary World" 211.
Lockhart (J. G.) 134.
Longfellow (H. W.) 134, 135, 136, 142.
Lowell (J. R.) 136.
Lyly (John) 246.
Lytton (first Lord) 160.
Lytton (second Lord), "Owen Meredith" 149.

McKay (John) 213 note, 222, 231, 263.
McKerrow (R. B.) 229, 244, 246.
Maclagan (E. R. D.) 243.
Macpherson (James) 81, 86, 98, (213).
Mahaffy (J. P.) 227.
Mainwaring. *See* Manwaring.
Malden (Henry), 137, 259.
Mangan (J. C.) 213.
Manwaring (Edward) 9, 11-12.
Mapes (Walter) 243.
Marlowe (Christopher) 169, 200, 263.
Marsh (G. P.) 161, 259.
"Martin Mar-prelate" 246.
Mason (John) 9, *13-16*, 33, 40, 53, 57.
Massinger (Philip) 203.
Masson (David) 146-7.

Mayor (J. B.) 166, 169, 170, 171, 172, 196 note, *198-201*, 215, 234, *235*, 261, 265.
Mead (W. E.) 208, 261.
Meredith (George) 158, 159.
"Meredith, Owen." *See* Lytton (second Lord).
Miller (C. W. E.) 234, 264.
Miller (R. D.) 266.
Milton (John) *passim* (about every third page).
Mitford (William) *42-7*, 49 note, 53, 57, 62 note, 71, 72, 88, *91-2*, 115, 129, 130, 131, 149, 155, 248.
Monboddo (Lord) *36-40*, 46, 53, 56, 62, 64, 65, 71, 72.
Moore (Thomas) 87 note, 129.
Morris (William) 183.
Munby (A. J.) 159 note.
Munro (H. A. J.) 157.
Murray (Lindley) 51 note, *78-80*, 103, 107, 123, 137, 233.

Nares (Robert) 62 note, 71-3, 77.
Nash (Thomas) 246.
Newman (Ernest) 235-6, 265.
Newman (F. W.) 157, 259.
Northcroft (G. J. H.) 237, 265.

O'Brien (William) 137, 150, 153, 259.
Odell (J—) 62, 91, *95-8*, 99, 102, 114, 117 note, 210, *247-8*, 250.
Omond (T. S.) 58, 216, 235, 237, 254, 265.
onomatopoeia 12, (52), (67), 74, (163), 174.
"Ormulum, The" 183, 207.
"Ossian" 86, 98, 213.
Oxenford (John) 250.

Palmer (G. H.) 261.
Parsons (J. C.) 209.
Patmore (Coventry) 6, 63, *149-56*, 187, 259.
Pemberton (Henry) *9-11*, 12, 15, 52, 57.
"Percy's *Reliques*" 86, 116.

"Piers Plowman" [*cf.* Langland, William] 127, 185 *note.*
Poe (E. A.) 6, 58, 63, *138-44*, 148, 163, 165, 177 *note*, 212, 213, 216, 259.
Pope (Alexander) 8, 10, 19, 23, 26, 27, 28, 29, 33, 35, 40, 52, 62, 71, 85, 92, 94, 102, 108, 116, 120, 129, 162, 189, 190, 208, (239).
Primatt (William) 25, 83.
Prior (Matthew) 191.
Puttenham (George) 210, 265.

Ramsay (Allan, junior) 65-7.
Raymond (G. L.) 195, 196-8, 261.
Redesdale (Lord) 149.
Rice (John) 33-4, 257.
Ritchie (Frank) 224, 263.
Robertson (J. M.) 216-17, 262.
Robertson (Joseph) 85, 257.
Roe (R. B.) 62, 91, 99-100, *113-18.*
Roscommon (Earl of) 8.
Rossetti (Christina) 186, 241.
Rossetti (D. G.) 186.
Rudmose-Brown (T. B.) 239, 266.
Rush (James) 63, 121-2, 258.
Ruskin (John) *175-6*, 211, 235.

Sabie (Francis) 247.
Saintsbury (George) 126, 201, 225 *note*, *239-40*, 243, 264, 266.
Sandford (James) 244-5.
Sanford (E. C.) 229-31, 264.
sapphics (Classic) 9, 36.
sapphics (modern so-called) 17, 81, 97, 99, 158, *247-8*, 250, *253*, 254.
Say (Samuel) 9, *12-13*, 15, 33, 51, 52, 57, 174.
Schelling (F. E.) 209, 261.
Schipper (Jakob) 238, 246.
Scott (F. N.) 196 *note*, *223*, *238*, 246, 265, 266.
Scott (John) 73-4, 257.

Scott (Walter) 86, 87 and *note*, 94, 119, 155, 176, 228.
Scripture (E. W.) 223 *note*, 229-31, 264.
Seeley (J. R.) 167-8, 260.
Setzler (E. B.) 237, 265.
Shadwell (Lancelot) 134, 249-50.
Shakespeare (William) *passim*, but less often than Milton.
Shelley (P. B.) 163, 177 *note*, 200, 218, 233.
Sheridan (Thomas) 29, 33, 37 *note*, 40, 41, *47-54*, 65, 68, 72, 75, 77, 78-9, 80, 82, 83, 84, 94, 114-15, 121, 153, 257.
Sidney (Philip) 8, 176 *note*, 245, 246.
Sievers (Eduard) 220.
Simcox (W. E.) 157.
Skeat (W. W.) 125, 126, 130, 166, 200, *205-6*, 243.
Smith (G. G.) 247, 265.
Southey (Robert) 81, 86, 87, 97, *108-11*, 112, 113, 116, 117, 119, 124.
Spedding (James) 92, *157-8*, 159, 160, *250-1.*
Spenser (Edmund) 13, 129, 191, 239.
Spingarn (J. E.) 245 *note*, 263.
Squire (C. R.) 229-31, 264.
Stanihurst (Richard) 244.
Stedman (E. C.) 209-10, 214, 262.
Steele (Joshua) 38, 40, 47, *55-64*, 65, 66, 68, 71, 76, 82, 87, 88, 91, *95-6*, 98, 99, *101-2*, *105-7*, *113-18*, 120, 121, *130 note*, 140, 150, *170 note*, 174, *179*, 194, 258.
Stevens (L. T.) 201 *note.*
Stevenson (R. L.) 188, 192-3, 260.
Stoffel (Cornelis) 224-5, 236, 263.
Stone (E. D.) 220 *note*, 253.
Stone (W. J.) 158, 159, 160, *219-20*, 229, 251, 252 and *note*, 253.

T

"stress-rhythm" 88, 132, 164, *202-3*, 232-3.
Surrey (Earl of) 200, 215.
Sweet (Henry) 166, 206-7.
Swift (Jonathan) 8.
Swinburne (A. C.) 110, 127 *note*, *144*, (148), *154*, 155, 158, 162, *177*, 183, 186, 213, 221, 248, *267*.
Sylvester (J. J.) 58, *164-5*, 193, 260.
Symonds (J. A.) *168-9*, 200, 227.

Tamson (G. J.) 219, 262.
Taylor (William) 81, 87, 117 *note*.
Tennyson (first Lord) 105, 127 *note*, 146, 154 *note*, *158*, *169*, 181, 186, 198, 199, 200, (210), 213, 234, 251, *252*.
Tennyson (second Lord) 251-2.
Thelwall (John) 62, 87, 91, 97, *99-102*, 105-7, 114, 130.
Thomson (James) 74, 108.
Thomson (William) 237-8, 266.
Tillbrook (Samuel) 112-13.
Tisdall (Fitzgerald) 208.
Todhunter (John) 265.
Tolman (A. H.) 204-5, 261.
Triplett (Norman) 229-31, 264.
Tucker (Abraham) 34-5.
Tyrwhitt (Thomas) 54-5.

van Dam (B. A. P.) 224-5, 236, 263.
van Dyke (Henry) 235, 265.
Verrier (Paul) 238.
Victory (L. H.) 235.

Wadham (E—) 163-4, 260.
Walker (John) *75-8*, 95, 114, 121, 257.
Walker (W, S.) 147.
Wallaschek (Richard) 214, 262.
Waller (Edmund) 19, 102, 108, 209, 256, 257, 263.
Wallin (J. E. W.) 229-31, 264.
Warner (John) 83-4.
Warton (Joseph) 17, 80.
Warton (Thomas) 20, *41-2*, 54, 108, 215, 246.
Watson (Thomas, the Bishop) 244.
Watson (William) 159.
Watts (Isaac) 12, 97, 247.
Watts-Dunton (Theodore) 177 *note*, *193-4*, 210, 218.
Webb (Daniel) *29-32*, 53, 80, 106.
Webbe (William) 41, 246, 265.
Webster (John) 203.
Whelpley (J. D.) 137-8, 259.
Whewell (William) 134, 135, 160.
Whitman (Walt) 148.
Wilson (John) 120.
Witcomb (Charles) 191.
Wood (Henry) 209, 261.
Woodford (Samuel) 256.
Woods (Mrs.) 234-5.
Wordsworth (William) 81, 86, 87, 99, 104, 110, 126, 228, 235, 259, 260.
Worsley (Philip) 160.
Wulff (Fredrik) 239.
Wycherley (William) 192 *note*.

Young (Walter) 74-5.

THE END

Trieste Publishing has a massive catalogue of classic book titles. Our aim is to provide readers with the highest quality reproductions of fiction and non-fiction literature that has stood the test of time. The many thousands of books in our collection have been sourced from libraries and private collections around the world.

The titles that Trieste Publishing has chosen to be part of the collection have been scanned to simulate the original. Our readers see the books the same way that their first readers did decades or a hundred or more years ago. Books from that period are often spoiled by imperfections that did not exist in the original. Imperfections could be in the form of blurred text, photographs, or missing pages. It is highly unlikely that this would occur with one of our books. Our extensive quality control ensures that the readers of Trieste Publishing's books will be delighted with their purchase. Our staff has thoroughly reviewed every page of all the books in the collection, repairing, or if necessary, rejecting titles that are not of the highest quality. This process ensures that the reader of one of Trieste Publishing's titles receives a volume that faithfully reproduces the original, and to the maximum degree possible, gives them the experience of owning the original work.

We pride ourselves on not only creating a pathway to an extensive reservoir of books of the finest quality, but also providing value to every one of our readers. Generally, Trieste books are purchased singly - on demand, however they may also be purchased in bulk. Readers interested in bulk purchases are invited to contact us directly to enquire about our tailored bulk rates. Email: customerservice@triestepublishing.com

You May Also Like

Éléments de la Grammaire Latine à L'usage des Collèges

Charles François Lhomond

ISBN: 9780649638321
Paperback: 250 pages
Dimensions: 6.0 x 0.53 x 9.0 inches
Language: eng

English Metrists, pp. 1-118

T. S. Omond

ISBN: 9780649486052
Paperback: 134 pages
Dimensions: 6.14 x 0.29 x 9.21 inches
Language: eng

www.triestepublishing.com

You May Also Like

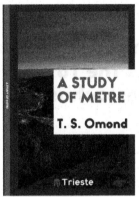

A Study of Metre

T. S. Omond

ISBN: 9780649470297
Paperback: 186 pages
Dimensions: 6.14 x 0.40 x 9.21 inches
Language: eng

Liége and the Ardennes

George W. T. Omond & Amédée Forestier

ISBN: 9780649292752
Paperback: 224 pages
Dimensions: 6.14 x 0.47 x 9.21 inches
Language: eng

www.triestepublishing.com

You May Also Like

1807-1907 The One Hundredth Anniversary of the incorporation of the Town of Arlington Massachusetts

Various

ISBN: 9780649420544
Paperback: 108 pages
Dimensions: 6.14 x 0.22 x 9.21 inches
Language: eng

Biennial report of the Board of State Harbor Commissioners, for the two fiscal years commencing July 1, 1890, and ending June 30, 1892

Various

ISBN: 9780649194292
Paperback: 44 pages
Dimensions: 6.14 x 0.09 x 9.21 inches
Language: eng

www.triestepublishing.com

You May Also Like

Biennial report of the Board of State Harbor Commissioners for the two fisca years. Commeneing July 1, 1884, and Ending June 30, 1886

Various

ISBN: 9780649199693
Paperback: 48 pages
Dimensions: 6.14 x 0.10 x 9.21 inches
Language: eng

Biennial report of the Board of state commissioners, for the two fiscal years, commencing July 1, 1890, and ending June 30, 1892

Various

ISBN: 9780649196395
Paperback: 44 pages
Dimensions: 6.14 x 0.09 x 9.21 inches
Language: eng

Find more of our titles on our website. We have a selection of thousands of titles that will interest you. Please visit

www.triestepublishing.com

Lightning Source UK Ltd.
Milton Keynes UK
UKOW06f0948231017
311488UK00005B/1010/P